THE DEVELOPMENT OF
MARKETING MANAGEMENT

The Development of Marketing Management

The Case of the USA *c.*1910–1940

KAZUO USUI

Saitama University, Japan and University of Edinburgh, UK

ASHGATE

Published by
Ashgate Publishing Limited
Wey Court East
Union Road
Farnham
Surrey GU9 7PT
England

Ashgate Publishing Company
Suite 420
101 Cherry Street
Burlington, VT 05401-4405
USA

Ashgate website: http://www.ashgate.com

British Library Cataloguing in Publication Data
Usui, Kazuo
   The development of marketing management: the case of the USA *c.*1910–1940. –
   (The history of retailing and consumption)
   1. Marketing – United States – Management – History – 20th century 2. Consumption (Economics) – United States – History – 20th century 3. United States – Economic conditions – 1918–1945
   I. Title
   658.8'00973'09041

Library of Congress Cataloging-in-Publication Data
Usui, Kazuo, 1953–
   The development of ideas in marketing management: the case of the USA *c.* 1910–1940 / by Kazuo Usui.
      p. cm. – (The history of retailing and consumption)
   Includes bibliographical references and index.
   ISBN-13: 978-0-7546-0606-2 (alk. paper)
   1. Marketing–United States–Management–History–20th century. 2. Marketing–United States–History–20th century. 3. Marketing–Management–Case studies. I. Title.
   HF5415.1.U88 2007
   658.8001–dc22

                                                                        2007035686

ISBN 978-0-7546-0606-2

Reprinted 2009

Mixed Sources
Product group from well-managed forests and other controlled sources
www.fsc.org Cert no. SA-COC-1565
© 1996 Forest Stewardship Council
FSC

Printed and bound in Great Britain by
MPG Books Ltd, Bodmin, Cornwall.

Contents

The History of Retailing and Consumption
General Editor's Preface

It is increasingly recognized that retail systems and changes in the patterns of consumption play crucial roles in the development and societal structure of economies. Such recognition has led to renewed interest in the changing nature of retail distribution and the rise of consumer society from a wide range of academic disciplines. The aim of this multidisciplinary series is to provide a forum of publications that explore the history of retailing and consumption.

Gareth Shaw, University of Exeter, UK

List of Tables and Figures

Tables

Figures

Publisher's Note

Acknowledgements

The original version of this book was published in Japanese by Otsuki-shoten in Tokyo in 1999, and was fortunate enough to be recognized with an award from the Japan Society for Distributive Sciences. It has been fundamentally revised, however, for foreign readers; the revision was needed because academic interest and common understanding are largely different in Japanese academia from those in other countries, even in the current globalized world. This is perhaps partly due simply to the language barrier, and partly to more complex considerations springing from the different history of the academic world, which has been accumulated under the different politico-economic, educational and cultural environments. The unique interest and understanding in Japanese academia are context-bounded and thus it is difficult for those outside these contexts to penetrate meanings and its significance. The revised work has made this book essentially different from the original version in Japanese.

I owe much to many people in making the publication of this book possible. Because English is not my mother tongue, I asked a few native speakers to check my drafts, particularly Ms Alison Bowers, who is a freelance professional editor. Without her support, the present publication would not have been realized. Mr Tim Bolt read earlier versions of my drafts, and Ms Kathleen King was also committed to this work.

In respect to the content of this book, I especially appreciate the contribution of Professor Gareth Shaw, who provided many valuable comments on my drafts. I also thank Professor John Dawson for providing me with much support to continue this work, as well as hosting me at the University of Edinburgh.

I always remember with honour meeting two of the leaders of the movement for historical research in marketing in the USA, now no longer with us, who encouraged my own research: Professors Stanley Hollander and Terence Nevett. Discussions with Terry (Nevett and Usui 1996) during his stay in Japan are among my vivid memories. I thank Professor Nikhilesh Dholakia for having introduced me to these experts and leading my path to cross with Western academia. Professor Brian Johns, Professor Terrence Witkowski, Professor Eric Shaw and the members of CHARM (Conference on Historical Analysis & Research in Marketing) in North America, Professor John Benson, Professor Gareth Shaw and the members of CHORD (Centre for the History of Retailing and Distribution) in the UK, and Professor Shigeo Mitsuzawa, Professor Makoto Miura, Professor Kazuyoshi Hotta, Professor Hiroshi Kohara and the members of JSSMH (Japan Society for the Study of Marketing History) in Japan, are among the historians who focus on the various aspects of the history of marketing and marketing thought. I learned much from the discussions with these groups.

Finally, I cannot forget the name of the late Professor Fujiya Morishita, who was strongly influential in the criticism of marketing in Japanese academia when I was a student in the period of campus unrest in Japan. While this book does not follow his paradigm, I derived many valuable insights from it.

Kazuo Usui

Saitama and Edinburgh, June 2008

Introduction

Marketing management and marketing management thought, now very often used practically as synonyms with marketing and marketing thought in general, are symbolized by the so-called 4Ps model. This signifies that the planning, implementing and control processes of marketing should not merely be concerned with sales and advertising, but cover the whole of the 4Ps (Product, Price, Place and Promotion). This idea is generally recognized to have become fully-fledged in the USA after the Second World War. At the same time, the idea was exported to Western European countries and Japan, wherever the USA enjoyed politico-economic power. As a result, marketing management, simply called marketing, became a popular discipline in business education across the world. Nonetheless, the history of such an influential idea has still many unexplored topics. This book focuses on the period around 1910s to 1940s, i.e., the pre-matured phase of this idea, and explores how it developed.

Historical analysis in marketing tends to be unpopular, especially among students of the marketing discipline itself, as much research in marketing has often been criticized as 'ahistorical' (e.g. Fullerton 1987a, Hollander and Rassuli 1993). Nevertheless, the situation has been changing gradually. In addition to early efforts, including seminal books (e.g. Converse 1959a, 1959b, Coolsen 1960, Bartels 1962, 1976, 1988, Schwartz 1963, Shapiro and Doody 1968, Wright and Dimsdale 1974) and pioneering conferences (Myer and Smalley 1959, Decker 1962, Greyer 1963, Smith 1965), earnest endeavours to form scholarly organizations to hold regular historical meetings have been made since the 1980s in North America, the UK and Japan (Jones and Shaw 2006, Marco 2006).[1] There have been numerous advocates of historical study (e.g. Myer and Smalley 1959, Williamson 1963, Stern 1963, Doody 1965, Savitt 1980, Nevett 1991, Nevett and Hollander 1994), and various methodological approaches have been proposed. These include 'historical relativism' that criticizes the ethnocentric idea that the North American way of marketing is the world standard (Kumcu 1987), German historicism that applies 'bounded relativism' (Fullerton 1987b), the interpretive/humanistic approach that considers 'reality as socially constructed' (Lavin and Archdeacon 1989), the 'interpretive research

---

1 In the USA, CHARM (Conference on Historical Analysis & Research in Marketing) has held conferences every two years since 1983, resulting in establishing a worldwide organization called the CHARM Society (see http://faculty.quinnipiac.edu/charm/). In the UK, CHORD (Centre for the History of Retailing and Distribution) was set up in 1998 to study the history of retailing and distribution to act as a point of contact between scholars (see http://home.wlv.ac.uk/~in6086/chord.html). Also in Japan, JSSMH (Japan Society for the Study of Marketing History) was organized in 1988 by marketing scholars focusing on the history of modern marketing and marketing thought, while the SSMH (Society for Studies in Market History) was set up in 1985 by historians in broader fields who especially focus on the history of traditional fairs and municipal wholesale/retail markets of perishable foods and daily necessities.

approach' to consumer research (Smith and Lux 1993), literary criticism meaning psychobiographic, editorial and structural approaches to historical marketing thought (Stern 1990), and postmodern critique of marketing history (Brown, Hirschman and Maclaran 2001). Although the view that historical research is insufficiently considered in marketing (e.g. Holden and Holden 1998, Church 1999) may still be prevailing, such changing conditions enable some academics to recognize that marketing history has emerged as an independent school of marketing thought (Shaw and Jones 2005) or even 'a major research stream' (Brown, Hirschman and Maclaran 2001).

This book contributes to historical research in marketing. The author originally began to be involved in historical study in the context of Japanese academia,[2] in which a leading scholar emphasized, 'Above all, marketing is a social and historical phenomenon', therefore, 'If social and historical factors are removed from marketing, what remains has no life and no soul' (Morishita 1968, p. 13). This spirit substantially coincides with a recommendation of historians in Western academia: 'the history of marketing thought cannot be studied in a meaningful way unless the writings themselves are linked to the historical context in which they were produced' (Nevett and Hollander 1994, p. 3). In accordance with these notable suggestions, this book will focus on the combined process of the developing thought and its contexts so as to explore and uncover how the globally-influential idea of the 4Ps type of marketing management was articulated and what the historical settings were. This approach can identify the historical implication of meanings that marketing

---

2   In Japan, when the idea of marketing management, simply called marketing, was imported in the late 1950s, Japanese marketing historians confronted a conceptual dilemma; that is, how the new idea of 'marketing' should be distinguished from the long-held traditional merchant activities in Japan. As a result, a custom has taken root in Japanese academia that the traditional activities of merchants are 'distribution' or 'commerce', while the new concept of American origin is called 'marketing' (written in Japanese *katakana* characters). At the same time, a leading figure, Fujiya Morishita (1913–2005), advocated the importance of the historical study of American marketing, so that several books written in Japanese were published dealing with the development of marketing and/or marketing thought in the USA (e.g. Miura 1971, Hashimoto 1975, Arakawa 1978, Mitsuzawa 1980, 1987, 1990, Kohara 1987, Kondo 1988, Japan Society for the Study of Marketing History 1993, Hotta 1991, 2003, 2006, Usui 1999), as well as Japanese translations of books from American historians (Converse 1959a, 1959b, Bartels 1976, 1888, Sheth, Gardner and Garett 1988).

A feature of Japanese research in US marketing history is the focus on the particular pattern of manufacturer's dominant distribution (called 'marketing'), which is different from the traditional pattern of merchant's dominant distribution (called 'commerce'). This unique terminology came from the critical theory on 'commercial capitals' proposed by Fujiya Morishita (1958a, 1958b, 1960), who defined dominance of oligopolistic or large-sized manufacturers in the distribution process as essential in the definition of marketing. His idea reflected the fact that the manufacturer's dominant distribution became the basis of the so-called rapid economic growth in Japan (1955–73). He was also critical of monopolistic behaviour among manufacturers, and his criticism was supported by the political mood at the time. Although this kind of criticism has almost completely disappeared among Japanese academia and society, his legacy remains in terms of the analytical perspective of the distribution system, and even the terminology of some textbooks (e.g. Harada et al. 2002, p. 78).

literature originally had, to complement the many distinguished works dedicated to marketing thought (e.g. Converse 1959a, Coolsen 1960, Bartels 1962, 1976, 1988, Schwartz 1963, Sheth, Gardner and Garett 1988, Shaw and Jones 2005).

This introductory chapter is composed of three sections: firstly, a discussion of a few basic concepts and views, such as marketing, marketing history, periodization of marketing history and modern marketing; secondly, a clarification of the relationship between entrepreneurship, marketing management and its thought, followed by a general overview of the history of marketing literature before the Second World War in the USA in order to identify the historical position of managerial literature. Then it will introduce the basic model adopted by this research and an explanation of the structure of this book.

What are Marketing, Marketing History and Modern Marketing? The Focal Point of Analysis in this Book

The Long History of Marketing

The content of marketing history naturally depends on how marketing is defined. The definitions often provided are so general that its history is inevitably assumed to be very long.

A popular definition comes from the exchange paradigm, which has been popular since the 1970s: that the history of marketing is as long as the history of humanity. Philip Kotler, an originator of the broadened concept of marketing (Kotler and Levy 1969), advocates the 'generic concept' (Kotler 1972, pp. 48–50), insisting that the core concept of marketing is 'transaction' or 'exchange of values' between any two parties or social units. The 'values' here include not only goods, services and money, but also other resources such as time, energy and feelings. The 'social units' involved need not be limited to business organizations, but may consist of any individuals, groups, organizations, communities or nations. The 'market' means the social unit whose response is sought by another social unit, namely the marketer. In this context, marketing is defined as 'the attempt to produce the desired response by creating and offering values to the market'.

Richard P. Bagozzi (1975, pp. 32–5 and 36–7), another influential scholar of the exchange paradigm, equates marketing with 'exchange' by identifying three categories: restricted exchange (two-party reciprocal relationships), generalized exchange (reciprocal relationships among at least three parties), and complicated exchange (mutual relationships among at least three parties). In addition, marketing involves both 'utilitarian' and 'symbolic' exchange.

The definitions of marketing as exchange used by both Kotler and Bagozzi substantially point toward the history of marketing being almost as long as human existence, because exchanges of things such as feelings and symbols are universal to all human behaviour. Kotler (2005, pp. 4–5) himself admitted, 'Marketing started with the first human being', insisting that the 'first marketer' could be said to be the snake in the Bible who convinced Eve to market the idea of eating the forbidden apple to Adam.

Although the exchange paradigm is now predominant, there are scholars who restrict marketing to 'market exchange', i.e., the economic and commercial arena. This is the view taken by this book. It is essentially consistent with traditional definitions of marketing, that 'marketing includes those business activities involved in the flow of goods and services from production to consumption', as defined by the National Association of Marketing Teachers in 1935 (p. 156), or that marketing is 'the performance of business activities that direct the flow of goods and services from producer to consumer or user', as defined by the American Marketing Association in 1948 (p. 209) and 1960 (Alexander and the Committee on Definitions 1960, p. 15).

Even adopting such economic definitions, however, it is still true that marketing has a long history. The historical study of commerce can be traced back to Adam Anderson (*c.*1692–1765) (1764), who explored the origin of commerce in the primitive ages of the world and constructed a detailed chronology that covered the whole period of human history, followed by the work of David Macpherson (1746–1816) (1805). Many successive historians such as Webster (1903), Day ([1907] 1908), Herrick (1917) and Stephenson (1924) told the story from ancient commerce, while Hotchkiss (1938), whose work has recently been highlighted (Jones 1995, 1998, Enright 2002), started his description from the fifth century. Generally speaking, economic exchange and commerce can be recognized as having ancient origins, recalling Max Weber's phrase ([1904] 2000, p. 22), 'the *auri sacra fames* [the greed for gold] is as old as the history of man'.

Therefore, no matter which definition of marketing – social exchange or economic exchange – is used, the historical study of the subject is wide-ranging. As for the history of the term 'marketing' itself, although Bartels (1962, p. 4) insisted that marketing was first coined as a new noun 'between 1906 and 1911' in the USA, this view has been strongly challenged. Lazer (1979, p. 654) recognized that *An American Dictionary of the English Language* in 1856 contained the word 'marketing'. The author of this book also identifies that in *A Dictionary of the English Language* published in 1832 in London, Noah Webster (1758–1843) defined 'marketing' as a noun, 'Articles in market, supplies', and in *An American Dictionary of English Language* published in 1836 in New York, 'Supply of a market; attendance upon a market' was the definition. Dixon (1979, 2000) emphasized that a verbal noun 'marketing', meaning 'buying and selling' could be traced back to the middle of the sixteenth century (see also OED). Whatever its changes in use, the term has been used as a noun over its long history.

A marketing historians' group in North America adheres to this long-ranging view. In its manifesto, it clearly professes that marketing history has no chronological or geographic limits (Nevett and Hollander 1994, pp. 5–6, see also Nevett and Usui 1995, pp. 117–19), and the topics at its conferences have actually covered the whole period of history in any country. Firat and Dholakia (1989) suggested an even more radical version, based on an idea of anthropological economics (see Polyani 1966), stressing that in addition to 'exchange', 'self-provision', 'reciprocity' and 'redistribution' were essential in marketing history.

It is true that some anthropological ideas, such as gift-giving, would be useful when one considers exchanges and consumer behaviour even in current society. However, historical study covering such a long time would also create confusion.

The usual image of marketing held by many people would perhaps be of new concepts and modern methods of exchange, but this image ignores a considerable variety of marketing revealed by historical research. These people are seemingly puzzled by what Baker (1976, p. ix) expressed as the 'enigma of marketing'; that is, marketing is 'one of man's oldest activities and yet it is widely regarded as the most recent of the business disciplines'. A way to avoid this trouble is to periodize the long history of marketing and assume marketing in the most recent period as 'modern' marketing, which signifies or implies that it is different from traditional or pre-modern marketing and has a direct connection with today's marketing. This view, however, still leaves a few questions to be solved.

Periodization of Marketing and its Modern Form

There have been many recent definitions of modern marketing. One definition provided by Alford (1981, p. 328) is: 'Marketing, in modern terms, involves deciding marketing objectives in relation to firm's products and then integrating research, production, advertising, selling and distribution into a policy and programme designed to secure these objectives.' This definition is sometimes referred to when historians consider the history of marketing (e.g. Corley 1987, p. 66, 1993, p. 100, Church 1999, p. 407). Fullerton (1988a) also coined the term 'Modern Western Marketing', which is operationally defined as 'the vigorous cultivation of existing markets and equally vigorous efforts to open up new ones through insistent promotion, frequent introduction of new products, careful study of market demand, and ongoing efforts to control and coordinate distribution channels' (pp. 73–4). These definitions are very likely to match with the current view of marketing. As a matter of fact, these are similar to the explanation of marketing in current marketing management textbooks, in that the definitions are basically composed of the 4Ps – although both cases exclude price – plus market research. Rather, it can be said that the reason why one can identify the modern form of marketing in the long history is that commentators already know the 4Ps approach to marketing management. In this sense, exploring the history of this idea is important. A problem confronted is that opinions vary regarding when modern marketing started.

A popular view is the so-called triadic model of the development of marketing. Although strongly criticized by some scholars (Hollander 1986, Fullerton 1988b), it is still predominant in introductory marketing textbooks (see Enright 2002). Believed to derive from Keith's (1960) concept of 'marketing revolution', with variants (see Hollander 1986, Church 1999), the triadic model divides the history of marketing into the production/product era (business must focus on increasing the volume of well-made products at low cost), the selling/sales era (aggressive sales, advertising and other promotional efforts); and the marketing era (focused heavily on consumers' needs and wants). The model assumes a historical development from production via sales to the marketing era. While 'modern' is not always explained, it is usually assumed to have begun in the 1950s in the USA.

The distinctions between production-, sales- and marketing-orientation are useful when one analyses the philosophical and/or strategic features of businesses, but it is obviously misleading to use these terms as a determinant for periodization of the history of marketing. Production-orientation and sales-orientation can co-exist with marketing-orientation in the same historical time, and even within the same firm at the same time (see Church 1999, p. 413). Furthermore, a philosophy of consumer-focus, although regarded as a core of the marketing era, can be recognized in different historical periods in different countries. This is basically because any voluntary exchange of goods and services has no guarantee of success in advance, so that the seller must consider what possible buyers want. Therefore, the consumer-focused philosophy itself can be identified in many different historical contexts (e.g. see Nevett and Nevett). Several examples will also be seen in this book.

A traditional view in general history regards the concept of 'modern' time as part of the three or four divisions of the history of humanity; that is, ancient, medieval and modern time, or ancient, medieval, early modern and modern periods. Traditional historians of commerce adopt this view. Day ([1907] 1908) typically divided commerce into ancient, medieval and modern commerce, while Stephenson (1924) partitioned the history into the period of antiquity, the medieval period, the period of geographical discovery and invention, and modern times. Webster (1903) and Herrick (1917) applied the same basic approach with some revisions. As a current scholar, Fullerton (1988b) takes a similar view, insisting that 'modern Western marketing' developed with the progress of capitalism, from pre-capitalism (1300–1500 A.D.), via early (1500–1800 A.D.), and high (1800–1929), to recent capitalism (1930–present).

A crucial time in such long-term commerce or marketing is the period of the Industrial Revolution in Britain (*c.*1760–1825). Jefferys (1954) pointed out the delay in development of the distribution sector compared with the advance in manufacturing: the wholesale and retail trades in Britain still bore the characteristics of the pre-industrial system even by 1850 (p. 1). His view provoked a debate over the features of the distribution system, especially in terms of food distribution (see Scola 1975, Shaw 1985, 1992, also Alexander 1970). No matter how the general picture in the distribution sector was, however, pioneering entrepreneurs in modern marketing were identifiable at least in such cases as Josiah Wedgwood and Matthew Boulton (see McKendrick 1960, Robinson 1963, 1986, McKendrick, Brewer and Plumb 1982). Fullerton (1988b, p. 112, see also 1988a, pp. 78–83) insisted that 'demand-enhancing marketing' spread from the UK to other countries.

Identifying entrepreneurship in marketing is an important task in the historical study. The focal analysis of this book is how marketing management thought was generated on the basis of such entrepreneurship. In this regard, just as Pollard (1965) once sought to determine whether 'a management science or at least a management technology' (p. 250) had been achieved in the field of industrial management, it would be valuable to ascertain whether these were objectives at any time during the Industrial Revolution in Britain. Otherwise, it can hardly be confirmed whether or not there was an actual historical process in which the idea of 'demand-enhancing marketing' spread originally from Britain to the rest of the world. This book, however, does not examine the Industrial Revolution, but the other key historical factor, managerial capitalism, as the general environment that fostered the creation of the idea of marketing management rather than entrepreneurship in marketing itself. A discussion of the relationship between entrepreneurship, marketing management and managerial capitalism leads to the main theme and the fundamental view of this book.

Entrepreneurship and Marketing: The Basic Model to Analyse Development of Marketing Management Thought

Entrepreneurship, Marketing and Managerial Capitalism

The concept of the entrepreneur has been vigorously discussed in economic theory since the work by Richard Cantillon ([1755] 1959) in the eighteenth century (see Hébert and Link 1988, also Long 1983). Entrepreneurs may be regarded, for instance, as the person assuming the risk associated with uncertainty (Knight [1921] 1957), as an innovator creating disequilibrium (Schumpeter [1934] 1961), or as the person restoring equilibrium (Kirzner 1979).

It should be noted that in any theoretical standpoint, making marketing decisions is an essential function of entrepreneurship. Cantillon ([1755] 1959, chapter 13) originally discussed the distributive dimension of entrepreneurship as referring to 'the circulation and exchange of goods and merchandise ... at a risk'. Many years later, Schumpeter ([1934] 1961, p. 66) listed the famous five types of 'new combinations' carried out by entrepreneurs, and two of them – the 'introduction of a new good' and the 'opening of a new market' – are apparently functions that are also included in marketing, or synonymously in marketing management. Similarly, Cole (1946, p. 6) enumerated a half-dozen spheres of an entrepreneur's actions, and the 'development of a market for a product, and the devising of new products to meet or anticipate consumer demands' are related to the function of marketing or marketing management.

Thus, marketing is an essential function of entrepreneurship in its origin. As recent scholars put it, 'Market opportunity analysis, new product development, the diffusion of innovation, and marketing strategies to create growing firms are at the heart of both marketing and entrepreneurship' (Hills 1994, p. 7); '"[M]arketing behavior" and "entrepreneurial behavior" are similar in nature' in that 'they are both boundary spanning, involve extensive interplay with the environment, require the assumption of risk and uncertainty, and inevitably interface the complexity of human behavior with commercial and other endeavors' (Hills and LaForge 1992, p. 32). In this respect, it should only be natural that scholars discuss the 'marketing/entrepreneurship interface' (e.g. Hills and LaForge 1992, Gardner 1994).

This book explores the historical relationship between entrepreneurship and marketing management, simply called marketing above. The basic premise of this analysis is that the idea of marketing management was extracted from entrepreneurship and applied to routinized behaviour. In other words, entrepreneurship in marketing emerged first. It was the entrepreneurs who made marketing decisions based on hunches, inspirations, initiatives, skills and experience. By the term used in the field of knowledge management (see e.g. Nonaka 1994, Nonaka and Takeuchi 1995, Krogh, Nonaka and Nishiguchi 2000), the situation is described that knowledge on entrepreneurship in marketing was 'tacit' in this early phase. The tacit dimension of knowledge was originally referred to the advocacy by Michael Polanyi ([1966] 1983, p. 4), that is, 'we can know more than we can tell'. Tacit knowledge is thus defined as human knowledge that is not articulated and expressed in language. This kind of knowledge is embodied in a human action and embedded in a specific context surrounding the action, so that 'tacit knowing', or 'a way to know more than we can tell', is necessarily 'indwelling' (Polanyi [1966] 1983, pp. 17–18). As such, the method of such entrepreneurial decision making on marketing would be difficult to learn.

However, as capitalistic economies progressed, the need to develop such tacit knowledge into explicit knowledge also increased. A general driving force of this transformation is assumed to be managerial capitalism. In contrast to traditional and personal capitalism, managerial capitalism developed, in which 'salaried managers decided on investment strategy and allocated the resources for the future' (Chandler and Daems 1974, p. 32). It required capable salaried managers instead of owners, who in turn required specialized higher business education. Along with the progress of this type of capitalism, the movement towards collegiate education in commerce grew from the 1880s onwards (Marshall 1928a).[3] In the case of the USA, after the Wharton School of Finance and Economy started at the University of Pennsylvania in 1881, around 183 departments, schools, courses or divisions were organized in

---

3   The movement towards higher commercial education was not limited to the USA, but can also be identified in some European countries and Japan at the time (Marshall 1928a, Locke 1985, Sugiyama and Nishizawa 1988, Nishizawa 1988). For instance, in Germany, after the Handelshochschule (Higher School of Commerce) was founded in Leipzig in 1898, many new colleges were organized in quick succession (Fehling 1926, Locke 1985). In the UK, a B.Com. (Bachelor of Commerce) course started at the Faculty of Commerce of the University of Birmingham in 1902, and several other universities also initiated it (Smith 1928, Nishizawa 1987, Nishizawa 1988). And in Japan, the B.Com. also began to be given at the Higher Commercial College of Tokyo in 1901 (Nishizawa 1987).

Based on these organizations, initial efforts were made to produce marketing thought, as well as business management, in each country. In Germany, Johann Friedrich Schär (1846–1924) (1911) published a famous pioneering work, *Allgemeine Handelsbetriebslehre (General Theory for Commercial Business)*; in the UK, William James Ashley (1860–1927) (1908) advocated the 'Enlargement of Economics' towards 'Business Economics' or 'Science of Commerce' in his paper; and in Japan, Renkichi Uchiike (1876–1949) (1906) brought out the first systematic book on the science of commerce in that country, *Shogyogaku Gairon (The Introduction to Science of Commerce)*. These facts raise an interesting academic task in the comparative and historical study of marketing thought at the turn of the twentieth century. Although this is beyond the scope of this book, it can be pointed out that American society was likely more appropriate than other societies in terms of developing the managerial idea. In Germany, in his pioneering book, Schär (1911, pp. v and 74) amazingly insisted on the necessity of eliminating *Gewinnprinzip* (the principle of profit) from commercial theory in order to make the thought scientific, as well as the necessity of subordinating private enterprise under the functions of national economy. A similar sentiment was expressed in Japan when a headmaster of the so-called '*maedare-ha*' (working-apron group) who sought only 'selfish prosperity of individuals' was expelled from the Higher Commercial College of Tokyo, and nationalist-minded businessmen were respected in education (Usui 1995, pp. 157–8). Meanwhile in the UK, although some pioneering efforts were made for 'national efficiency' (Searle 1971, Brennan 1975), it has been indicated that there was a general reluctance to utilize the idea of scholarly training for business at the universities (Keeble 1992, p. 93, Nishizawa 1994, p. 353). The cultural environment in the USA likely allowed business theorists to develop their managerial thought more easily and form direct comparisons with other countries at the time.

universities and colleges by the start of 1925 (Marshall 1928b, pp. 3–4, see also Jones and Shaw 2002, pp. 51–3). The goal of this movement was clearly expressed by E.J. James (1901, pp. 156–7), an economist strongly influenced by the Younger German Historical School and the first director of the Wharton School (1883–96): 'I believe the American university ought to take the same attitude toward the higher training of the future merchant, railway or insurance manager, as it has so long taken toward the education of the future lawyer, physician or engineer'.

Under such circumstances, attempts were made to transform tacit knowledge on entrepreneurship in marketing into explicit knowledge for future professional managers. The result was the idea of marketing management, now simply called the idea of marketing. This book explores the detailed historical process of articulating the managerial idea of marketing. Before explaining the basic model of this book, another easily misunderstood issue should be cleared up: the synonymous usage of the ideas of marketing and of marketing management is fundamentally the one that prevailed after the Second World War. This was not the case before that.

The Historical Position of Managerial Thought in Marketing Discipline

It has been generally recognized that as far as the USA is concerned, large amounts of dedicated literature related to 'marketing' began to appear around the turn of the twentieth century, although some earlier contributions are recognizable such as *The Retailer's Manual* in 1869 uncovered by Hoagland and Lazer (1960, also Lazer 1979) and advertising books (Coolsen 1947, see also Jones and Shaw 2002, p. 51). The massive body of literature, however, was not simply limited to managerial issues, but also embraced wider economic and societal issues. In terms of the micro/macro dichotomy, where micro generally suggests the managerial discussion and macro is the socio-economic one in terms of the aggregation criterion (Hunt 1976, Hunt and Burnett 1982) and/or the perspective criterion (Shawver and Nickels 1978), the body of marketing literature before the Second World War was a mixture of the two (see also Shaw and Jones 2005). Therefore the term 'marketing', which was often interchangeable with 'distribution', did not always imply the managerial idea, and much less the idea of 4Ps.

Around the turn of the twentieth century, some empirical economists faithful to the *laissez faire* doctrine began to write dedicated marketing literature (Coolsen 1958, 1960). Almost at the same time, some students of R.T. Eli, who was strongly influenced by the Younger German Historical School and led the organization of the American Economic Association in 1885 (Eli 1886), began to discuss farm and industrial product marketing (Jones and Monieson 1990). Thus, discussion of economics-based marketing started. In these works, the managerial idea was not the main focus.

It is well known that there existed three classical approaches or schools from the early twentieth century to the Second World War; that is, the commodity, the institutional and the functional schools of marketing, as classified by C.S. Duncan (1922, pp. 7–8). These approaches were either basically macro-oriented or combined macro and micro discussions.

The commodity approach was defined as examining 'separately the marketing system for say wheat, cotton, coal, petroleum, meats, industrial machinery, telephone service, etc.' (Breyer 1931, p. 2). This discussion was basically macro, as the purpose was to explore the distribution structure or trade flow for the commodity concerned, which was on the aggregated level of an industry far beyond the individual marketing system of a firm, and/or because the discussion was made from the societal point of view. At the same time, however, the commodity approach embraced the famous classification of goods – into convenience, shopping and specialty goods – which will feature in later chapters of this book. This idea originated with Charles Coolidge Parlin (1872–1942) in 1912 (see Gardner 1945, Parlin [1914b] 1978, 1916) and was developed by Melvin Thomas Copeland (1884–1975) (1927). This discussion can be described as micro at least in terms of the perspective criterion, as it was made to prescribe a 'marketing recipe' (Sheth et al., 1988, pp. 36–7) for an individual company. Thus, 'commodity-based classification', which is at the heart of the commodity approach (Zinn and Johnson 1990), can provide in itself both bases of macro and micro discussions. In this sense, the commodity approach was conceived as a child of the debates concerning managerial topics.

The institutional approach 'leads to a consideration of the various types of middlemen or agencies engaged in the marketing of goods and services' (Converse 1930, p. 363) in order to identify what types of middlemen existed, what types of commodities they handled and how they operated. The discussion was primarily macro because the analysis was made on an aggregate level of middlemen beyond the level of an individual firm, and/or because its purpose was a study on a societal scale; for instance, '[t]heir operations may be criticised with a view to increasing their efficiency' for society (Converse 1930, p. 363). It is only natural, however, that knowledge provided by the institutional approach would become the basis of micro or managerial considerations, for example managerial discussions for a specific type of institution such as the retailer (e.g. Nystrom [1914] 1986a, [1917] 1986b). It also provided basic knowledge for selecting or eliminating some types of middlemen when manufacturers established their marketing channels. Therefore, as Duncan (1922, p. 6) indicated, the 'professional busness man' had to 'study not only the art and science of selling and buying, but also the whole mechanism of trade organization' in order to develop a 'broad, sound business policy'.

With respect to the functional approach, the story is slightly more complex, and has a direct relation to the exploration in this book. As Vanderblue (1921) stated, the functional study of marketing was started by Arch Wilkinson Shaw (1876–1962) (1912, p. 731, [1915] 1951, p. 76): he defined the 'functions of the middlemen' as: 1. sharing the risk, 2. transporting the goods, 3. financing the operation, 4. selling (or communication of ideas about the goods), and 5. assembling, assorting, and re-shipping. Then Louis Dwight Harvell Weld (1882–1946) (1917, p. 306) expanded it to the 'marketing functions', including 1. assembling, 2. storing, 3. assumption of risks, 4. financing, 5. rearrangement, 6. selling, and 7. transportation. These discussions were a mixture of macro and micro since the functions were assumed to be performed both by the whole distribution structure and by any individual marketers when some middlemen were selected or eliminated.

In the meantime, a different type of micro- or management-oriented discussion was introduced under the same heading of 'marketing functions'. In his list that enumerated 16 'functional categories' and 120 'functional elements', Ryan (1935) included 'administration of personnel' and 'general management and strategy'. These factors apparently belong to the so-called management functions, which should be distinguished from the original discussions on the middlemen or marketing functions that were performed in the distribution process or marketing channels. Nevertheless, historical discussions generally confounded these two different types of functions, or at least were unconcerned about these differences. It was the managerial functions that decisively affected the development of the managerial idea of marketing. Therefore, this book will focus on the birth and development of managerial functions in marketing.

En masse, classical marketing literature was a mixture of different kinds of discussions. The managerial idea always existed; Hunt and Goolsby (1988, p. 35) recognize that the managerial approach, in addition to the three traditional approaches, was a historical one in marketing. Nevertheless, this approach often intermingled with other types of discussions. This book will identify the 4Ps type of managerial knowledge among the traditional three approaches and various types of managerial discussions, and explore how it developed and what its basis was.

The Basic Model and the Structure of this Book

Figure I.1 shows the basic model to analyse both birth and development processes of the 4Ps type of managerial idea in marketing and the historical context that prompted its development.

The model assumes entrepreneurship in marketing emerged first, based on tacit knowledge acquired by personal inspiration and skills developed in individual situations. In response to increasing demand for knowledge for the future managers in managerial capitalism, theoretical pioneers began transforming some aspects of tacit entrepreneurship into explicit knowledge, usually based on the successful experiences of entrepreneurs in marketing. Thus, primitive knowledge on marketing management was articulated. This is shown as 'Process A' in Figure I.1. The process embraces two dimensions; that is, generalization and abstraction of successful activities by entrepreneurs so as to make the idea adaptable to different situations on the one hand, and decontextualization which extends the lessons beyond their original, actual contexts on the other hand.

At almost the same time, some managerial ideas and specialized knowledge originating outside the marketing world began to be introduced and adapted to make it much more systematic and scientific. This process is shown as 'Process B'. The process represents what is called the combination of different types of explicit knowledge in the field of knowledge management, and advances the two dimensions of generalization and decontextualization of the idea.

In the meantime, changing environments, such as business conditions, law and politics, features of society and consumer preferences, and the relationship between manufacturers and merchants called for new types of entrepreneurial decision-making and behaviour by marketers. In this process, some knowledge utilized in

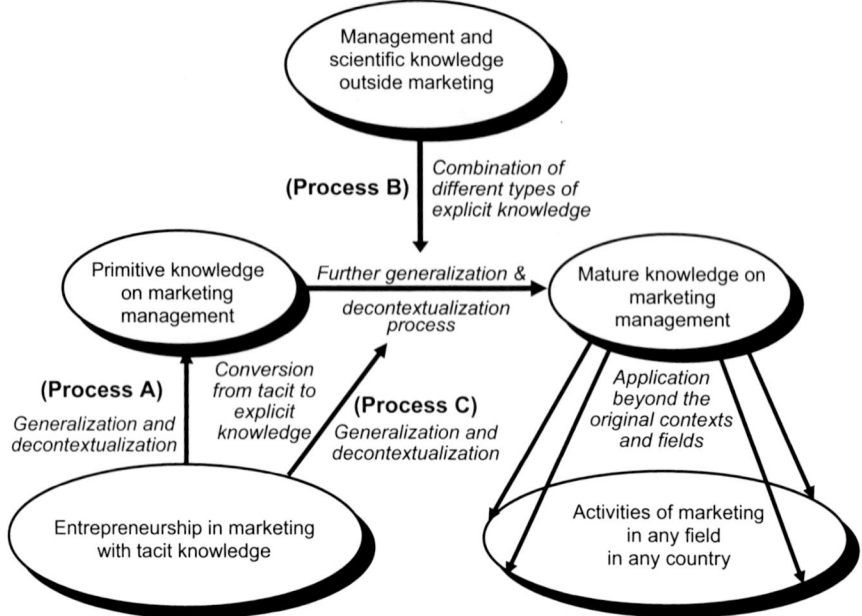

Figure I.1   Development model of explicit knowledge on marketing management

these new practices could be made explicit, and new content added to the existing explicit knowledge of primitive marketing management. This process completes the generalization of ideas that could be applicable in different situations, as well as decontextualization from their original situation. This is represented as 'Process C'. Thus, the idea could progress to its mature form.

Adopting the above model, this book explores how the explicit knowledge on the 4Ps type of marketing management developed from primitive roots to a mature form, based on the interrelationship between the idea and its historical context. The book is composed of six chapters, in addition to this introduction and the concluding chapter.

Chapter 1 deals with 'Process A' shown in the model, the generation of explicit but primitive knowledge based on entrepreneurial behaviours of marketers. The chapter throws special light on advocacy by Ralph Starr Butler of an early version of explicit knowledge on the 4Ps type of marketing management. His idea reflected and directly represented the actual and historical backgrounds. In this sense only, his idea should be called 'primitive'.

Chapters 2 and 3 address 'Process B', combining different types of explicit knowledge. Individual attempts are identifiable, such as combining psychological idea and advertising (e.g. Scott [1903] 1985, [1908] 1987), and statistical idea and market analysis (e.g. Shaw 1912, 1915, 1916). The movement to apply the idea of 'scientific management' raised by F.W. Taylor exerted the most important influence on development of the 4Ps concept, and this book will focus on this topic.

The attempts to apply scientific management to marketing can be recognized in the 1910s and 1920s (LaLonde and Morison 1967), but the contents were misleadingly varied. Therefore Chapter 2 will discuss, first of all, what the application of scientific management exactly means, identifying two types of application – the strict and the broad. Chapter 2 will consider the former type, that is, the idea proposed by Taylor's immediate disciples and Charles Wilson Hoyt, while Chapter 3 will analyse the latter case, including the work of Arch Wilkinson Shaw and Percival White, as typical historical examples. The concluding part of Chapter 3 provides an overview of the development of literature covering the whole 4Ps area in the period between the two world wars.

The last three chapters focus on 'Process C', by which new factors were added to the existing explicit knowledge based on development of entrepreneurial practices. These chapters are different from the preceding chapters in two ways. Firstly, the discussions focus on product policy in Chapters 4 and 5, and channel policy in Chapter 6, not on the whole area of the 4Ps. This is because these two policy areas can be considered as essential elements in the 4Ps. Among the four factors, Promotion is the subject of literature dedicated to sales force management and advertising; inclusion of factors other than Promotion is fundamental to identifying an idea as being of the 4Ps type. In contrast, Product, to which Price was sometimes historically combined, and Place (or channel) are essential in the 4Ps type of idea. These three chapters will explore in depth how the idea in these fields further developed on the basis of new practices emerging. Secondly, while earlier chapters explore in depth the ideas by well-known scholars in previous historical research, the latter three chapters include the literature that earlier researchers rarely focused on. As such, Chapter Four explores how the historically unique concept of 'sales engineering' and 'merchandising' arose as a function of product policy. Chapter 5 focuses on the so-called redesign movement in the 1930s, which added some new considerations to the concept of 'merchandising'. Chapter 6 provides an overview of the channel structure between the two world wars and identifies old and new features in channel discussions.

The whole process shown in Figure I.1 is the generation of mature, explicit marketing management knowledge, which is so influential that it becomes, consciously or unconsciously, synonymous with modern marketing or marketing itself. The whole process also reflects both dimensions of generalization and abstraction of the way of entrepreneurship in marketing, and decontextualization that loses the actual and unique contexts. The mature idea of marketing management is so well generalized, and decontextualized enough, that it appears applicable to any marketing activity for any occasion in any country.

Chapter 1

An Archetype of Marketing Management: Butler's Ideas and their Background

When massive amounts of literature related to marketing emerged in the USA around the turn of the twentieth century, managerial or micromarketing literature existed from the beginning. These included the works by Scott ([1903] 1985, [1908] 1987), Calkins and Holden ([1905] 1985), Hollingworth ([1913] 1985), Cherington ([1913] 2002), Casson ([1914] 2002) and Calkins (1915) in the field of advertising, Macbain et al. (1905), Hoyt (1913), Shively (1916) and Brisco (1916) on sales force management, Parlin (1914a, [1914b] 1978, 1916) on market research, and Nystrom ([1914] 1986a, 1915, [1917] 1986b), Fisk (1916) and Swinney (1917) on retail salesmanship and management. These works made an outstanding contribution to each specialized field, but did not necessarily articulate the 4Ps type of idea itself. There were only a few who substantially covered the whole area of the 4Ps and contributed to the fundamental framework of marketing management, particularly Butler (1911a, 1911b, 1914, 1917) and Shaw (1912, [1915] 1951, 1916). While Shaw's idea will be explored later in this book, this chapter sheds light on Butler's. It was Butler who explicitly articulated an archetype of the 4Ps idea. This chapter explores his management thinking and the historical background that encouraged him to formulate it.

Managerial Definition of Marketing and the Activities of the New Type of Manufacturer

Butler's Definition of 'Marketing'

The contribution by Butler was his definition of marketing. When marketing literature was emerging, the definition of this term was much more vague (see Lichtenthal and Beik 1984), as exemplified by the fact that many pioneers tended to use the term 'distribution' synonymously with 'marketing' (Coolsen 1958). Butler introduced a clear definition that was apparently management-oriented.

Butler's (1914, p. 1, 1917, p. 3) definition of marketing was the 'plan behind the campaign', suggesting that there were some important factors other than salesmanship and advertising to be included in sales campaigns. He wrote,

There is no name in general use to indicate those activities that are included in the complete campaign. The word "selling" properly includes everything that is done by the man who has anything to dispose of in a commercial way. In general practice, however, this word is quite frequently restricted in its meaning so that it applies only to personal salesmanship. In its stead the word "marketing" is gradually coming into popular use to apply generally to the distribution campaign. It is this word that we shall usually employ. *Marketing methods*, in a sense, are inclusive of everything that is done to influence sales. Ordinarily, however, the study of marketing methods excludes the consideration of the technique of advertising and technique of salesmanship, and includes only those sales considerations that are not concerned solely with one or the other of the two distinct ways of disposing of commodities (Butler 1914, p. 2, double quotations and italic are original).

What Butler recognized as the essential factors in the 'plan behind the campaign', or marketing, were the 'goods that are to be sold', the 'market for the goods' and the 'methods of reaching the desired market'. These are now called product policy, market research and channel policy. Butler (1914, p. 5, 1917, p. 25) called them 'trade factors' or the 'cogs in the machinery of marketing', which were to be studied 'prior to the actual selling campaign'. The inclusion of product policy and channel policy, as well as market research, as part of the 'plan behind the campaign' was essential in the 4Ps type of idea and distinguished it from sales management or sales force management. Although his treatment of pricing policy was initially weak, Butler (1917, p. 228; see Butler and Swinney 1918, p. 164) later began to recognize it as an important step in the planning of a campaign.

Bartels (1962, p. 213) indicated that these ideas shaped an early version of the 'marketing mix'. While this comment hits the point, another evaluation would be possible: Butler advocated the separation of the planning function from implementation not merely in personal selling or advertising, but in marketing activities as a whole. It is natural to say that even though the function of planning was not clearly separated, any planning activities were always carried out by someone, usually the owner of the business and/or high ranked officers. In this case, however, the planning was based on implicit knowledge embodied in entrepreneurs and embedded in the contexts. The appropriate division of labour in management and the factors that should be considered in planning were very vague. Against such old-fashioned planning, Butler's advocacy marked the first steps in establishing a rational approach to decision making in marketing. As a genealogy of marketing management thought, Butler's definition was the first suggestion of the management process in marketing, which was to evolve via White as will be seen in Chapter 3, toward the so-called 'analysis, planning, implementation and control paradigm' (Brown 2001, p. 465). The paradigm is widely utilized in current marketing textbooks, as typically exemplified by Kotler (1997, 2000, 2003) and Kotler and Keller (2006). The factors of 4Ps are now essential components of the planning function in marketing.

The Integrated Manufacturer as the Context

The remarkable definition introducing separation of planning from implementation in marketing was generated from Butler's experiences at the Procter and Gamble Company (P&G). He wrote in his memoirs that when he went to Cincinnati to serve as an assistant to the eastern sales manager of P&G, he had his first experience in the field that he later called 'marketing'.

> My experience with the Procter and Gamble Company had convinced me that a manufacturer seeking to market a product had to consider and solve a large number of problems before he ever gave expression to the selling idea by sending a salesman on the road or inserting an advertisement in a publication (Butler's reply to Bartels in Bartels 1962, p. 225).

His memoirs show the experience at P&G had a direct influence on the development of his ideas.

Butler also stated in his books (1914, p. 149, 1917, p. 228) that his discussion was made 'primarily from the manufacturer's standpoint'. This was because he believed that the manufacturer had 'a more complex selling problem to solve' than the retailer or the jobber (Butler 1911b, p. 305; see Butler 1911a, p. 19). In addition, Butler emphasized (1914, p. 150; 1917, p. 229) the importance of watching the timing when 'the manufacturer' was about to start business because it was the logical time for a complete analysis. In his later book, Butler even went to the extreme that the only discussion from a manufacturer's point of view should be considered under the heading of 'marketing', whereas discussions about wholesalers and retailers should fall under the heading of 'merchandising' (Butler and Swinney 1918, p. v).

Thus, adherence to the manufacturer's standpoint was consistent in Butler. As will be seen below, his discussion on product policy or 'the goods that are to be sold' and channel policy or 'the methods of reaching the desired market' was apparently formulated as manufacturer's marketing policy. From the current perspective in marketing, it is easy to discard this view as too narrow and myopic. Nevertheless, this book makes the assertion that it was such a narrow and limited view that enabled Butler to develop his ideas on marketing management. Generally speaking, it would be natural to suppose that product policy, including strategies such as new product development and national brands, and channel policy for selecting merchants for marketing channels, was originally a manufacturer's issue.

It should be remembered that from the late nineteenth century onwards a new type of manufacturer, including companies such as P&G, which launched their own marketing initiatives, was emerging. As revealed by business historians (Chandler 1962, 1977, Porter and Livesay 1971), these manufacturers vertically integrated their mass production with mass distribution by setting up their own sales offices or branches. This new tendency was recognized by Butler's contemporaries. Jones (1905, p. 1) described 'the tendency of American manufacturing concerns to take up a variety of mercantile functions, by means of which they are increasing their dominance in the domestic market'. Shaw's (1912, p. 727, [1915] 1951, p. 71) concept of 'merchant-producer', as Chapter 3 illustrates, represented the same tendency. Thus, citing the words of Porter and Livesay (1971, pp. 12 and 228), one can say that the 'marketing revolution occurred between the mid-1890 and World War I', at which time 'the end of [wholesale] merchant's dominance and the beginning of the manufacturer's predominance' became 'the new order in American marketing', in that 'the manufacturer of goods had also become their distributor' in many industries. This was the fundamental context producing Butler's managerial definition of marketing.

The First Idea of Product Development and the Experience of Crisco by P&G

Introduction of Crisco to Market

To establish the managerial idea of marketing it was essential to embrace the function of product policy, distinguishing it from sales management. From the current perspective, it is only natural to classify product policy as a part of marketing management. However, this was not so easily defined since product policy is also a function in production. A feature to bridge production and distribution is essential in product policy, and it was continually discussed during the period between the two world wars, as will be seen later. The discussion by Butler was the very first step. It was a simple abstract from his experience with manufacturers, especially P&G.

The history of P&G, established in Cincinnati in 1832, is well documented, in particular regarding the 1879 development of its floating soap, 'Ivory' (Procter & Gamble 1944, pp. 10–11, Lief 1958, pp. 3–13, Editors of Advertising Age 1988, pp. 9–10). P&G launched nationwide marketing and became a listed company in 1890. When Butler was involved in the company, between 1907 and 1910, P&G was growing into a large-sized enterprise. This reflected the trend towards the increasing dominance of large-sized manufacturers evident in the soap industry at the time. If we define large-scale producers (manufacturing establishments) as those with an output of more than one million dollars worth of soap a year, in 1904 there were only 13, or 3.0 per cent of commercial soap manufacturers, who produced a total of 38 million dollars worth of all soap, or 55.9 per cent (Department of Commerce 1913, p. 670). By 1919, this rose to 36, or 10.3 per cent of commercial soap manufacturers, who were large-sized establishments and who produced a total of 280 million dollars worth of all soap, or 88.5 per cent (Department of Commerce 1923, p. 769). Such dominance of the large manufacturers, however, did not mean a reduction in competition. On the contrary, competition in this industry remained keen and vigorous, not only from traditional soap manufacturers such as Colgate and Co., B.T. Babbit, Inc., N.K. Fairbanks and Co., and D.S. Brown and Co. (Colgate 1968, p. 426), but also from some large-sized manufacturers from other industries who could produce soap as a by-product. These companies included Swift and Co. and Armour and Co., the dominant manufacturers in the meatpacking industry, and American Cotton Oil Co., one of the trusts consolidated in the 1880s. The census described 'a very large quantity of soap' made by establishments engaged in slaughtering and meatpacking and in the manufacture of grease and tallow, cotton oil seeds, and other oil-related products (Department of Commerce and Labor 1907, p. clxxvii, Department of Commerce 1913, p. 667). Facing such fierce competition, P&G began to adopt a diversification policy, which naturally led the company to enter unfamiliar markets with development of a new product. This was the strategy in place when Butler joined the company.

The story of Crisco attracted a great deal of attention among contemporary researchers as a successful case of P&G entering the food market. This case also had a strong impact on Butler's perspective. P&G established one of the earliest industrial research laboratories in the USA and brought in a UK chemist, a patentee of the process whereby liquid oil could be converted into a solid fat by addition of hydrogen. The company launched a commercial hydrogenation plant in 1909 and introduced the first all-hydrogenated pure vegetable shortening, branded Crisco, in 1911 (*Printers' Ink* 1916, p. 73, Procter and Gamble 1944, pp. 14–19, Haynes 1949, p. 344; Lief 1958, pp. 103–5). The process was accompanied by ingenious marketing activities.

When P&G was about to introduce Crisco, they recognized that there was a strong reluctance among consumers in many places to use any substitute for natural lard as a cooking-fat (*Printers' Ink* 1916, p. 78). Some shortening manufacturers had mixed shortening with cottonseed oil and oleostearin because of the high price of lard, but the final products, called 'lard compounds', left much to be desired in flavour and colour and storage quality (Haynes 1949, p. 344). P&G had to tackle two problems: to change the cooking habits of America's women who 'were wedded to the use of lard', and to show their new product was different from anything else (Lief 1958, pp. 106–7). In order to solve these problems, they did much more than elaborating the brand name and the style of the straight-side tin container to differentiate it from all other lard compounds (*Printers' Ink* 1916, pp. 73–4, Lief 1958, pp. 105–6). They also established an experimental bakery and created recipes using Crisco and inaugurated week-long cooking schools in large hired halls in many cities, at which well-known lecturers on domestic science used Crisco, without making explicit commercial reference to it, in their performances, providing the audience with positive impressions of the product (*Printers' Ink* 1916, p. 74, Lief 1958, p. 107). In combination with these activities, P&G carried out sophisticated advertising campaigns, and dispatched retail-store demonstrators and house-to-house canvassers (Hoyt 1913, pp. 171–2, *Printers' Ink* 1916, p. 74). The Crisco marketing campaign was thorough, artificially planned and one of the most outstanding campaigns of its day. Recently, Strasser (1989, pp. 7–8 and 14) considered that although the famous marketing of Ivory Soap could hardly be called a 'campaign' as it lacked a careful design of procedure, the marketing of Crisco looked 'strictly modern'.

The Concept of 'Making the Product Sure' in Product Policy

As part of the 'plan behind the campaign', or marketing strategy, Butler (1914, pp. 161–2; see 1917 pp. 241–2) enumerated many factors in his discussion of the 'goods that are to be sold' or product policy. These included the choice of product, manufacturing conditions, business capital, product name, trademark, packaging, selling points and demand. Butler did not fully organize these points and offered only rather primitive descriptions with some simple references to actual cases. Among them, however, the concept of 'making the product sure' is worthy of additional attention. The idea was a direct outcome of his experience with the Crisco campaign.

> First there should be a technical test to prove the product is right. Before Crisco was put on the market, the manufacturers experimented for years to get it exactly right. Literally, hundreds of times the company thought that the product was ready for the market, only to find that after exhaustive tests had been made some changes were still necessary (Butler 1914, p. 151; see Butler 1917, pp. 229–30).

[Crisco] was given a series of tests lasting over a period of two years before it was accepted as a saleable product. During this time it was tried out in chemical laboratories, cooking schools, private homes in different sections of the country, restaurants and many other places. Many changes were made in its composition as a result of the experience (Butler and Swinney 1918, p. 27).

Thus, 'making the product sure' meant the efforts to improve the 'technical' quality of a new product to fit the consumers' preferences before fully introducing it to a market. Although the discussion was simple and neglected the relationship between production and marketing, his remark was just the first step to show that product policy as part of marketing management should include consideration of product development. The discussion of the production–marketing relationship progressed between the two world wars.

Defining the Channel Options: Conflicts and Cooperation between the Manufacturer and the Merchant

The Declining Importance of Middlemen

The inclusion of channel policy, or what Butler called the 'method to reach to the desirable market' or 'the analysis of the various trade channels and the selection of the right way to reach his chosen market' (Butler 1914, p. 179; see Butler 1917, p. 263), was another essential feature of marketing management. While Bucklin (1966, p. 2) considers that Butler's discussion was the first serious effort to define the marketing channel, his historical contribution to this discussion was also remarkable.

The discussion on channel can be recognized as Butler's original interest, as his earlier books delved into this issue, although neither his outstanding definition of marketing nor the discussion on product had yet appeared (Butler 1911a, 1911b). In these books Butler emphasized the 'declining importance of middlemen' (Butler 1911a, [p. 27], 1911b, p. 314).

Recent years have witnessed many changes in manufacturers' selling method. The number of manufacturers who are leaving the middleman entirely out of their schemes of distribution is constantly increasing. ... [M]any manufacturers have abandoned the policy of relying exclusively upon the wholesale merchant for the distribution of their products. They are seeking more and more to find a direct market among the retail trade (Butler 1911b, p. 314).

This tendency was apparently the result of the new type of manufacturer who engaged in marketing by setting up his own sales offices or branches. At almost the same time, Shaw (1912, p. 728; see Shaw [1915] 1951, p. 72) identified the same tendency: 'recent years have shown a growing tendency to decrease the number of successive steps in distribution'.

However, the intervention in the distribution process by these manufacturers did not progress trouble-free: it was accompanied by many conflicts with both traditional and innovative merchants. The traditional merchants were supposed to assume the distribution functions legitimately, whereas the innovative retailers often competed vertically or sometimes came into conflict with the manufacturers. Butler recognized the issue of channel selection as 'the hardest part' (Butler 1914, p. 179) because of the existence of 'trade relations', which meant 'the complicated relations that modern marketing has developed among various factors in trade' (Butler 1914, p. 2) or the relations that 'the producer establishes with the jobber, the retailer and the consumer' (Butler 1919, p. 25). Among Butler's discussions of 'the complicated relation' between manufacturers and merchants, four topics deserve to be explored here to understand the historical contexts that encouraged him to articulate the issue of channel selection: (1) the problems of chain stores, (2) resale price maintenance, (3) private brands and (4) the concept of a 'real merchant'.

The Chain Store Problem: an Ambiguous View by the Manufacturer

A serious conflict was caused by the emergence of the chain store retail format. As is well known, following the development of department stores and mail order houses from the late nineteenth century to the early twentieth century, the chain store began to boom as a new retail format in the 1910s, especially after the launch of the 'Economy Store' by Great Atlantic & Pacific Tea Company (e.g. see Tedlow 1990, pp. 191–3).

Table 1.1 shows the list of chain stores with more than fifty outlets, based on the 1914 investigation by *Printers' Ink*, a leading weekly journal in the advertising world. There are a few distinct categories recognizable in this table. One is the co-operative chains such as 'Rexall' stores affiliated with the United Drug Company and the stock-holding stores of the American Druggist Syndicate (Hurd and Zimmerman 1914a, p. 3). Another group was the manufacturers' own retail chains, essentially subsidiaries or branches of the manufacturer, including the United Cigar Stores Company (Poor's Manual 1910, Porter and Livesay 1971, p. 210), and branches of Burroughs Adding Machine Company and of the Underwood and Remington Typewriter Companies (Hurd and Zimmerman 1914f, pp. 64 and 66). However, the bulk of the chain stores were independent retailers, which included the grocers. Along with tobacco chain stores, these were the 'four important fields' in this category (Hurd and Zimmerman 1914d, pp. 36–7).

The rapid growth of these chain stores, especially of the independent type, created a sensation and caused many disputes in the marketing world. From the point of view of national advertisers – who were in essence the manufacturers that launched marketing to distribute their branded products nationally – the rapid growth of independent chain stores represented a 'menace' (Fieux 1913). Many grew rapidly and resorted to price cutting of the national brands advertised by the manufacturers and/or providing substitutes for the national brands with so-called private brands. A series of articles in *Printers' Ink* focused on chain stores and defined them as 'a new and formidable power in business', emphasizing 'Unusual ability, no doubt, from the start; from that to system and standardization; thence to direct buying in quantity, and special discounts; then on to price-cutting and the promotion of private brands – these are the undisputed means and methods of the majority of them' (Hurd and Zimmerman 1914a, p. 4). There were some companies which refused to sell

Table 1.1   Chain stores with more than 50 stores reported by *Printers' Ink* (1914)

Grocery Chains	*Stores*
Great Atlantic & Pacific Tea Co. (Jersey City)	... 807
Acme Tea Co. (Philadelphia)	... 315
James Butler Grocery Co. (New York)	... 238
Child & Co. (Camden, N.J.)	... 230
Grand Union Tea Co. (Brooklyn)	... 200
Kroger Grocery & Baking Co. (Cincinnati)	... 182
M. O'Keefe, Inc. (Gardner, MA)	... 146
Wm. Butler (Philadelphia)	... 140
Bell Co. (Philadelphia)	... 130
Robinson & Crawford (Philadelphia)	... 130
National Grocery Co. (Jersey City)	... 126
Direct Importing Co., Inc. (Boston)	... 125
Thos. Roulston (Brooklyn)	... 121
John T. Conner Co. (Boston)	... 110
G.M. Dunlop Co. (Philadelphia)	... 106
Valley Supply Co. (Pittsburgh)	 65
Union Supply Co. (Pittsburgh)	 63
Voss Grocery & Co. (Cincinnati)	 62
C.F. Smith & Co. (Detroit)	 61
Federal Supply & Co. (Pittsburgh)	 57
James Vandyke & Co.	 55
S.K. Ames (Boston)	 55
Daniel Reeves, Inc. (New York)	 52
Mohican Co. (New York)	 50

Drug Chains	*Stores*
Riker-Hegeman Corporation (New York)	... 105
Lois K. Liggett Co. (Boston)	 52
American Druggists' Syndicate (New York) (retailers' co-operative manufacturing and jobbing corporation)	...about 16,000
United Drug Company (Boston) (retailers' co-operative manufacturing and jobbing corporation)	...about 5,000
Philadelphia Wholesale Drug Co. (retailers co-operative jobbing house)	...about 550

Cigar-store Chains	*Stores*
United Cigar Stores Company (New York)	...over 1,000

5, 10, 25-cent-store Chains	*Stores*
F.W. Woolworth Company (New York)	... 774
S.H. Kress Company (new York) and S.H. Kress & Co. (Texas)	... 147
S.S. Kresge Company (Detroit)	... 124
L.G. McCrory Company (New York)	... 115

Restaurant Chains	*Stores*
Baltimore Dairy Lunch (New York)	... 140
John R. Thompson Co. (Chicago)	 81
Waldorf Lunch (Boston)	 55
Fred Harvey (Topeka, Kan.)	 55

Drug and Department Stores	*Stores*
J.C. Penney Co. Inc. (New York) (formerly Golden Rule Stores)	 71

Men's Clothing Chains	*Stores*
Scotch Woollen Mills (Davenport, Ia.)	... 117
Gateley's Credit Clothing Co. (St. Louis)	... 115

Boot and Shoe Field	*Stores*
R.H. Long (Waldorf) (Framingham, Mass)	 82
W.L. Douglas Shoes Co. (Brockton, Mass)	 79
Hanover Shoe Co. (New York)	 52

Oil and Gasoline	*Stores*
Standard Oil service station (New York)	...over 600

(There are probably four or five such groups, with 2,000 stations in all.)

In Dairy Field	*Stores*
Sheffield Farms-Slawson-Decker Co. (New York)	 83
Borden Condensed Milk Co. (New York)	 77

Chain of Coal Stores	*Stores*
Consumer's Co. (Chicago)	 96

Theatrical Chains	*Theaters*
John A. Cort (New York)	 92
Marcus Loew (New York)	 69

News Stands, etc.	*Stands*
Union News, Co. (New York)	... 900
Ward & Gow (New York)	... 125

Hardware Fields	*Stores*
Singer Sewing Machine Co. (Jersey City)	...1,600
(800 are run directly by the company)	*Districts*
National Cash Register (Dayton, Ohio)	some 500
	Branches
Burroughs Adding Machine Co. (Detroit)	... 125
Underwood Typewriter Co. (New York)	... 220
Remington Typewriter Co. (New York)	... 200

Motor Truck	*Branches*
International Harvester Company of America (Chicago)	 88

Automobile Supply	*Stores*
H.W. Johns-Manville Co. (New York)	 58
B.F. Goodrich Co. (Akron, Ohio)	 58
Diamond Rubber Co. (Akron, Ohio)	 57

their branded products to the chain stores, such as Kellogg Toasted Corn Flake Co. (Collins 1910, Kellogg 1911, [*Printers' Ink*] 1914e, Hurd and Zimmerman 1914b, p. 63, Lebhar 1959, p. 112). Butler shared this concern:

> The manufacturer perforce must take a keen interest in the development of chain stores. If he is a national advertiser he often looks on the chains with distrust and suspicion. So many chains have built business on the basis of cut prices, particularly on nationally advertised goods, that the manufacturer often considers them a menace. Furthermore, the common practice of chains of putting out and pushing their own brands of package goods means a decreasing market for the advertised goods with which the private brands are in competition. Again, some manufacturers often insist on prices lower than those that independents will pay (Butler 1917, p. 105).

Nevertheless, there was not always friction in the relationship between the manufacturer and the chain store. It was undeniable that the rapid spread of chain stores provided a great opportunity to expand the sales possibilities for national brands that were engaging in mass production. Therefore, some manufacturers with enormous production capacity and who were looking for competent retailers looked favourably upon the opportunity to sell through the chain stores as well. The discussion of chain stores by *Printers' Ink* was not always critical; it also expressed the view that not every chain was a 'menace' (Hurt and Zimmerman 1914e, p. 38). '[W]e have "good and bad" chains, just as we are said to have good and bad trusts' (Hurt and Zimmerman 1914b, p. 68). The focal point of blame was the so-called 'bad methods', that is, price cutting of national brands and pushing private brands to consumers. Again, Butler shared this view.

> On the other hand, the chains unquestionably provide a tremendous outlet for an enormous variety of manufactured products. ... Thousands of manufacturers find in the chain quick, sure and profitable markets for their products; and, because of their size and their great influence in merchandising, the chains are bound to be carefully considered as possible channels of distribution by every manufacturer who has anything to market that the chains will handle (Butler 1917, pp. 105–6).

Therefore, the attitude of the national brand manufacturers was ambiguous. Current thinking on marketing channel would assume that this problem and the ambiguous standpoint of manufacturers must have been the basis of the theory of power and conflict in channels. Nevertheless, the idea of power/conflict relationships was introduced to marketing literature only after the managerial idea became mature, especially from the end of the 1960s as will be discussed in the end of Chapter 6. In its early phase of the managerial idea on channels, this ambiguity only raised a question for the manufacturer: whether or not to sell to the chain store as one of the marketing channels.

Resale Price Maintenance to Protect 'Goodwill'

While the so-called big businesses grew rapidly from the late nineteenth century onwards, there was strong public opinion against 'monopolies' in the USA, resulting in the first anti-trust law, the Sherman Act, in 1890. Although the first section of this

Act did not directly refer to the term resale price maintenance (RPM) (Murchison 1919, p. 156), it was used in practice as a basis for defining RPM in inter-state trade as unlawful (e.g. Cammelgaard 1958, p. 31, Matsushita 1982, p. 197). RPM was called 'the biggest issue of the mercantile world' (Collins 1910, p. 3) and supporters and critics debated vigorously.

Many traditional merchants, threatened by the aggressive price-cutting of the new-format retailers, were eager supporters of price maintenance or the 'one price policy'. Many manufacturers who were selling their branded products nationally were also keen to maintain the resale price. As mentioned above, Kellogg refused to sell their products to the chain stores in order to support RPM. The American Fair Trade League was organized in 1913 to protect the sales prices and profits of small retailers (Federal Trade Commission 1945, Nakano 1975, p. 150) and shortly thereafter submitted a bill to legalize RPM, which many manufacturers supported (*Printers' Ink* 1914a). In 1912 the Association of National Advertising Managers (ANAM), whose membership base covered over 200 firms including some of the largest in the nation, distributed a questionnaire (*Printers' Ink* 1912a, b, c, d). Among the 97 companies responding on whether they regulated prices of their goods throughout the country, about 60 per cent did so, about 7 per cent did so only by establishing a minimum price at which their goods could be sold, and 33 per cent did not (*Printers' Ink* 1912a, p. 73).

Nonetheless, some firms and organizations were not in favour of RPM. Famously, department stores like Macy's and the National Retail Dry Goods Association were strongly opposed to it (*Printers' Ink* 1910, *Printers' Ink* 1915). The National Trade Association was formed in 1915 in order to oppose RPM (Federal Trade Commission 1945, Nakano 1975, pp. 150–51).

Generally speaking, the legal status of RPM was becoming more and more tenuous. Under a political movement called Progressivism, the Federal Government attacked vertical price maintenance policies ([*Printers' Ink*] 1913a). Some judicial decisions by the US Supreme Court against RPM exerted a strong influence on the business world (*Printers' Ink* 1913b). These judgements included the case of Dr Miles Medical Co. *v.* Park & Sons Co. in 1911, in which the contracts for RPM were judged to be *per se* illegal in terms of the Sherman Act (*Printers' Ink* 1913c, p. 72, Murchison 1919, pp. 188–91, Neal 1960, pp. 340–42, Hollander 1966, p. 68, Matsushita 1982, pp. 197–8), and the case of Bauer *v.* O'Donnell (the Sanatogen Case) in 1913 where it was decided that the manufacturer of patented goods could not fix the price of his goods by notice ([*Printers' Ink*] 1913c, p. 72, Murchison 1919, pp. 167–70). The severe legal constraints on RPM continued until the 1930s, when 44 states passed resale price maintenance acts and the Miller-Tydings Amendment (1937) to the Sherman Act was passed to allow price maintenance at the federal level (Palamountain 1955, pp. 235–6).

Such contradictory conditions of RPM exerted a strong influence on the decisions on channel selection by manufacturers. An example was P&G. They originally bound wholesalers to sell at the list prices to retailers, and refused to sell to any wholesaler who cut prices. After the Supreme Court condemned RPM, however, many wholesale grocers, especially in New York, engaged in cutting prices. Therefore, P&G decided to adopt the direct-to-retailer channel in New York in 1913, although they were hesitant at first to try out direct selling in a wider area (Lief 1958, pp. 117–18, Editors of Advertising Age 1988, pp. 16–7). Nevertheless, while P&G was accused of price maintenance by the Federal Trade Commission in 1918 (*Printers' Ink* 1918), the direct-to-retailer channel continued to expand, overcoming boycotts by some wholesale grocers (Editors of Advertising Age 1988, pp. 17 and 40).

Butler's view concerning RPM was clearly from the manufacturer's standpoint. He pointed out that price cutting itself was nothing new, but that this practice increased with the advent of national advertising. 'If an article is widely advertised, universally known, and in constant demand, some retailers believe it good policy to offer it at an unusually low price in order to get people into the store and to create the impression of a general low level of prices' (Butler 1914, pp. 197–8; see Butler 1917, p. 294). So the problem of price maintenance is one of protecting 'goodwill', that is the 'favourable attitude of the public' towards the brand concerned. '[G]oodwill is often the manufacturer's or the dealer's most valuable asset. Goodwill is not easily built, and it is very easily destroyed. Accordingly the protection of goodwill, acquired slowly or expensively, is one of the most important problems in marketing. For the manufacturer this problem is largely one of price maintenance' (Butler 1914, p. 196; see Butler 1917, p. 293). One can hear similar sentiments nowadays when discussing brand equity.

A Ubiquitous Problem of Private Brands

Private brands or the 'substitutes' for the national brands were everywhere in Butler's time. The ANAM questionnaire in 1912 reported 95 members responding to the question, 'Have you had any trouble through substitutions?': about 25 per cent of companies reported 'much', about 6 per cent 'some', while about 8 per cent responded 'little' and about 31 per cent, including the automobile trade, reported 'no substitution' (*Printers' Ink* 1912a, p. 73).

While the chain store has been well known as the cause of the private brand problem historically, other retail formats such as department stores, mail order houses and some specialty stores also actively utilized private labels (see for example Barney 1910, *Printers' Ink* 1914b, Anderson 1917). A seriously disputed dimension of private brands was the problem of the loss leader. Some aggressive retailers were often condemned for using nationally advertised goods only as 'leaders' and paying their clerks premiums to switch customers to private brands or 'long-shot' goods when the customers asked for an advertised brand (Hurd and Zimmerman 1914e, p. 41). Butler indicated the same problem existed with mail order houses (Butler 1914, pp. 79–80) and chain stores (Butler 1917, p. 94).

The dispute covered some wholesalers and jobbers as well. The jobbers who sold private brands to retailers were called 'manufacturing jobbers'. Some actually established factories for their own branded products, and others utilized independent manufacturers, who were often called 'private-brand manufacturers' (Savage 1914). Still other jobbers bought various products without labels and attached their own labels at their warehouses. Whilst some large-sized jobbers used local and national advertisements, the majority of jobbers and manufacturers did not advertise their products directly to consumers (Barney 1910, p. 10, Butler 1914, pp. 132–3, 1917, pp. 190–91). There was a dispute in the marketing world between the critics of private-brand jobbers and manufacturers (e.g. Barney 1910, Simpson 1911) and their supporters (e.g. Brown 1910, Anderson 1917).

Butler always supported the 'advertising manufacturers' who essentially engaged in national advertising for their national brands. Butler (1914, p. 131, 1917, pp. 187–8) explained, 'There is no private brand problem as long as the jobber puts his own label only on the kinds of goods that are not generally branded and advertised by the manufacturers', because this kind of practice brought no conflict with manufacturers. 'The problem arises when the jobber comes into direct conflict with the advertising manufacturer by putting his own brand on the same kind of goods that are branded by the manufacturer'.

The Concept of a 'Real Merchant': an Obstacle

As national advertising of national brands by the manufacturers prevailed, so traditional retailers became bewildered or antagonistic towards national advertising and nationally advertised products. Butler wrote:

> Some merchants believe, or say, that advertised goods are really sold by the manufacturer, the dealer acting merely as a slot-machine; therefore, to the extent that dealer refuses to handle such goods he becomes a real merchant, an independent business man, and not a mere machine, a mechanical distributor of goods which he stocks and sells only because the manufacturer creates a consumer demand for them (Butler 1917, pp. 152–3; see Butler 1914, p. 101).

Interestingly, Charles Coolidge Parlin, a famous pioneer of market research who worked as head of market research organization at the Curtis Publishing Company, dealt with the same issue in his speech at the Associated Advertising Club of the World. Parlin (1916, p. 99) indicated, 'A dealer sometimes says: "If I handle advertised lines I become only a slot-machine. I am not a real merchant at all."' This speech offers supporting evidence that the concept of a 'real merchant' was not unique to Butler, but was shared by many traditional merchants at the time. Their complaint is understandable because the legitimate freedom of assorting the products at their stores began to be undermined at that time as a result of the so-called pre-selling effect of national advertising on the mind of consumers. It was only natural that many traditional merchants felt they were being forced to supply the advertised national brands.

From the manufacturer's point of view, however, a concept such as a 'real merchant' was unfavourable. Parlin continued from the above citation:

> That man has misunderstood the definition of merchant. He thinks that a merchant is a student of merchandise who should judge and determine what his community should buy. But if he looks up the definition of a merchant he will find that a merchant is a man who buys and sells – not a student of merchandise, but a *student of human wants* (Parlin 1916, p. 99, italic from the original).

The recommendation of studying not merchandise but human wants sounds in line with the modern philosophy of marketing, although this speech implied that the traditional merchants had to cooperate with the manufacturers and supply the national brands that consumers demanded as a result of national advertising.

Butler took the same view as Parlin. He admitted that the complaint by the merchants contained 'a germ of truth' since each merchant tried to build up individuality and personality in his business wherever possible, but this was 'untenable'. 'In a certain sense, every retail dealer and every other kind of middleman is a machine; at least he is part of the machinery of marketing. Yet no retailing can be machine-like. Irrespective of the kind of goods carried, every successful storekeeper is a real merchant' (Butler 1917, p. 153; see Butler 1914, p. 101).

The concept of a 'real merchant' was, in a sense, nostalgia for the good old days of traditional merchants, but had to be overcome to establish cooperation with the manufacturers now vertical marketing activities were becoming the norm.

Channel Selection as Discussed by Butler

In these conflicting contexts, Butler produced the concept of channel selection purely from the manufacturer's point of view. In his earlier books, Butler had included possible options for the manufacturer to reach the desired market by comparing advantages and disadvantages. He developed these ideas in his later books, as shown in Table 1.2. Butler emphasized:

> The possible combinations of trade channels are almost numberless. Whether a manufacturer is to sell through one or more channels, whether he is to use salesmen or the mails or both, depends partly on custom in the trade, partly on the nature of this product, and partly on his ability to see new methods of marketing, to overcome tradition, and to adapt to his own use all marketing plans that appeal to him as offering new opportunities for the sales of his goods (Butler 1914, p. 181. See 1916, p. 165).

It should be noted that the table substantially embraced all three essential criteria for selecting the channels, that is, long-or-short, wide-or-narrow, and open-or-closed (Furo 1968).

The long-or-short criterion represents how many steps exist between the manufacturer and the consumer. Butler drew his table primarily based on this criterion; the heading A was the shortest, D the opposite. This classification is still the core of channel selection thought in current marketing management textbooks. Butler (1914, p. 182, 1917, pp. 265–6) indicated that the shortest channel enabled the manufacturer to have 'absolute control of his market' and 'no problem of price-cutting, substitution, or lack of dealer cooperation', as well as to have exact data on his goods, although opposed to these advantages, the manufacturer must have faced 'the greatest expense of direct selling' and 'the antagonism of dealers' at the same time.

Table 1.2   Possible trade channels suggested by Butler

A. Manufacturer direct to consumers.

    1. Through solicitors or canvassers.

    2. By mail.

    3. Through the manufacturer's own retail stores, usually conducted on the chain store principles.

B. Manufacturer direct to retailers.
He may reach the retailers either through salesmen or by mail.

    1. He may deal with one or more of these kinds of retailers:

        a. Country general stores.

        b. Specialty Stores.

        c. Department Stores.

        d. Chain Stores not owned by the manufacturer.

        e. Mail-order houses.

        f. Cooperative buying organizations or retailers.

    2. He may sell generally to all retailers in a selected class who will buy.

    3. He may confine sales to one retailer in a community.

C. Manufacturer direct to jobbers.
He may reach the jobbers either through salesmen or by mail.
His goods may be distributed to any desired class of retailers by:

    1. All jobbers who will cooperate with him.

    2. Selected jobbers having exclusive jobbing agencies in restricted territories.

D. Manufacturer direct to special representatives.
He may reach them by salesmen or by mail.
They are called special representatives because they are not normal parts of the marketing chain.
These special representatives may sell to jobbers, retailers, or consumers.
They are:

    1. Agents.

    2. Commission men.

    3. Brokers.

Source: Butler (1914), pp. 180–81. Also see Butler (1917), pp. 263–4.

The wide-or-narrow criterion shows how many sales outlets dealing with the product or brand concerned exist within a certain area; the wider channel means that almost all sales outlets freely sell it, whilst narrower means that some outlets are selected to resale it according to some criteria. Even in the case of the same length of marketing channel, therefore, there can be a difference in terms of the wider-or-narrower criterion. The criterion is often called 'market coverage' or 'exposure frequency' of the product or brand (Furo 1968, pp. 206–8). As Butler included under B the option whether the manufacturer should sell to all retailers or confine to one in a community, Butler's table apparently included this criterion although he did not directly refer to these terms. The table suggests that the types of retail formats should influence wide-or-narrow selection. Furthermore, Butler (1914, pp. 186–8, 1916, pp. 270–71) focused on Parlin's ([1914b] 1978) idea on distinction of products between '"shopping" line' and '"convenience" goods' as a basis of channel selection. For instance, Butler (1914, p. 187, 1916, pp. 271–2) indicated, 'If a manufacturer is marketing something that can be classified as a shopping line and which is bought chiefly by women, it is often advantageous for him to confine its sales to one of the three competing stores in each shopping center.' As will be seen in Chapter 6, the idea of wide-or-narrow selection based on typology of products became popular between the two world wars. In this sense, Butler's advocacy was far-sighted.

Finally, the open-or-closed criterion is whether or not the sales outlet exclusively sells the specific manufacturer's products (Furo 1968, p. 209). Even if only a few sales outlets are selected in a certain community, there can still be a distinction in terms of open or closed. The closed channel limits the store to stocking only the specific manufacturer and prohibits it from handling competing products/brands; the open channel does not. Closed channels were adopted by manufacturers who wanted to exclude the competing national and private brands and establish intimate cooperation with the merchants. This channel also provided the manufacturer with a stronger position from which to maintain resale prices. The exclusive dealing contract was, however, delicate in terms of its legality especially after the passing of the Clayton Act in 1914. Therefore, in his later book, Butler brought up the legal questions regarding selling through exclusive agencies (Butler and Swinney 1918, p. 103). The discussion was followed by some scholars in the interwar period, as will also be explored in Chapter 6.

Conclusion

Butler's idea of marketing management was apparently extracted directly from the experiences and observations of the new type of manufacturer who launched marketing with the integration of mass production and mass distribution from the late nineteenth century onwards. His writings drew heavily on this background, and he also always adhered to the manufacturer's perspective. It can be said, however, that this narrow view enabled him to articulate an archetype of discussion on the 4Ps marketing management. His managerial definition of marketing that separated planning from implementation in marketing, his attention to making the product attractive, and his consideration of conflicts and possible options in marketing channels were to be developed in later years, although most of his successors did not recognize this precedent but developed their own ideas to cope with their current situation.

Butler's ideas were the starting point and rather primitive as his explanations were often supported by undeveloped actual examples rather than structured and abstracted categorization. Butler included market research as part of the 'plan behind the campaign', the function of which is, of course, essential in marketing management, and he also actually engaged in research activities at the US Rubber Co. after resigning from his academic position in 1918 (see Butler 1918). Nevertheless, his opinion in this field was not necessarily as advanced as contemporary counterparts such as Parlin and Shaw. In the early twentieth century interest grew in related research. For instance, after the establishment of a private research organization, the Business Bourse, in 1908 by J.G. Frederick, some institutes started their own similar programmes (Lockley 1950, pp. 733–4). In 1911, the commercial research division was set up at the Curtis Publishing Co., for which Parlin worked. In the same year the Bureau of Business Research was organized at the Harvard Business School based on the recommendation of Shaw. The US Rubber Co. organized a department for commercial research in 1915 under the leadership of P.H. Nystrom, and Swift & Co. also established a department for commercial research guided by L.D.H. Weld (Lockley 1950, p. 735).

With such developments in the marketing field, the 1910s saw the initial study of 'scientific management'. This substantially encouraged the efforts to make marketing more scientific. This is the theme in the following two chapters.

Chapter 2

Scientific Management and Sales Management: The McDonaldization of Sales Activities

It was after the Eastern Rate Case in 1910 that the principles of scientific management advocated by F.W. Taylor attracted attention in American society. The case was well described by Drury (1915, pp. 15–21) and Copley ([1923] 1969, pp. 369–77): Louis D. Brandeis, who was known as 'the people's lawyer', spoke against advance freight rates, the inefficient management system of the railroad companies, and presented many supporters of Taylor's system to the hearings before the Interstate Commerce Commission. This event created a sensation and a mania for scientific management in American society. At the time, the name 'scientific management' was officially adopted instead of other names, such as 'functional management' or 'Taylor's system'.

In such a setting, some pioneers naturally tried to begin adapting the principles to the marketing world. This chapter focuses on attempts in the 1910s to apply them to sales management and sales force management. Similar attempts were also made to apply this to marketing management in both the 1910s and 1920s. These will be considered in the next chapter. The attempts considered in these chapters can be evaluated as the combination of different types of explicit idea from the standpoint of knowledge management.

To begin exploring this issue, it is useful to discuss exactly what scientific management means. The query was posed historically (e.g. Sheldon 1925, pp. 130–31, Devinat 1927, pp. 2–4), but the meaning is still often vague. To avoid confusion, this problem should be considered first in the context of the analysis in this book. Such a discussion can provide an analytical point of view applicable to both this and following chapters. Then this chapter will consider two typical applications of scientific management to sales management from the 1910s; one is an attempt by Taylor's immediate disciples and the other is the idea of 'scientific sales management' advocated by Charles W. Hoyt.

Two Levels of Meaning for Scientific Management

Scientific Management and scientific management

It was Taylor himself who strongly emphasised that the 'fundamental principles of scientific management' were 'applicable to all kinds of human activities' or 'all social activities', including management of homes, farms, business of large and small tradesmen, churches, philanthropic institutions, universities, and governmental departments (Taylor 1911, pp. 7–8). What this application meant was misleadingly vague, however, resulting in the emergence of many self-proclaimed applications of scientific management. One reason was that scientific management embraced various kinds of tools, such as time study, motion study, instruction cards, functional foremanship, stores system, inspection, and so forth. Criticism at the time suggested that 'many a false prophet' came to businessmen and brought 'only the shell of Taylor's methods and not the principles', leaving in their wake a heterogeneous assortment of cards, filing cabinets, and record sheets that involved endless clerical labour and in many cases constituted useless red tape (Shaw 1911, p. 330).

There followed an important substantial shift in Taylor's own commentaries about the 'principles' of the management system (Thompson 1914, p. 14). In his early book, Taylor emphasized four factors as 'principles': (1) many daily tasks, (2) standard conditions, (3) high pay for success and (4) loss in case of failure (Taylor 1903, pp. 63–4). However, he later advocated four completely different factors as the 'underlying principles of management': (1) the development of a true science, (2) the scientific selection of the workman, (3) his scientific education and development and (4) intimate, friendly cooperation between the management and the men (Taylor 1911, p. 130). This shift in emphasis by Taylor himself made it recognizable that there were at least two different levels of meaning in scientific management.

The first was the narrower and stricter definition, denoting a particular management system of productive operation, which he advocated in earlier works (Taylor 1895, 1903). The second was the broader and more generalized definition oriented towards 'science in management' in general, emphasized during his later years (Taylor 1911, 1912). The latter level went beyond operational management in production and was more oriented towards general management covering a whole organization. The influence of this broader meaning was so immense that Taylor has often been considered the 'father' of management theory. Nevertheless, as indicated by Koontz and O'Donnell (1959, p. 20), Taylor's original idea was 'not on the general management of enterprise but on management at the shop level'. In this respect, the first strict level of meaning could be presented as a proper noun with capital letters, Scientific Management, or Taylor-system, whereas the second broader meaning could be presented as a common noun with small letters, scientific management. Thus, the shift in emphasis by Taylor himself was a change from Scientific Management to scientific management or from Taylor-system to science in management.

The attempts to apply scientific management to the marketing arena included both definitions, and references to them have been inconsistent according to each particular historical commentator's point of view. Therefore, this book generally uses lower case to show both S/scientific M/management unless it cites a historical commentator directly.

The Strict Level in Application

When one tries to apply the strict definition of scientific management to the marketing field, the production management or shop management that Taylor originally discussed should be replaced by the equivalent in the marketing arena, that is, sales management or sales force management. The salesman is the counterpart of the productive worker.

As with the strict meaning of scientific management, the idea of task management, 'a large daily task' represented by Taylor (1903, pp. 63–4), is essential among the four principles he outlined in 1903 (Mohri 1965, p. 51). It should be noted that the 'task' that Taylor called for never meant a general 'goal'. On the contrary, Taylor strongly criticized the setting of goals on the basis of the piece-rate system, known as the Town–Halsey systems (Town 1889, Halsey 1891). This was because the 'goals' in these systems were based purely on 'previous experience' (Halsey 1891, p. 759), not on any rational or 'scientific' grounds. Thus Taylor was critical that as a result a worker's performance might 'drift' gradually to the goal due to some incentives, but could not result in the same optimal performance that the 'first class man' could accomplish (Taylor 1903, p. 41). In contrast, the tasks in Taylor's system were to be set more rationally: the manager intervened in the worker's activities, investigated both the method and the conditions surrounding them, and set the 'one best way' as the standard. The task was 'a full day's work', which the worker could complete if he did his best according to the standardized best method that the manager gave him. In this context, standardization is *sine qua non* for the task, whereas high pay for success and loss in the case of failure were the supplements to accomplish the task. As Taylor emphasized, 'complete standardization of all conditions and methods is not only desirable but absolutely indispensable' (Taylor 1903, p. 123).

A problem arises, however, when one tries to apply such strict conditions to the marketing arena. Setting a salesman's sales quota, the marketing equivalent of the goal, based not on past experience but on standardization of both the method and its conditions, causes unique difficulties that do not exist in the production field. Even though sales activities can be standardized, the conditions surrounding them cannot, because they are composed of various factors which the marketer cannot control, such as the customers with whom the salesman talks, the location of sales activities, and the atmosphere surrounding them which are affected by psychological, cultural, social, political and many other miscellaneous elements. Thus the results of sales activities will always vary and setting a sales quota for the salesman would be closer to 'drifting management' rather than the Taylor-system.

To overcome this problem, it is necessary to standardize these conditions as much as possible. When considering any McDonald restaurant, one can see the extreme standardization of not just sales activities but also the surrounding conditions such as the layout and atmosphere of the restaurant. In this sense, attempts at a similar situation in sales resemble the so-called McDonaldization (Ritzer 1996), although this concept is not necessarily limited to sales and business activities, but embraces consumer culture and society. Not all self-confessed scientific management practitioners actually tackled this problem, and only a few pioneers, consciously or unconsciously, have even addressed it directly.

The Broader Level in Application

In the broader and generalized meaning, scientific management is a scientific approach to management or a seeking of science in management. The principle of 'development of a true science' that Taylor mentioned in 1911 reflected this meaning, as did Taylor's insistence on a 'mental revolution' that substituted scientific knowledge for the old rule-of-thumb methods (Taylor 1912, p. 31). The influence of this interpretation is tremendous. Although there was strong opposition and Church (1911) suggested that scientific management had no science, it has been generally recognized that scientific management was a landmark in the history of science in management (see Drury 1915, Copley [1923] 1969, Taylor Society [1929] 1972). The application of scientific management to the marketing field in this broader sense is not limited to sales management, but can be expanded to marketing management. In this case, it is necessary to identify the elements composing the 'science' in scientific management so as not to fall into a tautology in that scientific management is scientific because it is defined as a scientific approach to management. Generally speaking, introducing some scientific methods such as statistical techniques into management has tended to be recognized as scientific. According to this interpretation, any of the ideas of marketing management that is based on market research can be called the application of scientific management. If one accepts this, almost all of the developments in marketing management from Taylor's period to the current time must be defined as the 'application of scientific management'. The most eminent historical commentators looked for much more specific relationships with the original concept of Taylor. In this case, the key was standardization.

At the end of the 1920s, the Taylor Society, which was originally established as the Society to Promote the Science of Management in 1911 and changed its name after Taylor's death in 1915, advocated a '1929 statement of principles' of scientific management: (1) management research, (2) management standard, (3) management control and (4) cooperation (Person [1929a] 1972, pp. 10–11). The 'standard' here was extended to many fields, from factory operation and factory standards via sales operating, merchandising and clerical standards to general administrative standards (Taylor Society [1929] 1972). As exemplified by budgetary control based on accounting of standardized costs, the broadened concept of standardization came to be utilized as a tool for general administration in the 1920s. Although standards in general management could not be as precise and rigid as those in productive operation, seeking 'one best way' as a standard in all spheres of business was the evident attempt to apply scientific management in the broader sense in the history of management. Arch W. Shaw and Percival White, both of whom will be discussed in the next chapter, followed this tendency in the field of marketing management, although in different ways.

Application of Scientific Management to Sales Management

A Shared Mindset

After the Eastern Rate Case in 1910, several works emerged that attempted to apply the principles of scientific management to sales and marketing management, including Frederick (1912), Shaw (1912, 1915), Hoyt (1913), Walker (1913), Brown (1914), IEED (1914), and Lewis (1916a–d, 1917a–c).

The mindset they shared was an awareness of the backwardness of management in the sales or marketing field compared to the production field. For instance, as Walker (1913, pp. 388 and 390) believed, the 'goods made under scientific management can and should be sold by scientific management', but the 'present condition of things in distribution is very nearly the same as in production when not under scientific management'. Similarly, Lewis (1916a, p. 841) pointed out, 'This was the era of Taylor, Emerson, and the trained analysers and observers, who applied the technique of the scientist to the study of the problem. But while production was increased, sales were not. It is no satisfaction to increase production and then build storehouses to keep the unsold product.' Shaw (1912, p. 705; see [1915] 1951, p. 43) also emphasized, 'we have built up a relatively efficient organization of production. … The recent introduction in many industries of so-called "scientific management" is only a partial crystallization of long years of progress. While we are but upon the threshold of the possibilities of efficiency in production, the progress thus far made has outstripped the existing system of distribution. If our producing possibilities are to be fully utilized, the problems of distribution must be solved'.

Despite similar concerns, the actual ways in which scientific management was applied varied, partly due to the different understanding of what scientific management really was and partly due to the differences in the actual problems they were tackling. This chapter considers two cases in depth: an attempt to apply scientific management by the sales department of the Tabor Manufacturing Company introduced by Brown (1914) and IEED (1914) and the idea of scientific sales management advocated by Hoyt (1913).

A 'Demonstration Shop' of the Taylor-system

The Tabor Manufacturing Co. manufactured moulding machines in Philadelphia. The company was famous for one of the two finest 'demonstration shops' of the Taylor system, the other being the Link-Belt Engineering Company in Philadelphia (Nadworny 1955, pp. 15–16). Therefore, the initiative at the Tabor Manufacturing Co. can be recognized as an official attempt by the so-called 'Taylor group' made up of Taylor's immediate disciples and followers. Published in the first bulletin of the Society to Promote the Science of Management (1914), the paper by Brown was the only one in the 1910s that discussed scientific management applied to a sales department. Many papers on this followed, in the 1920s.

Brown (1914, p. 3) described a problem that the Tabor Manufacturing Co. faced: 'Formerly each salesman was given a certain territory, and as is customary practice, was allowed to cover it as he pleased. An investigation of each salesman's territory and reports showed that the salesmen were reaching but a fraction of the prospects in their respective territories.' An anonymous paper estimated it to be only '50 per cent' (IEED 1914, p. 386).

A remedy for the problem was what was called a 'routing system'. The core element of the system was a 'route map' indicating the most convenient routes for each salesman, arranged with consideration of railroad connections such that the salesman could reach the different towns in his territory. Several potential customers in each town were listed in the reports and for each the information provided included who the officials of the company were, the number of employees, nature of its products, character of equipment in the factory, etc. (Brown 1914, [p. 4], IEED 1914, pp. 386–7). This approach became a popular topic in sales force management (see e.g. Jones [1917] 1922, pp. 174–82 and 307, Russel 1922, p. 110, Tosdal 1927, Chapter X, Hay 1929 p. 85), and was also the opinion of a contemporary scholar, J.G. Frederick (1912, p. 205, see also [1919] 1978). Tosdal ([1925] 1978, p. 680) indicated that among 20 sales manuals he investigated, five included the issue of 'routing' as the 'subject-matter'.

The concept of 'routing' used here was suggested by Taylor in his *Shop Management* as the 'route clerk', one of the eight species of functional foremen. According to Taylor (1903, p. 102), the route clerk works in the planning department to lay out 'the exact route which each piece of work is to travel through the shop from machine to machine in order that it may be finished at the time it is needed for assembling, and the work done in the most economical way'. As described in other words by Thompson (1914, p. 37), a contemporary of Taylor, the term routing had to do with the 'analysis of the sequence of operations on the work and the determination of the place and time for each operation and group of operation'. The routing system was the application of this concept to sales activities, while the same concept was naturally also applied to the manufacturing department of the Tabor Manufacturing Co. (Carter 1917, pp. 19–27).

The idea of routing is still utilized in sales management (e.g. see Stanton and Buskirk 1974, pp. 607–9, Bennett 1988, p. 175), and in this respect the initiatives at the Tabor Manufacturing Co. can be considered a historically significant step. From the perspective of the application of scientific management, the sphere of standardization was limited to the peripheral part of sales activities and did not cover the core, even though the idea of routing can be seen as part of standardization.

The paper introducing the Tabor Manufacturing Co. also explained that the 'setting of definite tasks for the men' and the routing system just described were the 'two principles' applied to the sales department of the company (IEED 1914, p. 385). Nevertheless, the fundamental difficulty of setting defined tasks for the salesmen was properly recognized by this company. The paper explained, 'In the sales department, it is a matter of some difficulty to determine what is a fair task' because the 'actual orders taken may depend upon circumstances over which the salesman has little or no control'. Therefore, it would be 'manifestly unfair' 'to rate a salesman altogether by the volume of his sales' (IEED 1914, p. 390). Applying this reasoning, the Tabor Manufacturing Co. made 'a moderate attempt to set tasks for the salesman' (Brown 1914, [p. 3]), which was based on factors that related to the schedule defined by the routing system, such as how well the salesman followed the schedule, the total number of calls made, and so forth (IEED 1914, p. 391, see Brown 1914, [p. 4]).

Thus, the attempts by Taylor's immediate disciples were very deliberate regarding setting tasks for the salesmen. The logic here was absolutely faithful to the Taylor doctrine. But the competitive business situation, especially among mass manufacturers, required more.

The Idea of Scientific Sales Management

Charles W. Hoyt was not an immediate disciple of Taylor, but published a book entitled *Scientific Sales Management* in 1913. This book was highly regarded in Taylor's time as the 'most ambitious attempt to apply the Taylor principles to selling' (Thompson 1914, p. 20), as well as being currently considered as the 'first "typical" sales management book' (La Londe and Morrison 1967, p. 10).

Hoyt accumulated experience as a travelling salesman and worked as a manager for the wholesale branch of Armour & Co. (Barton 1929, p. iii). The company was one of the two biggest companies in the meat packing industry, the other being Swift & Co. As is well known, the meat packing industry was one of the typical industries in which manufacturers vigorously launched marketing with the integration of mass production with mass distribution from the late nineteenth century, and the wholesale branches were the cornerstone of their vertical behaviour (Porter and Livesay 1971, pp. 168–73, Chandler 1977, pp. 391–402). In this sense, Hoyt's experiences were supposed to be more advanced in terms of marketing compared with the 'demonstration shop' of the Taylor-system. As a matter of fact, the materials of Hoyt's discussion were extracted from his observations of many integrated manufacturers, including National Cash Register (NCR) and P&G, as mentioned below.

A problem Hoyt tackled was 'the "big" salesman', highly experienced and skilful in selling, but who did not accept the control of the sales manager.

> The old kind of salesman is the "big me" species. He is the "little you" (meaning the house) sort. He works for himself and, so far as possible, according to his own ideas. He resents anything coming from the house except checks for salary and expenses. The house may tell him what territory to cover, even to the extent of naming the town. In many cases, however, the "big" salesman only permits the house to name the States or counties which he is to cover. In other words, they assign him a territory. He has his own customers. Mind you, I speak with wisdom when I say they are *his* customers. At any rate, he considers them as such. If a newly appointed sales manager attempts to tell him of some firms on whom he must call, he is "peeved". Sometimes it is his practice to suggest that the sale manager better come out and do it, while he (the "big" salesman) will take his customers with him to another house (Hoyt 1913, pp. 3–4, italic and parentheses are original).

As a background to this remark, it should be remembered that there were many travelling salesmen, usually called 'drummers', at the turn of the twentieth century in the USA. They were basically independent salesmen working on their own accounts (Hollander 1964, Moore 1972, ch. 2, Spears 1995, esp. ch. 4). However, as the manufacturers launched marketing campaigns, they also began to hire the salesmen and require more loyalty from them. Hoyt's remark has to be understood within this historical context. Therefore, it was only natural that Hoyt's purpose was to create 'the new type of salesman', 'the sort who works for a house', instead of the old type who were 'rapidly decreasing in number' but were 'still the larger' (Hoyt 1913, pp. 5 and 3). He emphasized, 'Many such manufacturers spend hours, and much money, reducing the "cost-to-make", while they permit the "cost-to-sell" to rest in the palm of the insufficient old type of salesman' (Hoyt 1913, p. 4). According to Hoyt, in order to create a new type of salesman the manager had to show how he could 'intelligently' support the salesman, who in turn would believe a better result was achievable if he cooperated with the manager. Here exists the connection between Hoyt and scientific management.

Hoyt enumerated a variety of items as management tools in his book, including bulletins, letters and house organs for salesmen, as well as councils, meetings and conventions for salesmen and the use of an expense account system. However, his emphasis on standardization of sales talks and salesman's behaviour deserves particular attention. 'One of the first principles of Scientific Management', he pointed out, 'provides scientific methods in place of rule-of-thumb methods for each element of the workman's work. ... Scientific Sales Management also provides for a careful study of the salesman's individual efforts' (Hoyt 1913, p. 165, capitalization from the original).

One of his prime examples was the famous attempt by NCR, which has also been well described in other works (Crowther 1923, ch. 2, Marcosson 1948, pp. 34–5). John H. Patterson, who bought NCR, began to standardize the salesman's talks from the mid-1880s. Patterson compiled the sales pitches of the company's best salesmen, which were taken down in shorthand by a stenographer hidden behind a screen, and distributed these in a sales manual called *The Primer*. Furthermore, he required every salesman to memorize and utilize these standardized talks. This was the start of the so-called 'canned talk'. Based on standardization of sales talks, Patterson established a training school for their salesmen and organized competitions among them. In due course, the NCR case study became popular through introductory articles in business journals (e.g. Gibbs 1911a, 1911b). Hoyt (1913, pp. 167–70) identified this attempt as a good example of the 'one best way' for salesmen.

Additionally, Hoyt also examined the sales campaign of Crisco by P&G, which was mentioned in the previous chapter. In contrast with NCR, the attempt by P&G to standardize sales activities is totally forgotten today. However, when reading the description below, one can recognize the steps in the McDonaldization of sales activities.

The canvasser knocked at the door of the house. When the door was opened, the canvasser immediately removed his hat, placing it on the floor of the piazza or on the rail if one were handy. Using a set phrase such as: "Madam, I am here to show you Crisco, the new shortening", he offered her with his two hands a pail of Crisco. At the same instant he tore from the pail the parchment paper wrapper which enclosed it, removed the cover, and handed it to her exposed. There is a delicate little touch in this of apparently spoiling a package to show it to the prospect. ... The instant that the woman took the pail from the canvasser's hands he drew the pencil from one pocket and held it in his right hand. At the same time, he drew from another pocket a coupon which he held in his left hand. This was done so that the woman could not hand back the pail to the canvasser. The most she could do was to drop or place it on the floor. Then the conversation started (Hoyt 1913, pp. 171–2).

Despite this standardization, the reactions of the customers must have differed between individuals since the salesman could not control all the circumstances surrounding his activities and the customer. This limitation was clearly recognized by the immediate disciples of Taylor (IEED 1914, p. 390). In the case of Hoyt, he did not necessarily realize this problem fully. Nevertheless, his advocacy of a thorough advertising campaign as the 'preliminary work' was to substantially reinforce the imperfect effects of standardized sales behaviour. In Hoyt's (1913, pp. 32–5) opinion, the salesman should not do the 'preliminary work', but be the 'closer' of the campaign. The manager must do the preliminary work; for instance, by making a mailing list of the possibilities in a territory and regularly sending them printed material like letters and coloured leaflets, perhaps six times over a certain interval, to lure a response. The ratio of response may be low, even a mere 1 per cent, but this is enough. In most cases, they were ready for a salesman's call.

Thus, the combination of the advertising campaign as the 'preliminary work' and standardized sales activities by the salesmen as the 'closer' was a key part of Hoyt's concept of scientific sales management. Hoyt himself recognized this combination as the 'co-operation' between the manager and the worker that Taylor emphasized. Hoyt's advocacy must sound like old-fashioned high-pressure marketing to modern readers. This is because the advertising campaign itself was not sufficient as preliminary work for sales activities. From the current perspective of marketing management, what Hoyt called the preliminary work must be assumed to be all of the factors of the marketing mix or the 4Ps. This means that the limitation of Hoyt's ideas was inherent in sales management in itself because it could not then cover all factors equivalent to the 4Ps. In this sense, the idea of sales management was so narrow that the effects of applying scientific management were not effective enough.

Conclusion

Sales management thought after Hoyt's articulation diverged from marketing management thought, as noted by Jones ([1917] 1922), Russel (1922), Hall (1924), Aspley (1929) and Hay (1929). These books dealt with salesmanship and personnel management of salesmen, including topics such as hiring, training, and payment, but did not cover other fields such as product policy, pricing policy, channel policy and market research. A controversial issue was the relationship of sales management with advertising; some of these authors insisted a closer link was needed, but others ignored the issue. In any case, sales management became established as an independent and distinct field from marketing management.

Although 'moderate' applications remaining faithful to Taylor's doctrine were suggested by his immediate disciples, the urgency for mass manufacturers launching marketing efforts to control sales activities required more vigorous action. The standardization of all possible elements of sales activities began not only in the talks and behaviour of sales people but also the environments in which they worked, a phenomenon that can now be seen everywhere and which is often called the 'McDonaldization' of society. As many examples shown by Ritzer (1996) suggested, it has come to be applied not only to sales of products, but also to sales of services. Service industries in both the private and the public sectors, including restaurants, hotels, education, health care, government services, etc., are now where the main applications of this McDonaldization can be seen. This is an example of applying an idea far beyond the original background that produced it, into new fields, as the integrated model suggests in the introductory chapter.

Meanwhile, the idea of marketing management progressed along a different path. A few intermediate attempts to bridge sales management and marketing management appeared, including L.S. Lyon ([1926] 1978), whose book utilized the concept of 'marketing strategy' although its main body remained as an analysis of sales force management, and J.G. Frederick ([1919] 1978), whose book mixed many factors of marketing management and sales force management despite the title, which utilized the term 'salesmanagement'. At the same time, however, much more marketing management-oriented works also emerged as a result of the attempt to apply scientific management in the broader sense.

Chapter 3

Scientific Management and Marketing Management: 'Science in Business' for Marketing

While some pioneers tried to apply the principles of scientific management to sales management, others did the same with marketing management. The latter case applied the broader meaning of scientific management, as set out in Chapter 2, and trials were continuously made in the 1910s and 1920s. Arch Wilkinson Shaw was the outstanding contributor in the 1910s, and Percival White during the 1920s. Their ideas were fundamentally different, but can be evaluated as a complement for development of marketing management thought.

This chapter first explores the ideas of Shaw, who had both a business and an academic background. As the editor of business journals published by his own company, A.W. Shaw Co., he collected and observed many cases of actual business activities during the 1900s. He worked at the Harvard Business School as a part-time lecturer in business policy and a board member, after being taught by F.W. Taussig in the 1910s (Copeland 1958a, 1958b, pp. 313 and 315). He contributed much to the School financially and in publications – in fact, the *Harvard Business Review* was published by his company from the first volume until Volume 7, No. 3 in April 1929 – as well as in teaching methodology; Chandler (1977, pp. 467–8) pointed out that the famous case method for instruction was introduced at Shaw's urging. After considering the general basis of Shaw's thought, this chapter analyses how Shaw understood the concept of scientific management and how he utilized this understanding. The exploration also investigates Shaw's social awareness, which had a significant effect on marketing management and society.

Percival White engaged in an early study of marketing research during the 1920s in the USA, the UK and Germany. He was an independent marketing advisor, whose customers included the Ford Motor Co., GM and the Burroughs Adding Machine Co. White first met scientific management in the 1910s when, as a newspaper reporter, he reported on its use at the Watertown Arsenal, and then again during the First World War when he worked as an automobile expert for the Rock Island Arsenal (Cowan 1927, p. 460, fn. 3). Continuing in the same line, White wrote a typical textbook of business administration in the 1920s, and his ideas became a bridge between the work in marketing and in management that were being expanded from the original ideas of Taylor. After considering the general conditions of business, marketing and American society in the 1920s which formed the basis of White's ideas, this chapter explores how White's approach, called 'scientific marketing management', is related to scientific management in the broader sense, and what the historical contributions of his writings were.

The Concept of Marketing Management by Shaw: Focusing on the Relationship with Scientific Management

The General Basis of Shaw's Ideas

Unlike Butler, Shaw was never explicit in his works that his view was from the manufacturer's standpoint nor that his ideas were only intended for the manufacturer. Nonetheless, the concept of 'merchant-producer' played an essential role in Shaw's thought, apparently reflecting the emergent type of manufacturers that launched their own marketing activities. According to Shaw, under the 'orthodox type of distribution' with numerous middlemen intervening between producer and consumer, the producer was not in any sense a merchant because the selling agent took upon himself the initial distribution of the entire output (Shaw 1912, pp. 731–40, [1915] 1951, pp. 76–88). Nevertheless, the 'growing tendency to decrease the number of successive steps in distribution' was becoming 'one of the most characteristic features of modern distribution', and resulted in a 'rapid adoption by producers of agencies for direct communication of ideas about the goods to the consumer' (Shaw 1912, pp. 728 and 730, [1915] 1951, pp. 72 and 75). Shaw's depiction is reproduced in Figure 3.1, which shows that the manufacturer was increasingly becoming the 'merchant-producer' although the extreme of actual direct selling was rare. Shaw's famous functional analysis of the middlemen, which was explained above in the Introductory Chapter and is considered the first functional analysis in US marketing thought, was needed to define which key functions were to be assumed by the manufacturer and which would be kept in the hands of the merchants when the merchant-producer launched marketing efforts (Shaw 1916, p. 163; see Shaw 1912, pp. 738–9, [1915] 1951, pp. 85–7).

In addition, Shaw articulated the concept of 'differentiation of commodities' or 'differentiation of the product', which was later used as the basis of non-price competition in the discipline of industrial organization. The policy was to be essentially assumed by the 'merchant-producer'. According to Shaw, while the 'orthodox type of distribution' was based on unbranded or undifferentiated commodities, the 'communication of ideas about the goods' by producers to consumers apparently depended on the 'differentiation of commodities' (Shaw 1912, pp. 707–12, [1915] 1951, pp. 45–51). Linking price policies of 'selling at the market plus', which Shaw defined as 'the most characteristic price policy of modern distribution', to product differentiation policies, i.e., the differentiation of commodities, Shaw pointed out that both of these were typically adopted by the 'present day merchant-producer' (Shaw 1912, pp. 712–21, [1915] 1951, pp. 51–9). Thus, although Shaw never limited his ideas to the manufacturer's standpoint, it should be apparent that the main body of his work, as with Butler's, was generated from studying the activities of the new type of manufacturers who launched marketing.

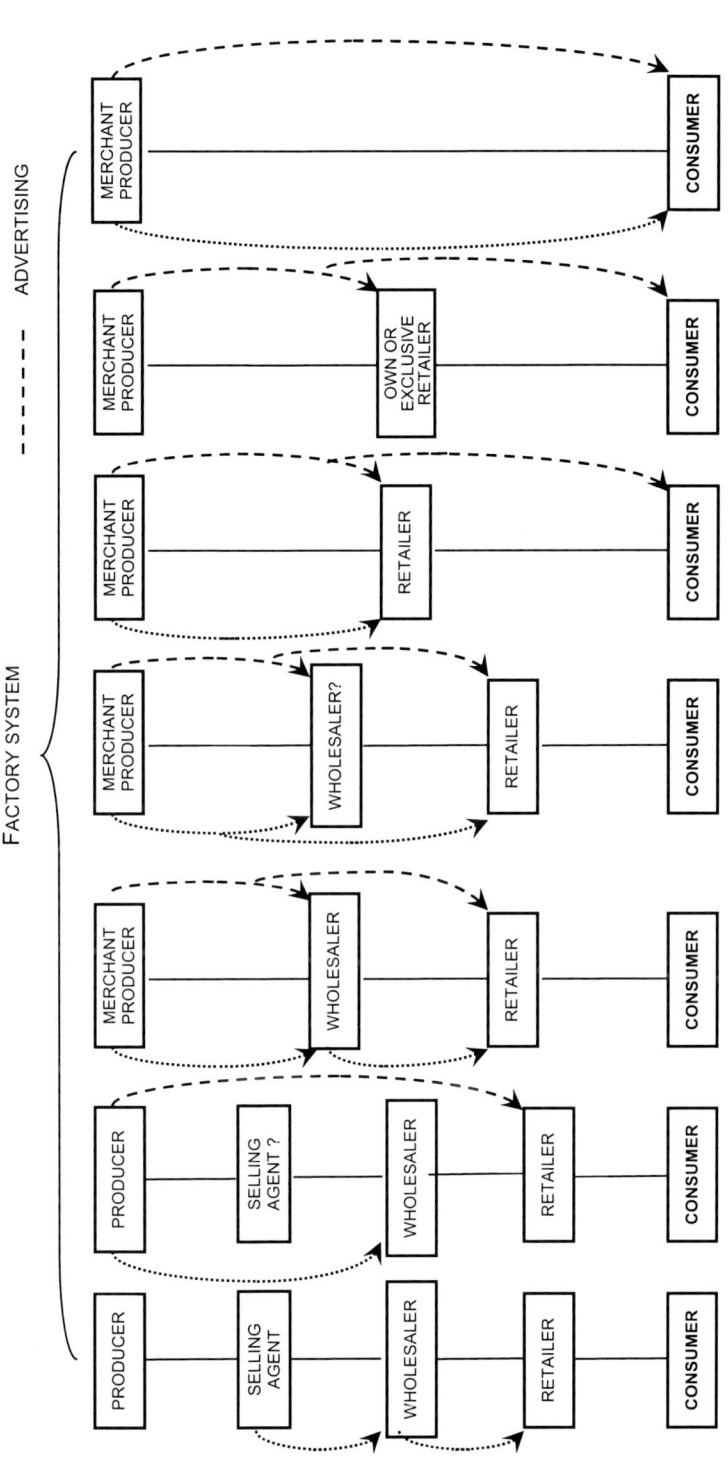

Source: Based on a figure from Arch Shaw's article 'Some Problems in Market Distribution', The Quarterly Journal of Economics, 26(4), 1912, p. 729.

Figure 3.1   Modern tendency to reduce successive middlemen described by Shaw (1912)

Shaw's Insight into Scientific Management

The relationship of Shaw's writings with scientific management has been controversial, especially among Japanese academics. Scholars in the USA have examined this relation (e.g. LaLonde and Morrison 1967), and the first Japanese scholar to do so was Miura (1951). He pointed out that Shaw's concept of 'laboratory point of view' meant Taylor's scientific management, and Shaw accepted the 'functional method of management organisation' from Taylor to eliminate the wasteful 'motions'. Although many scholars followed his opinion, a few doubted it in part (Nishimoto 1974) or strongly opposed linking this with scientific management, calling it 'shallow and wrong' (Mitsuzawa 1977; see Usui 2000, p. 133). This book raises an alternative view.

Firstly, it is evident that Shaw was greatly interested in Taylor's scientific management. This is shown by the fact that Shaw invited practitioners including F.W. Taylor himself as outside lecturers to the course on Industrial Organization that he set up at the Harvard Business School in 1910 (Chandler 1977, p. 467), and Shaw became a senior member of the Taylor Society in 1920 (BTS, 1920, p. 13). In addition, Shaw wrote a paper on scientific management, entitled '"Scientific Management" in business', which was originally published in 1911 and reprinted by Thompson (1914) with some omissions. At the outset of the paper, Shaw praised Taylor and his management system:

> The much-discussed "Scientific Management," reduced to simple terms, is a particular form of industrial management that develops the individual worker to the highest state of efficiency and of prosperity and at the same time secures greater prosperity for the factory owner by getting his product made at the lowest possible cost. Its principles have been slowly but accurately formulated by Frederick W. Taylor, the first investigator in the field of industrial management whose work may rightly be termed scientific (Shaw 1911, p. 327; see Shaw 1914f, p. 217).

Despite offering a complimentary appraisal, Shaw was very careful in applying it in its original form. According to Shaw, 'the exact systems' that Taylor devised 'should be introduced, in their entirety, in no factory except under the direct supervision of Mr. Taylor or of men trained by him or trained directly under his influence' (Shaw 1911, p. 330; see Shaw 1914b, p. 220). Instead, Shaw advocated 'the steps toward Scientific Management', which Shaw himself acknowledged 'not, perhaps, as Mr. Taylor would designate them, but as they might be taken by a business man who, having studied the literature of Scientific Management, would apply its principles to an individual problem' (Shaw 1911, p. 330; see Shaw 1914f, p. 219).

1. To separate from the 'line organization' or to add to the line organization a staff officer or 'staff organization'.
2. To set up tentative standards of performance.
3. To correct these standards by scientifically working out the best methods of performance.
4. To determine the best inducement to the employee to attain these standards.
5. To equip the employee with clear, complete, and exact knowledge of the best way of doing work (Shaw 1911, p. 330; see Shaw 1914f, p. 219).

As a matter of fact, these steps were never the same as the 'exact systems' of Taylor's. For instance, the first step, an advocacy for the line-and-staff organization, was not the same as functional foremanship that Taylor originally identified as management organization (Taylor 1903, pp. 92–109); the line-and-staff system is generally recognized as being derived from Emerson (Emerson 1908; see Wren 1979, pp. 182–3). The fourth step, the method of inducing employees financially, was not confined only to Taylor's idea of a differential piece rate system (Taylor 1895), but could be adapted to other specific compensation systems. In addition, there was no mention of the idea of tasks as an essential step of application.

Thus, Shaw deliberately avoided the direct application of the 'exact systems' that Taylor himself raised, let alone many surface and peripheral applications by 'many a false prophet', who brought 'only the shell of Mr. Taylor's methods and not the principles' and made businessmen mistake 'the form for the substance' and ignore 'the real system'. Shaw emphasized,

> A system is not a card or a filing cabinet; it is the right way of doing a thing. Similarly, Mr. Taylor's method of Scientific Management does not consist of forms or charts or of sets of rules and regulations. It is a big policy of establishing after scientific study and research a standard way of performing each industrial operation with the best possible expenditure of materials, capital, and labor (Shaw 1911, pp. 330–31; see Shaw 1914f, p. 220).

This remark represented the essence of Shaw's understanding of scientific management. It makes clear that Shaw recognized the business policy of establishing a 'standard way' after 'scientific study and research' as the quintessence of Taylor's scientific management. Among the steps towards scientific management cited above, the second, third and fifth steps explained this feature in detail. Establishing the 'standard way' was the core of the relation between the ideas of Shaw and Taylor. Therefore, when Shaw emphasized, for instance, 'Production is relatively well standardized', but '[T]here are few trained experts in distribution and administration, and few absolute standards of practice, except perhaps in the specific field of accounting' (Shaw 1916, pp. 4 and 6), Taylor's influence is identifiable.

At the same time, Shaw emphasized 'scientific study and research' itself, which was to be the premise of standardization. The reason was that Shaw recognized different features in the marketing process and in the production process, and indicated,

> [T]he problems of marketing are even more complicated than the problems of manufacturing, because the human factor is of more direct importance (Shaw 1912, p. 704; see Shaw [1915] 1951, p. 42).
> The present lack of standards is due largely to the difficulty of analyzing a structure so intricate as our system of distribution, complicated further by geographical, seasonal, and other physical conditions, and by the presence of the changing human factor in every individual transaction (Shaw 1916, p. 102).

He focused on 'scientific study and research' because of an absence of established standards, caused precisely by such variables, seeing the essence of scientific management as the scientific approach or science of business. Shaw wrote,

[F]rom a study of the principles of "Scientific Management" the business man can get a new business viewpoint – a new mental attitude toward his specific business problem (Shaw 1911, p. 332; see Shaw 1914f, p. 223, double-quotations and capital letters are original).

The adoption of a new point of view was the starting place in the development of the Taylor system of shop management. ... Scientific management may be nothing but applied common sense, as some of its critics have declared. It is important, however, because it is common sense applied in a new way (Shaw 1916, pp. 21–2).

Thus Shaw's recognition of scientific management as a great business policy of establishing a 'standard way', and as a basis for standards, especially in marketing, based on 'scientific study and research'. Here Shaw was a typical pioneer who attempted to apply scientific management in the broader meaning, which was defined in the previous chapter.

Finally, it should also be noted that Shaw's standpoint can be explained by his original enquiry in 'systems'. Shaw recognized that the concept of a 'system', defined as the 'right way of doing a thing', was treated equally with Taylor's scientific management (Shaw 1911, pp. 330–31; see Shaw 1914f, p. 220). In fact, when he wrote about the importance of 'picking out ... the right way of doing things, or as Mr. Taylor had expressed it, the only right way of doing things – system' (Shaw 1911, p. 332; see Shaw 1914f, p. 223), Shaw apparently treated the two concepts as synonymous: the 'standard way' was often rephrased the 'one best way' and 'system'.

The concept of 'system' was Shaw's original concern. A business journal that Shaw edited from 1900 was named *System*, which was in turn merged with *Business Week* when his company was bought by the McGraw Company. Therefore, the term 'system' was especially important for Shaw. According to him, 'system is a general principle', and his journal, *System*, 'stood for fewer forms, fewer tools, less of the red tape, and more of the principle – system' (Shaw 1905, p. 308). 'Honesty, or promptness, or politeness, or diligence, or perseverance are worthless without system, and so with truthfulness, and attentiveness and tact, and economy. System is the key. If we aspire to succeed, then let us combine our good qualities, which are natural, generally, with the system, which can be acquired' (Shaw 1904, p. 142).

The concern with 'system' apparently had to do with the so-called systematic management movement started in the latter decades of the nineteenth century (Litterer 1959, 1961b, 1963). As a matter of fact, Haber (1964, p. 20, fn. 5) indicated that the journal *System* played a central role in the movement, especially focusing on the office system. Thus, Shaw had sought the principles of business or what he called 'system', before he encountered Taylor's scientific management, so that he recognized Taylor's idea as a concrete instance of 'system'. In this sense, Shaw's 'system' or the 'right way of doing a thing' was essentially equivalent to Taylor's 'standard way' or the 'one best way'.

The Laboratory Standard for Marketing

Despite his recognition of the complexity of the marketing process, Shaw was optimistic about 'establishing standards comparable with the laboratory standards so common in the industries' (Shaw 1916, p. 142). '[E]very step in the selling process can be standardized, from analysis of the product and its market to the closing argument which clinched the order', emphasized Shaw (1916, p. 195).

Marketing, or distribution as Shaw often interchangeably referred to it, was composed of the activities of 'demand creation' and 'physical supply' (physical distribution in current terms) in Shaw's view. Although clear distinction of physical distribution was a feature of Shaw's thought, the most important part of his ideas were the activities of demand creation. 'The activities of demand creation focus on the consumer. Their purpose is to communicate to his mind such ideas about the product as will arouse desire for it and cultivate willingness to pay the price and make the effort required to secure possession of it', defined Shaw (1916, p. 100; see Shaw [1915] 1951, p. 11). The 'materials' of demand creation, according to Shaw, were the 'ideas about the product', while the 'agencies' that transfer these ideas were middlemen, direct salesmen and advertising. These activities were conducted in accordance with 'organisation' for demand creation, that is, 'analysis of market', 'price policy' and the 'combination of agencies' (Shaw [1915] 1951 pp. 11–12, Shaw 1916, pp. 13–14). In order to set up the laboratory standards for these activities, Shaw advocated the 'laboratory study of distribution' (Shaw [1915] 1951, p. 107).

This study ought to make full use of what Shaw called the 'method of "sampling"' (Shaw 1916, p. 145) or the 'testing method' (Shaw 1912, p. 762; see Shaw [1915] 1951, p. 117). The method was the application of the so-called large sample theory, which was state-of-the-art in statistics in his time. 'In making these tests the manufacturer can borrow the methods by which statisticians in many fields of social and business endeavor arrive at their results', Shaw pointed out (1916, p. 144),

> He [the statistician] is familiar with what are termed mass phenomena. ... Provided that the smaller group is not so selected as to prevent being typical of the larger body, and provided the group is large enough to render the law of averages applicable, the statistician knows when he has determined the average height of the smaller group that it will roughly coincide with the average height of the larger group (Shaw 1912, p. 757, Shaw [1915] 1951, pp. 110–11; see Shaw 1916, p. 144).

According to Shaw, the 'idea about the product' (defined as the 'materials' of demand creation), could be handled as an almost tangible thing; the effectiveness of each marketing approach could be tested, measured and compared, for instance by mailing the various forms of 'copy', so that the manager found that his problem of demand creation became to a great degree one of definite measurement rather than of opinion and personal judgement (Shaw 1912, pp. 754–60, see Shaw [1915] 1951, pp. 107–15). This method was assumed to be applicable to every activity of demand creation, including the choice of advertising media and copies, sales talks, and the efficiency of the middleman ('agencies' of demand creation), as well as the combination of agencies and the effect of different price policies ('organisation' of demand creation) (Shaw 1912, pp. 760–64; see Shaw [1915] 1951, pp. 114–19,

1916, p. 255). Therefore, he emphasized, 'an entire selling campaign can be directed on the basis of what may be termed laboratory study' (Shaw 1912, p. 763; see Shaw [1915] 1951, p. 118).

The method of laboratory study to set up the laboratory standard was the connecting link between Shaw's idea of marketing management and Taylor's scientific management in the broader sense. Thus his ideas of marketing management took a big step towards the more mature versions now applied.

Beyond Scientific Management: Politics Surrounding Marketing

Current discussions of marketing management do not confine their analysis only to the management system inside a company, nor to the immediate environment of the marketer including customers, marketing intermediaries (wholesalers, retailers, advertising agencies etc.), competitors and providers. They are also concerned with the so-called interested parties such as shareholders, mass media, consumer activists, politicians and government that can enact miscellaneous laws and rules, and public opinion, because these can exert a strong influence on the marketing strategies of a company. No matter how polished the 'scientific' system of marketing management was, it could not be successful if the environment was antagonistic to the company. Furthermore, gathering data necessary for marketing management needed a supportive attitude, rather than an accusatory attitude, from government. Discussion on the relationships between marketing management and society is not, in itself, an issue in the application of scientific management, but is a necessary premise. The originator of this discussion was Shaw.

The early twentieth century is often called the Progressive Era, in which many monopolistic businesses were strongly criticized by the public. The Federal Commission Act and the Clayton Act in 1914 were the result of anti-monopolistic politics at the time, supplementing the Sherman Act of 1890 and completing preparation for the fundamental framework of anti-trust laws in the USA. The same period was also called the 'high cost of living era' (Converse 1959b, p. 7). It has been shown by statistics of the US Department of Commerce (1975, p. 200) that the wholesale price index (1926=100) of all commodities rose remarkably from 46.5 in 1896 to 68.1 in 1914. Although it is evident that the price index soared during the First World War to 138.6 in 1919, it had already been rising rapidly before the War. The war accelerated the price rises, but was not the initial cause, as was suggested at the time (Howe 1917, p. v). Hofstadter (1955, p. 168), a leading scholar of the history of politics, wrote, 'Just as the falling prices of the period 1865–96 had spurred agrarian discontents, so the rising prices of this era added to the strength of the Progressive discontents'.

Many political disputes focused on the high prices. It should be noted that the Eastern Rate Case occurred within such a political environment. This case provided momentum for the spread of Taylor's scientific management because its supporters insisted that they could avoid advanced freight rates by introducing an efficient system. The dispute led to the establishment in the Senate of the Select Committee on Wages and Prices of Commodities, usually known as the Lodge Cost-of-Living Committee, in February 1910. The purpose of this committee was to investigate the cost of living and to ascertain whether the price of necessities had increased, and if so, to ascertain the causes. The committee's majority report (Senate 1910a) and minority report (Senate 1910b) both found many causes, and some of them were substantially related to marketing by business organizations, such as the increased cost of distribution, advertising, and the higher standard of living (Senate 1910a, pp. 10–11). As a matter of fact, the problem of increases in the cost of living evoked much discontent among consumers and resulted in the setting up of consumer movement organizations. Starting with the Chicago Housewives League in 1910, similar organizations were set up in many cities (Sorenson 1941 [1978], p. 7, Beem 1973, p. 15). Julian Heath, with the title of the Founder and the President of the National Housewives League in New York, insisted that because of the high cost of living problem, 'The housewife has become class conscious, and with this class consciousness came the demand for organization and there has been a great uprising of women all over the land' (Heath 1913, p. 122).

The blame was often straightforwardly directed at marketing policy. 'For instance', insisted one critic, 'Gillette sells his safety razor for $5. It is stated by many with whom I have conversed that the actual cost of the razor, including the manufacture and advertising, is at the very most $1' (Hess 1913, p. 242). The case of Gillette's safety razor was also discussed by Shaw in order to justify the differentiated product sold at the price of 'market plus'. Shaw emphasized,

> When the first widely advertised safety razor was put upon the market at $5.00 a considerable margin of profit was left the producer. It was often said at the time that the actual cost of manufacture of that razor was less than $1.00. Now this wide margin made possible an extensive advertising campaign. The new device was brought to the attention of the entire consuming public. Everyone, whether in the large centers or remote districts, learned of the safety razor and its uses. Great numbers purchased the razor because the subjective valuation which they placed on the commodity, when it was brought to their attention, exceeded the price asked. The large reward received by the distributor may perhaps properly be regarded as compensation for bringing about a better adjustment to meet human needs (Shaw 1912, p. 719; see Shaw [1915] 1951, p. 60).

This defensive remark can be understood fully only when one recognizes the political context during this period of high cost of living.

It should be noted at the same time that Shaw was absolutely confident that social problems, including the high cost of living, could be solved by introducing the 'science of business' into each company. However, he believed that this could not be achieved only by the individual companies. 'Seven years ago,' Shaw wrote as of 1914, 'I came to the conclusion that the work SYSTEM [the journal Shaw edited] had begun was too big and too vital to American business to be carried on solely by a private institution' (Shaw 1914a, p. 444, capitalization is original). This was the reason that Shaw contributed financially and intellectually to the foundation of the Harvard Bureau of Business Research in order to gather useful information to support business management. Nevertheless, the main purpose of this institute within the university was to collect information for use in its courses, rather than keeping its instructors in touch with practical business. In addition, it was obviously impossible for even as great an institution as Harvard to cover the whole field of business.

'Hence,' Shaw concluded, 'it has always seemed inevitable to me that this work must be taken [on] by the Government' (Shaw 1914a, p. 446). Therefore he advocated establishing the Federal or the Government Bureau of Business Practice in order to support business activities.

According to Shaw, this organization especially ought to support marketing activities. '[T]he American business man', he explained, 'has been playing the game alone. ... This is notably true of distribution. We have not even a census of wholesale and retail merchants.' '[T]he Government should concern itself first with the study of distribution. This is the great uncharted jungle of business' (Shaw 1914a, pp. 445 and 447). As will be mentioned again below, support to marketers by publishing a census of distribution was realized in the late 1920s. In this sense, Shaw's advocacy was far-sighted. Interestingly, Shaw was strongly confident that if the managerial problem could be solved in each company, the societal problems including the high cost of living would be solved as well.

> The work of the proposed Bureau, therefore, while of immediate interest to the business man, would be of tremendous social importance as well – to the farmer and the consumer, no less than to the man who makes or sells things. Fewer motions in production, distribution and administration will mean lessened costs and lower prices – a wider margin for the specialization of commodities and opportunity to shape the products of the land more closely to the needs and uses of consumers – a lower level of living costs, but a higher standard of living.
>
> By solving the problems of waste in Manufacturing and retailing, the Bureau would find the only permanent way of reducing the high cost of living (Shaw 1914a, p. 448).

This represented the fundamental way of thinking: 'National efficiency and national well-being are the sum of individual efficiency and individual well-being' (Shaw 1914a, p. 448) – this was an essential feature of Shaw's perspective on the relationship between individual companies and society, and was in turn shared by many American scholars of business and marketing.

Discovery of the Macro-environment for Marketing Management

Despite Shaw's advocacy and expectations, the political tendency led to the establishment of the Federal Trade Commission, which was seen as antagonistic to, not supportive of, businesses. Just before the final passage of the bill in the Senate, Shaw began to offer serious warnings through his journal about the ongoing anti-trust legislation. 'It involves an external problem important to the business man' (Shaw 1914c, p. 109).

According to him (1914c, pp. 109–10), although size had originally nothing to do with the honesty of business, the phrase 'big business' no longer meant the ordinary business grown big, but 'unfair business', because some big businesses had undoubtedly over-reached. Thus, the legislation was prepared in the spirit of retribution or in a desire to punish. However, it overlooked the interests of 'non-combatants' or the 'average business man'. Shaw expressed grave apprehension and anxiety, stating, 'The average business man will be policed by the methods for regulating unfair business' (1914c, p. 110) '[a]nd clean-cut expressions of the attitude of business men, definitely and frequently presented at Washington, mean better government' (1914c, p. 112). Just a month later, the journal *System* not only reported many echoes of Shaw's article, but also reported an event with a picture of Shaw himself visiting the White House with other business men from Chicago, including the executives of Marshall Field and Co., Cudahy Packing Co., and the Chicago Chamber of Commerce, to hold a conference with the President (Shaw 1914d).

Despite Shaw's lobbying, the Federal Trade Commission was nevertheless established. However, the experience bore fruit: Shaw realized the importance of the 'external problems of business' and described this in the closing remarks of his 1916 textbook: 'In a word, the external problems of business thus become internal problems in the sense that no intra-organization policy can safely be determined without taking into account the attitude of society toward the activities involved' (Shaw 1916, p. 333).

This remark can be said to be the first discussion about the macroenvironment of marketing management. The remark also played a substantial, conclusive role in the attempts to seek the 'science of business' in marketing management in the 1910s.

White's Idea of Scientific Marketing Management and the Progress of Science in Management

The Hedonistic Age and Rationalisation Thinking in the 1920s

White's concept of 'scientific marketing management' was created in the context of the 1920s. He confessed in the preface of his book that 'The undertaking was inspired by Frederick W. Taylor's books on scientific management' (White 1927, Preface), leading many scholars to analyse his idea as an application of scientific management. Nevertheless, White was not simply attempting to apply Taylor's principles. As he indicated elsewhere, 'The science of management has developed largely since the earlier days when "scientific management" was introduced' (White 1926a, p. 81). As the discussion of management was progressing in the 1920s, so the concept of scientific management was embracing many more factors than it had in the 1910s. White was one eminent discussant on management thought at the time, so that his ideas were a mixture of Taylor's influence and a developing classical view of management.

White tackled wasteful marketing in the 1920s. After the First World War, American society enjoyed a period of economic boom and prosperity, although as the Hoover Committee indicated, 'Acceleration rather than structural change is the key to an understanding of our recent economic developments' (Hoover [1929] 1966, p. ix). During this decade, numerous new products spread rapidly among consumers, including consumer durables such as phonographs, radio sets, washing machines, vacuum cleaners, oil-burning and gas furnaces, and clothing such as furs and fur-trimmed garments, short skirts, silk hosiery and novelty styles in shoes (Copeland [1929a] 1966a, pp. 322–8 and 394–402). In order to support the marketing of these products, a great amount of advertising was conducted through the new medium of radio in addition to traditional media, so that pre-World War II advertising expenditures peaked in the 1920s (Department of Commerce 1975, pp. 200 and 856). Exaggerated expressions were frequently used in these advertisements (Allen 1931, ch. 8). Installment selling was a widespread practice to lure immediate buying of these products (Seligman 1927, p. 14). Styles and fashions were rapidly changing, and the use of branding and packaging was everywhere (Borsodi [1927] 1967, pp. 159–64 and 227–33), along with a demand for curious ornaments with superficial decorations; buyers were criticized later as 'misguided decalcomaniacs' (Streichler 1963, p. 36). The decade saw growing colour consciousness and demand for colour in everyday life (Keppel 1933, p. 979). Artificial 'colours' were introduced to many products, such as red beds, yellow alarm clocks and blue trains (*Fortune* 1930a). 'From toothbrushes and overshoes, umbrellas, pots and pans, towels, etc., up to motor cars and office buildings, we see this demand for color', indicated one commentator (Keppel 1933, p. 980).

All of these tendencies were accompanied by changes in consumer culture. As symbolized by a famous phrase, 'The United States took to wheels' (Rostow 1990, p. 77), the 1920s saw the 'age of the mass automobile' and the 'age of high mass-consumption'. The feeling of high-speed living also spread (Copeland [1929a] 1966a, p. 322, Updegraff 1929). Consumer culture was becoming increasingly dependent on the 'ethics of hedonism, of pleasure and play', far from the tradition of the 'Protestant ethic and the Puritan temper' (see Bell [1976] 1996, pp. 54–80). '[A] hedonistic age is a marketing age', indicated Bell ([1976] 1996, p. 165).

In the meantime as the 1920s continued, there was increased criticism of 'the era of high pressure marketing' that in turn raised the 'cost of distribution' (Borsodi [1927] 1967). Although the problem of the high cost of distribution posed by the Twentieth Century Fund in the 1930s (Stewart and Dewhurst 1939) was historically well known, the same problem was already recognized as early as the 1920s. As a commentator described at the time, 'The well-known slogan of "The high cost of living" has practically disappeared from popular favor and the daily comic strip. In its place there has developed another phrase typifying an apparent economic maladjustment, "The High Cost of Distribution"' (Mazur 1925, p. 7, capitalization is original). White shared this awareness of the problem. According to him, 'There are greater wastes in marketing than in any other form of business activities' (White 1927, p. 3), and 'The marketing wastes … ultimately have had to be assumed by the consumer' (White 1927, p. 21).

It should be noted that despite the hedonistic mood in this decade there existed an undercurrent seeking rationality in business and industry. Just at the outset of the decade, the movement on the Elimination of Waste in Industry (CEWI 1921) lead by Herbert Hoover overcame the post-war depression to drive the recovery and economic boom. The advocacy of 'standardization of product' (CEWI 1921, p. 26) was part of this movement, and was substantially inherited from the drive for simplification during the war that was led by A.W. Shaw – who was the chair of the Conservation Division of the War Industrial Board (Copeland 1958a, p. 315), and was admired as the 'father of simplified practice' in the 1920s (Chisholm 1927, p. xii). The Simplified Practice Division was set up in the Bureau of Standardization, Department of Commerce and recommended reducing the numbers and varieties of basic products such as milk bottles, beds, tissue paper etc. especially during the earlier half of the decade (Chisholm 1927, pp. 43–4). Although Hollander (1986, p. 16) indicated that the simplified practice was considered not to have been effective in the realm of consumer goods, the practice paved the way for the prosperity of the 1920s by overcoming the traditional sectionalism in the US economy (see Mori 1976, p. 262).

In addition, the federal government began supporting the activities of businesses during that decade. The Domestic Commerce Division, which had been organized within the Bureau of Foreign and Domestic Commerce in the Department of Commerce in 1923, enlarged its activities. The *Annual Report of the Secretary of Commerce* stated,

> Prior to 1926 the Bureau of Foreign and Domestic Commerce was known throughout the country almost wholly as an organization acting for the promotion of our foreign trade. During the last fiscal year just ended there has been strong evidence that business interstates throughout the United States have awakened to the importance of the bureau's activities as an agency for the promotion of better domestic business methods (Department of Commerce 1927, pp. 72–3).

The Division focused on the 'problems of waste in domestic trade', and took the initiative in 1926 to hold a conference of delegates from all parts of the country engaged in market research in order to reduce duplication of effort through the organization of a central committee and various subcommittees; they began to publish *Market Research Agencies* giving a regular annotated list of all market-research studies available from research agencies throughout the United States. The Division also studied the marketing problems for particular commodities, and launched an "experimental 'census of distribution'" in 11 cities, cooperating with the Bureau of the Census and the Chamber of Commerce (Department of Commerce 1927, pp. 73 and 76–7, 1928, p. 98). Thus, the advocacy of the federal government providing census data as a basis of rational decision making in marketing, as encouraged by Shaw in the 1910s, was finally being realized.

White's ideas were an expansion of such a rationale in terms of business and marketing management. White recognized there were three primary causes of marketing waste: (1) distributive confusion (too many middlemen, too many retailers, and multiplicity of services), (2) destructive competition (excessive merchandising efforts, excess advertising, and trade abuses), and (3) company mismanagement or unscientific management (lack of information, lack of understanding, failure to functionalize marketing, and failure of coordination), and he indicated the last factor was 'more culpable' 'because it could be corrected' by individual companies and 'because it is now laid as a direct tax on the consumer in the form of higher prices' (White 1927, p. 14). In this way, just as with Shaw, White believed that related social problems could be solved by introducing the science of management into individual companies. In the case of White, however, the content was different mainly due to further developments of business management thinking during the intervening decade.

The Principle of 'Functionalization'

A key concept in White's approach to scientific marketing management was 'functionalization'. This concept was termed 'a basic assumption' of his book and was 'at the root of scientific marketing management' (White 1927, pp. 141 and 64). White often called his 'scientific marketing system' the 'functionalized system of marketing', the 'scientific functional system' or the 'functional system of marketing management'. What in fact was 'functionalization'?

In essence, it represented the concept of functionalization that was widely advocated in management organization thought at the time. The point of the concept was that management organization had to be built based on the 'function' or the 'work to be done' (see Mohri 1965, pp. 406 and 428); it presumed that management organization had often been built based on factors other than function – usually individuals who happened to have some skills or abilities (see Person [1929b] 1972, pp. 28–29). 'The organization should be built around the main functions of the business and not around an individual or group of individuals' (Cornell 1928, p. 26). As a business increased in size, there was a mathematical subdivision of work into unspecialized departments, the assignment being made to individuals and according to personal capabilities, not according to the functions to be performed, which resulted in the multiplication of departments and individuals, the duplication of work, and inefficient performance of functions (see Robinson 1925a, pp. 321–2). In order to counter this, the concept advocated was, 'The idea is first to determine the functions of the business, and then to find men who can fit them' (Robinson 1925b, p. 42).

It should be noted that White recognized the same problem in marketing management and attempted the same remedy. 'As the selling function has grown in importance new departments have been added without proper attention to function, but purely with regard to the operating expediency of the moment. The result has been great confusion and a total lack of uniformity in the practices of different concerns' (White 1927, p. 108). Or, 'Division of labor has been applied to marketing on the basis of chance and guess, rather than on that of scientific test. … The result has been waste – tremendous waste – which can be overcome only by functionalization' (White 1927, pp. 7–8). White attempted to apply this concept in order to 'to erect a working organization or system' in marketing management: 'According to scientific procedure this is done by separating marketing activities into a logical series of functions, and then by departmentalizing the personnel in accordance with these functions'…'The day is gone when the man is greater than the system. With present day large-scale operations, it is essential that organization be put before the personality' (White 1927, pp. 108 and 140).

The concept shared the same mindset as Taylor – and Shaw also – in that it strictly distinguished between the human and the non-human elements and attached greater importance to the latter (Person [1929b] 1972, pp. 28–9). In this sense, the concept fell under the classical school of management thought. Nevertheless, it was not directly inherited from Taylor because Taylor's views on 'function' were realized only in the form of functional foremanship. It has been indicated (Litterer 1961a, Inamura 1985) that the principles of managerial function of entire businesses originated from A.H. Church ([1914] 1977), and many classical theorists of managerial organization in the 1920s discussed the concept of functionalization as key (Gon 1970, p. 81). Thus White's advocacy was not directly derived from Taylor's principles, but based on the developing idea in managerial organization at the time. As can be seen in current textbooks of marketing management, functional organization is the most basic form of organization in this field. White's attempts can be seen as the first steps in the development of this concept.

Advocacy of Setting Up the Position of 'Marketing Manager'

White criticized the old idea of sales management, in which a 'sales manager' is responsible for everything, as typically presented in Frederick's book ([1919] 1978, pp. 36–7). Instead, he advocated setting up a 'Marketing Division', in which a 'marketing manager' was the executive head and each 'primary function' of marketing was organized as a department with its manager or director within the division. White (1927, p. 126) insisted on including a marketing manager, stating 'It is he who is, in the final analysis, responsible for the success of scientific marketing; he forms the pivot of the system.'

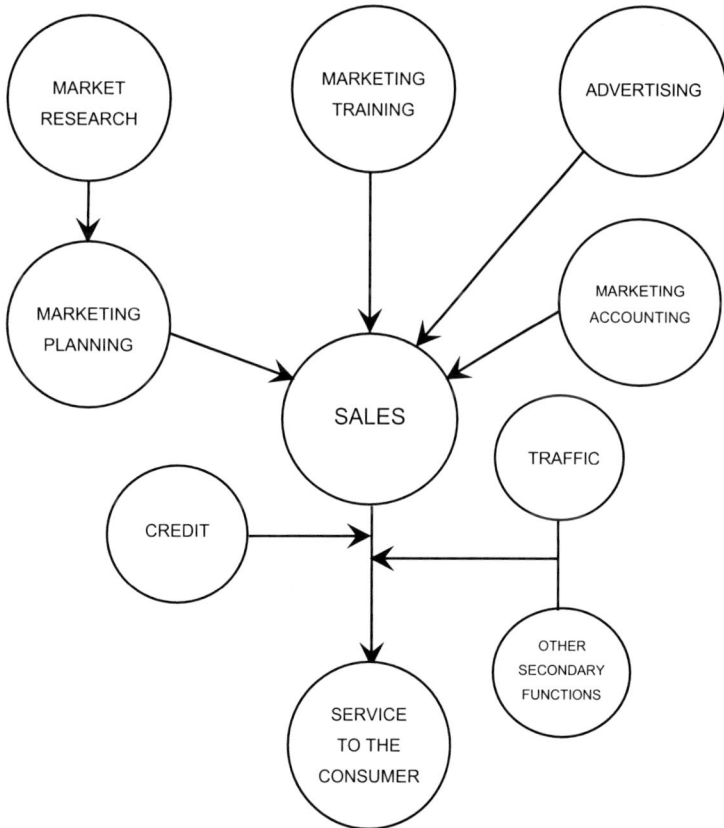

Source: White (1927), p. 110

Figure 3.2   Elements of the scientific marketing system by White

Figure 3.2 is White's illustration of the basic marketing functions, which constituted the 'logical basis for departmentizing the Marketing Division' (White 1927, pp. 110–11). White emphasized that marketing planning must be of 'the highest strategic importance' (1927, p. 164). He also pointed out the importance of market research as an independent function. Although such advocacy had already begun in the 1910s (see Parlin 1914, p. 4), the actual practice was only starting to be implemented in various forms. According to a questionnaire survey of large-sized enterprises by Weld (1923), only 29 per cent (18 among 62 responding companies) had an independent department for market research, whereas some companies conducted market research within departments such as accounting, sales or advertising and others relied on outside organizations such as advertising agencies. In this sense, progress towards scientific management in marketing was still incomplete. 'In the ideal plan of scientific marketing, a market analysis should and must constitute an integral part of the Marketing Division', insisted White (1927, p. 147). The research should include product data, market data, a distribution study and its data, and so forth (White 1927, pp. 153–63). White himself had been one of the earliest authors of market research books (White 1921, 1925), which covered broad research items such as the industry in general, competition, the company's customers, the ultimate consumer, the nature and size of the market, potential and limitation of the market, distribution, sales, and advertising. Thus, market research was the key to the marketing division. In this sense, White moved the idea of marketing management forward to a more scientific approach.

Cyclical Process of Management in Marketing

Another contribution by White was that he advanced the idea of the management process of marketing by shaping it into a cycle. 'These activities, in sequence, form a sort of cycle', insisted White (1926a, p. 97). He drew Figure 3.3 to illustrate this.

White advocated dividing all managerial activities into two sorts, the 'organizing' and the 'control' activities, in other words, the 'staff functions' and the 'line functions'. The component functions of 'organizing' are (1) analysing the situation, (2) initiating the idea, (3) planning the steps necessary to carry out the project, and (4) promoting the plan or persuading others of its merit, whereas 'control' is composed of (5) directing the newly organized work, (6) coordinating the activities of each, (7) maintaining the programme and the policy to carry them out, and (8) measuring the results (White 1926a, chapters 6–7). This is considered the earliest version of a cyclical approach to the management process (Inamura 1985, p. 225). White assumed the same cycle in each sphere of managerial activities, not only marketing but also accounting, finance, production and research (White 1926a, pp. 283–4, 491–3, 588–9 and 618–19).

The cyclical definition, which marked a new stage of development of the managerial thinking that substantially evolved from Butler's idea of separating planning function from implementation, has continued until now. As already mentioned in Chapter 1, current marketing management is the paradigm of analysis, planning, implementation and control which Brown characterized (2001, p. 465),

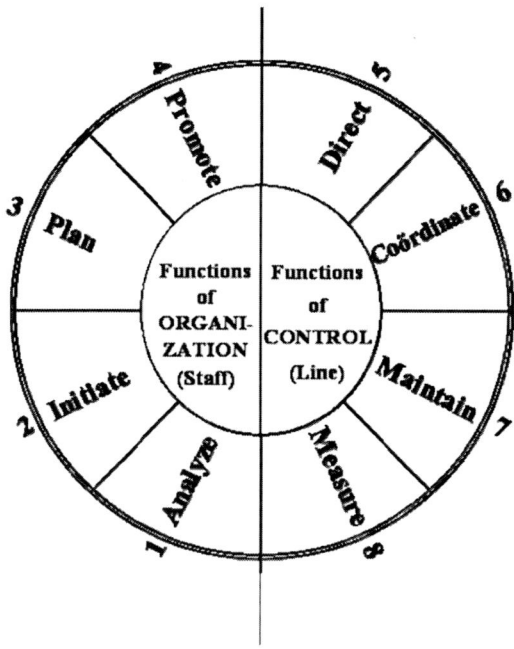

Source: White 1926, p. 97

Figure 3.3   Cycle process of management by White

in which cyclical steps of management generally provide the fundamental framework for marketing management, as typically exemplified by Kotler (1997, 2000, 2002) and Kotler and Keller (2006). White's advocacy connected Butler's idea of separating planning from implementation and the current concept of marketing management.

It is interesting to note that White assumed the principle of standardization as the basis of the cyclical process of management: 'Planning in marketing, as elsewhere, means setting up policies and objectives, establishing standards, proving suitable methods of procedure, and arranging for actual steps involved in carrying out the work in hand' (White 1927, p. 101). This feature of his ideas demonstrated the influence of scientific management.

Consumer Orientation and Standardization

For White, a premise of applying the principle of standardization to marketing was addressing the consumer's needs and wants.

> Marketing centers in all cases around the needs of the consumer. This is an absolute shift from the old practice of making the producer the focus of all business relations. It provides a definite goal based on the logic of cold facts rather than the subjective wishes of the industrial autocrat (White 1927, pp. 97–8).

Scientific marketing is based on the theory of finding out what the consumer *wants* and then giving it to him. ... Production exists in order to serve consumption, and for no other purpose. ... Consumption is primary, production is secondary; yet it is rare to find a business which boldly faces this fact and which produces goods always with a view to the requirement of consumption. In the future these requirements will have to be met, consciously and effectively, by business men. "What does the consumer need?" This question will stand at the beginning of every business problem (White 1927, pp. 99–100, italic is original).

Apparently, the text he stressed here was the same philosophy of consumer orientation that became popular after the Second World War as part of the marketing concept, the philosophy of marketing. This philosophy was based on his optimistic belief in the 'principle of the objectivity of demand' (White 1927, p. 97). He always emphasized, 'Markets are measurable' (White 1921, p. 1).

Markets do not happen. They follow and are governed by certain economic laws. That we are unable to solve marketing problems more accurately and readily is not due to any irregularity in the nature of the markets themselves, but rather to our ignorance of the facts which bear upon the situation. If we were in possession of all the data, it is safe to say that markets would be as measurable, as certain, and as determinable as any other phenomenon which obeys fixed laws. Markets are real, tangible, and things (White 1921, pp. 1–2).

As an expert in market research, White always recommended actual surveys of markets (White 1921, 1925), and especially utilizing statistical methods such as analysis on 'correlations' with the business barometer index (White 1926b, esp. ch. 9). Sharing the mood among contemporary statisticians, who for instance discussed the 'B curve' of the Harvard Business Index of General Business Conditions, in the 1920s, White was quite optimistic about the forecasting not only of business cycles but also of sales volumes using statistical methods. This belief was the basis of the 'principle of the objectivity of demand'. For White, once marketers can measure the objective demands, marketing must be able to centre around consumers' needs and wants.

Standard as a Goal

The statistical forecasting method was also the basis of the principle of standardization. The feature of White's concept of standard was to favour the setting of scientific goals rather than standardization of implementation.

[P]roduction has become fairly well standardized. ... The emphasis has shifted to marketing, and the endeavor is being made to apply those same principles of scientific management which have worked so successfully in production. Important among these is the principle of task setting and the measurement of accomplishment according to a scientifically determined standard (White 1929, p. 2).

One of the best methods of eliminating marketing waste is by setting up proper standards of accomplishment and then holding to them. These standards may be of various kinds. The quota is one form of standard (White 1927, p. 108).

By 'quota' White not only meant those for individual salesmen and each sales territory, but also for the entire company. Regarding the latter, he explained, 'This is practically a summary of sales expectations for a coming period, as correlated with production capacity, general business conditions, distribution facilities, the advertising program, competition, and many other factors which enter into this complicated problem. This major quota is at the same time the basis for all the minor quotas. It is equal to the sum total of all other quotas' (White 1929, p. 3).

Thus, the 'quota for the entire company' substantially meant the budget for the company. As is well known, it was budgetary controls that strode ahead in business management in the 1920s, as exemplified by publication of the book by McKinsey (1922). According to a survey of outstanding manufacturers that produced in excess of 100 million dollars in 1927 and had an AAAA credit rating, conducted by the National Industrial Conference Board in the summer of 1930, 55 per cent or 162 of the 294 surveyed companies had budgets of some kind; 48 per cent or 141 companies had sales budgets and 41 per cent or 121 companies had budgets for marketing, but in contrast 45 per cent or 132 had no budgets. Only 13 per cent or 37 companies had a complete set of budgetary systems as defined by the Board – a budget for sales, production, manufacturing expenses, marketing expenses, administrative expenses, capital outlays, cash, profit and loss, and balance sheets (NICB 1931, pp. 17–18). Thus, the budgetary system was still in the process of spreading among US businesses at the time. Under such circumstances, budgetary controls with a standard costing system were considered an extension of the idea of standardization that Taylor brought to business administration as a whole. This was one of the main reasons why the Taylor Society presented the '1929 statement of principles' of scientific management, which was referred to in Chapter 2.

Taking these tendencies into consideration, White advocated setting the sales quota for the company or sales budget as a standard to be accomplished and broken down into territorial and individual standards of performance (White 1929, p. 143). This method was still different from task-setting in production, in which tasks would be set based on standardization of operating methods and the conditions surrounding workers. However, a method based on production engineering was completely impossible in marketing, so other 'rational' grounds, rather than purely relying on past experiences, must be sought. Sales budgets, which were to be combined with profit management in the 1930s (see Knoeppel and Seybold 1937) and provided a meaning for sales volume that could realize target profits for a company, were considered a 'rational' ground for setting tasks for salesmen, at least by their managers. In this sense, sales quotas controlled by sales budgets and profit targets can be considered as reflecting the progress of scientific management in marketing management.

It should be noted that such opinions were held by not only White, but also by other contemporary commentators such as Frederick ([1919] 1978, pp. 241–3), Smith (1927, p. 196) and Reed (1929, p. 191). Nevertheless, White's advocacy was most typical. White combined the idea of setting standards with his cyclical management process. 'The standards must be the outgrowth of the marketing policy. The task outlined for every man in the organization must be built upon these standards.' In this sense, 'the whole structure of scientific marketing depends upon standards which are absolute and measurable' (1927, p. 113). According to White, standards were important in planning and control processes of management: 'Standards serve both as goals of accomplishment and as methods of measurement' (1927, p. 173).

Development of the 4Ps Idea during the Two World Wars: A Bridge to the Following Chapters

The Progress towards the 4Ps Idea

During the interwar period, several books appeared which took a similar line in progressing the science of marketing management that substantially covered the 4Ps.

For instance, in his first case book at Harvard Business School, Tosdal (1921) adopted the term 'marketing management' perhaps for the first time (see Mitsuzawa 1980, p. 77, fn. 106, 1987, p. 77, fn. 42): 'the writer is inclined to favor "marketing management" as indicating more clearly the scope of the field' although usual business 'usage favors the term "sales management"' (p. xx). Sharing the scientific approach (pp. xix and 5) with Shaw (1916, p. 22), Tosdal clearly identified the importance of 'the separation of planning from performance' (p. 3), and included 'policies as to product' and 'policies regarding use of marketing agencies' (p. 6) among the planning problems. As Tosdal continued to release updated editions (1925, 1931, 1939) and introduced new books on sales management (1933, 1940), the major groups of problems in sales management that Tosdal identified grew closer to the 4Ps. In the second edition of his case book (1925, pp. 7–8), Tosdal listed 10 areas of problems in sales management, including 'Sales policies relating to product policy', 'Distribution policies, relating to the channels of distribution utilized by the manufacturer or wholesaler' and 'Price policies', as well as 'Sales methods – methods of combining forms of personal salesmanship and advertising'. Here can be clearly identified the 4Ps. In his 1933 book (p. 7), Tosdal reduced the number of issues to six: (1) What to sell (merchandising policy [product policy] and its organizations), (2) To whom shall products be sold? (marketing channels, market research and analysis), (3) At what prices and terms shall products be sold? (price and credit terms), (4) How shall the product be sold? (sales methods, sales promotion, sales campaign), (5) By whom is the work to be done? (sales organization, management of sales force), and (6) Planning and control of sales operations.

A book by Hayward (1926) adopted the words 'sales administration' in order to distinguish itself from sales management, which usually meant sales force management. He covered the issues of the product, the market and marketing methods (channels, sales force and advertising), as well as the management of sales force and sales promotion. Although the position of price policy is not clear, Hayward's idea was close to the 4Ps. Similarly, Reed (1929) discussed a 'market plan' with considerations of the company and its setting, the product, the market, distribution, and advertising and the coordination factors (Part II). Ronald (1931) edited a *Handbook on Business Administration*, at which 'Marketing' was set as Section I. While each chapter was contributed by different authors, the section included 'Market Research and Analysis', 'Merchandising: Adopting the Product to the Market', 'Price Making and Price Policy' and 'Choice of Marketing Channels', as well as 'Setting Sales Quotas', 'The Sales Force', 'Sales Promotion', 'Retailing' and 'Export Management'. The structure of chapters clearly included the 4Ps factors.

In the meantime, Pyle (1942) wrote the second book that had the title of 'Marketing Management'. He discussed the 'Functional Classification of Policies' in business (p. 22) and defined 'Marketing Policies' including policies related to: (1) the Market, (2) the formation and development of an effective Marketing Organization, (3) Marketing Research, (4) Planning, (5) Administration and operation, (6) the Product, (7) Pricing, (8) Buying and (9) Sales Promotional activities (p. 28, capitals are original). The early collection of definitions of marketing terms by the NAMT (1935) included 'marketing policy', which was defined as 'A course of action predetermined in order to insure consistency of marketing procedure under recurrent and essentially similar circumstances' (p. 157), although it did not include 'marketing management' – which also did not appear in the definitions by the AMA (1948), but appeared in the 1960 definitions (AMA [1960] 1963, p. 16). Therefore, a few early books discussed a similar idea of 4Ps under the heading of sales or marketing policy. For instance, Converse (1927) published a book of *Selling Policy*, where he defined a policy as 'a line, a course, or a plan of action to be followed consistently over a considerable period of time, usually several years' (p. 4) and covered the issues on: (1) market research, (2) product and policy, prices, (3) method of distribution (choosing a method of distribution, some problems in distributive method, physical distribution), (4) demand and creation (advertising policies, policies in the use of salesmen, sampling and speciality men, dealer helps), (5) purchasing and (6) credit. Here again an equivalent to the 4Ps idea is clear. Agnew and Houghton (1941) also put out a book of *Marketing Policies*. It included product analysis, policies with distributors and price policies among many other factors, while this book apparently advanced compared with the previous books in terms of inclusions of newly raised issues in the 1930s such as teamwork with distributors, industrial marketing, public relations and the consumer movement. It is clear that these discussions of sales or marketing policy substantially derived from discussions on business policy (to which Shaw contributed in his 1916 book), and were made purely from a managerial point of view.

In addition to these tendencies, as exemplified by the book by Alexander et al. (1940, see also Shaw and Jones 2005, p. 256), the managerial issues were becoming increasingly clear among marketing textbooks based on the traditional approaches that were more or less a mixture of the macro and micro points of view. Thus, the 4Ps framework was progressing towards dominance after the Second World War.

Two General Backgrounds

While individual interests and backgrounds can be assumed in each contributor, there were two general background factors encouraging such development. The one was the progress of managerial professionalism (Chandler 1977, pp. 464–8) as the essence of managerial capitalism. The movement to collegiate education in commerce started in the late nineteenth century, as the Introduction describes.

This was accompanied by the appearance of professional associations, journals and consultants. Nevertheless, the progress was gradual. As Chandler put it,

> In the 1920 the societies were still small, the journals not too widely read, and the business school graduates still in the lower rank of management. By the mid-twentieth century, however, professionally oriented, salaried career managers were the men who had taken charge of the large multiunit enterprises dominating the critical sectors of the American economy (1977, p. 468).

It was only natural that such further progress of managerial capitalism led to a clearer articulation of explicit knowledge on entrepreneurial decision making in marketing and made it more scientific. The contributors mentioned above, although unconsciously in most cases, followed the pioneering works from before the First World War and attempted to articulate and progress the 4Ps type of thinking in marketing management.

The other factor was that diversification tended to become a main strategy of growth for manufacturers, who had vertically integrated to marketing, from 1920 onwards: 'since 1920, the large firms have increasingly followed a strategy of growth by diversification rather than vertical integration' (Chandler 1969, p. 274, see also [1962] 1969, pp. 42–9, 1977, pp. 473–4). The impact of diversification strategy was already shown in Chapter 1 with the case of Crisco from P&G and also will be seen in the two cases presented in the next chapter. Because diversification strategy meant entering a new market with a new product even though the company utilized existing technology and/or resources, the managers generally confronted the problem of 4Ps type of decision making: which product to introduce, at which price, and via which channel to distribute it, as well as judging whether the new market would be profitable. Professional and salaried managers increasingly needed explicit knowledge to make these decisions.

Features of Development of the Ideas

The progress of the above ideas was made taking a broadly similar line to Shaw and White; that is, making the explicit knowledge more scientific. This process generally suggests that the ideas were being separated from the factual circumstances of the decision and advancing towards generalization and decontextualization.

Nevertheless, some books, especially those in the 1920s, still sometimes reflected the same direct context that produced Butler's primitive idea of marketing management. Typical of this was Hayward (1926), whose book was subtitled 'a study of the manufacturer's marketing problems'. Reed (1929) implied the same standpoint: 'a practical guide in planning the marketing of manufactured goods' (p. iii). In a series of books, Tosdal stated: 'the scope of this book is limited to sales management in wholesale and manufacturing enterprises' although he thought the principles 'may be applied to retail stores' (1921, p. 1, see also 1933, p. 1). His limitation did not suggest that his arguments focused only on the integrated manufacturers, but showed that retail marketing was not yet included in the scope of his arguments.

Conclusions

Although both Shaw and White were influenced by scientific management in the broader sense and attempted to apply its principles to marketing management, the actual content of their work was different, partly due to different individual perspectives and partly to differences in the actual conditions of marketing and society and theoretical conditions of management during the 1910s and 1920s. Fundamentally, both considered the principle of standardization as the essence of scientific management, but the spheres they examined were different; whereas Shaw focused on standard ways of establishing marketing policies based on utilizing large sample theory in market research, White advocated setting standards in terms of quotas and linking tasks to budgetary control of a company, based on statistical forecasting. In addition, both also included elements that went beyond Taylor's scientific management. Shaw considered the importance of the macroenvironment of marketing, especially political movements and public opinion, in order to ensure a stable environment for marketing management. White's remarkable contribution was giving a cyclic form to the management process. In addition he found a clue for rationalizing the division of labour in managerial organization in the principle of functionalization that was being developed in management theory. Although both Shaw and White were over-optimistic that they could find the 'one best way' – and in this sense, both were classical thinkers of marketing management – it is evident that from a current point of view, both contributed to establishing the framework of scientific marketing management. The progress towards the formation of the 4Ps idea mentioned in the final section arose mainly along the same lines as the Shaw and White contributions.

In the meantime, progress in actual practice was being made in each individual field of the 4Ps. As new practices became popular, they in turn became the context that encouraged the articulation of further explicit knowledge and enriched the knowledge of marketing management. The following two chapters will focus on product policy, and the last chapter will address marketing channel policy, both of which are indispensable and unique features in marketing management. The books from the interwar period mentioned above will be explored in depth at relevant points in these chapters.

Chapter 4

'Merchandising' as a Missing Concept in the History of Marketing Management Thought

'Merchandising' was a historically unique concept. It existed between the two world wars, especially in the 1930s, to signify product policy or product planning. This concept has been popular among Japanese historians who explored marketing history in the USA.[1] This chapter recognizes that the existence of the concept offers evidence to show the development in practice of marketing management; therefore, it will analyse the interactions between evolving activities and the notion of 'merchandising' as an example of 'Process C' in the analytical framework shown in the introductory chapter.

This chapter first verifies the concept of 'merchandising' by looking through historical definitions primarily from the 1930s; then it explores the generation of this historical concept before that decade. The analysis will show that this concept was not unique to the 1930s, and will uncover the process of development in the idea of marketing management in terms of the function of product policy. The next chapter will identify product policy features in the 1930s in respect of this concept.

---

1 The existence of the concept of 'merchandising' in the 1930s was revealed uniquely by Japanese historians who explored US marketing history (e.g. Tokunaga 1957, Miura 1958, Morishita 1959a, 1959b, Arakawa 1960, Furo 1962, Mitsuzawa 1966, Hashimoto 1966, Tamura 1977, pp. 135–8, Yamamoto 1977, Kometani 1978). Based on Morishita's (1959a) paradigm (see also Usui 2000), many of them believed that in contrast with the 'high pressure marketing' of the 1920s when American business enjoyed prosperity, the 1930s saw a change towards 'consumer-oriented' marketing due to the more sluggish conditions as a result of the Great Depression in 1929. The existence of the concept of 'merchandising' was recognized as the key to this transformation in marketing philosophy.

This book disputes this Japanese version of the stage model. As was shown in Chapter 1 exploring Butler's ideas, marketing management included the idea of product policy, in other words, the idea of making products acceptable to consumers, from the outset. Shaw's concept of product differentiation discussed in Chapter 3 also sought to give products attractive features. In addition, White's comment in the 1920s explicitly formulated the idea of consumer orientation, although based on a classically optimistic opinion on forecasting consumer demands and the principle of standardization. Although it is true that the 1920s saw the term 'high pressure marketing' (Borsodi [1927] 1976), it must be said that hard-sell and soft-sell can be found existing in parallel at any time in marketing history (see Hollander 1986, p. 19).

The Historical Definitions of Merchandising: An Overview

As Duddy and Revsan (1953, p. 34) indicated, the term 'merchandising' was equivocal and difficult to define. This term has often been used to mean the promotional activities by marketers, or buying activities for resale to provide suitable assortments of products for merchants. The dictionary of marketing terms published by the AMA stated, 'It can (1) relate to the promotional activities of manufacturers that bring about in-store displays, or (2) identify the product and product line decisions of retailers' (Bennett 1988, p. 176).

The 1930s definition was totally different, typified by Copeland and Learned (1933):

> Merchandising is product planning. The job of merchandising is to ascertain the characteristics of the merchandise for which there is a potentially profitable demand, to prepare instructions for the manufacturing plant in order that it may be able to produce goods for which a demand exists, to aid in developing plans for promoting the sales, and to supervise various routine operations in connection with these activities. It includes the determination of what to make, how much, at what time, and at what price (Copeland and Learned, 1933, Glossary of Terms).

It is evident that the definition assumed the manufacturer as a marketer, and defined merchandising as product planning for the manufacturer. The Definition Committee of the National Association of Marketing Teachers, one of the former organizations of the AMA, defined it as follows:

> Merchandising – The adjustment of merchandise produced or offered for sale to customer demand. It involves the coordination of selling with production or buying for resale.
>
> *Comment* – This term has been used with a great variety of meanings. The definition recommended is practically that set up by the Harvard Group. The spade work already done by its originators in popularizing it should go far toward the attainment of some degree of uniformity in the usage of this much abused term. As set forth above, *merchandising* involves such activities as selecting the product to be produced or stocked and deciding such details as the size, appearance, form, dressing the product (packaging, etc.), quantities to be bought or made, time of purchase or production, price lines to be carried or made, etc. (NAMT 1935, p. 158, italics are original).

The characteristic of this definition was to coordinate selling with production for manufacturers although, significantly, it was not limited to manufacturers' activities.

These two definitions are unusual from the current point of view on this term. Even in the 1930s, such definitions confused many business people, so questions were often raised in business journals (see *Printers' Ink* 1928, 1932a, 1932d, 1936). Nevertheless, this kind of definition was gradually disseminated at the textbook level – by Richmond, for example:

> Retail merchandising is now generally defined as the *selection* of merchandise which will meet needs, wants, and desires of consumers.
>
> Manufacturers are more and more thinking of merchandising in terms similar to the retail usage. The main distinction is that for "select" the manufacturer must substitute

"create." For him merchandising is the creation of goods which people will want to buy. ... It is through merchandising that production and selling come closest together. Merchandising implies that a definite effort has been made, in advance of producing goods, to determine their sales possibilities. It signifies the coordination of manufacture and sales, taking into account consumer requirements and demands and the manufacturing facilities of the plants (Richmond 1931, p. 69, italic is original).

Similarly, Tosdal, who had been publishing marketing management textbooks from the 1920s, newly defined it in 1931: 'As used in this volume, merchandising includes the adjustment of the product to market demands, both qualitatively and quantitatively. ... The merchandising is used, therefore, in a narrower sense than that which has frequently been accorded it' (Tosdal 1931, p. 8). This explanation was not included in his books from the 1920s (Tosdal 1921, 1925), and thus can be seen as characteristic of the 1930s.

Elder (1940, p. 118), citing the NAMT definition, repeated this opinion: 'the function is primarily a matter of planning and controlling merchandise in order to adapt it to market demand'. Pyle (1942, p. 99, underline is original) adopted basically the same definition: 'Merchandising is that part of the marketing process which has to do with the determination of <u>what</u> to produce, add to or take from a line of goods or merchandise; the discovery and development of new uses for old products as well as new products for old uses; and the scientific pricing of the product.'

The 1948 definition by the AMA (1948, p. 211) maintained the 1930s terminology although the definition committee at the time added a slightly modified comment, 'The activities described here might also be called merchandise, or product, planning.' In due time after the Second World War, the term 'product planning', rather than 'merchandising', became more and more preferable. The 1960 definition by the AMA adopted the 1948 definition in essence, but the committee gave a much clearer recommendation for the limited usage of the term 'merchandising' to the area of merchant's trade: 'The term is most widely used in this sense in the wholesaling and retailing trade. Many manufacturers designate this activity as Product Planning or Management' (AMA [1960] 1963, p. 17). The original definition of 'merchandising', which meant manufacturer's product planning, has now totally disappeared, as shown in the beginning of this section.

Was such a changing process in terminology a meaningless confusion? No, this chapter argues. Rather, the process occurred because of serious efforts to give a suitable weight to product planning in manufacturers' marketing management. Analysing this process can reveal the development of this aspect in marketing management. It should be noted that the historical concept of 'merchandising' did not suddenly emerge in the 1930s but in the 1920s, based on the actual experiences of manufacturers and repeated discussions, mainly in the Taylor Society. Two historical concepts, 'sales engineering' and 'merchandising', were advocated there, and as the former quickly disappeared, the latter spread widely in the next decade.

The Concept of 'Sales Engineering' and Marketing by the Winchester Repeating Arms Company

The Concept of 'Sales Engineering'

In May 1920, what the Taylor Society (1920a, p. 229) called 'a little acorn', a round table conference on scientific management applied to the sales department, was planted. It was 'grown into a healthy sapling' when the Conference of Sales Executives was held in New York on 25 June. This was a big jump for the Society, to expand their view fully to the sales and marketing process. Although the first step had already been taken as early as the 1910s, the article that was explored in Chapter 2 was the only one carried in the Bulletin during that decade. After the conference in 1920, the Board of Directors of the Taylor Society (1920e) announced the establishment of a Sales Executives' Section. Three Preliminary Reports were submitted to the Annual Meeting of the Society in December 1920 by the committees which had been appointed by the resolution of this Conference. The reports were carried in the Bulletin twice, exceptionally (Taylor Society, 1920b–d, 1921a–c). Thereafter, the Bulletin carried many articles related to sales and marketing.

A leading figure who reported on 'Coordination of Sales with Scientific Production' at the June Conference and acted as the chairman of two of the three Preliminary Reports was Willard F. Freeland. He worked for the Winchester Repeating Arms Company. His idea of sales engineering, which was dominant both in the June Conference and the Preliminary Reports, reflected directly on his experience as 'sales engineer' (Williamson 1952, p. 285) at his company.

One of the points of Freeland's idea was separating the so-called engineering function from the operating function. Freeland reported at the Conference of Sales Executives,

> Now there is a wide-spread recognition of the function of engineering in production. We recognize, most of us, the essential difference between the planning – which is the engineering – and the production groups in the factory organizations. ... It has not been so well recognized, however, that there is a definite function for engineering in sales; and I want to interject here that when we use the term "Sales Engineering" in our factory, we do not use it in the sense so frequently used in the technical papers, of a salesman who goes out to do technical planning for the installation of a manufactured product or a machine. We use it in a sense analogous to that of manufacturing engineering (Freeland 1920, pp. 202–3).

In accordance with his speech, the Preliminary Report indicated,

> For convenience in this report the term Sales Engineering is used as descriptive of the major function discussed. Work of this character, in whole or in part, is now being carried on in organizations under such titles as Sales Technical Division, Sales Promotion, Merchandising, Merchandising Control, Sales Research, Sales Planning, Development Department, etc. It is not important at this time to discuss the name, as the choice of a name will depend upon the organization, personnel and character of the individual enterprise. ... Every modern sales manager has of necessity been compelled to carry on

some or all of the phases of distribution outlined herein. The subject matter is new only in the attempt to segregate into a distinct major function that part of his work which has to do with research, master planning and master scheduling (Taylor Society 1920c, p. 235, 1921a, p. 205).

The Report concluded, 'Master planning and scheduling can properly be considered sales engineers, delegating detailed planning and scheduling as secondary functions of operation.' This was 'a comparatively new phase of the work of a distributing or marketing organization' (Taylor Society 1920c, pp. 235–6, 1921a, pp. 205–6).

Despite the self-confidence in the Report, the advocacy would not sound so new at least to this book's readers, because Butler had presented similar views in the 1910s. However, one can understand this kind of advocacy was still effective at the time, when considering the historical context. The questionnaire by the Taylor Society to the manufacturing firms, which were 'fairly representative of the best general management rather than of the average' (Taylor Society 1920b, p. 231, 1921a, p. 202), reveals that the actual situation in business in terms of organization for the planning function in marketing was still in transit. According to this survey, nine firms or 36 per cent of firms responding had no independent department or staff responsible for devising 'sales plans' (Taylor Society 1920b, p. 232, 1921a, p. 203).

The Preliminary Report gave the definition that the 'sales engineering function represents at least three distinct phases', that is, (a) 'field research' on products, marketing policies and methods including trade channels, and general research, (b) 'technical assistance' to the entire business organization, and (c) 'master planning and scheduling' (Taylor Society 1920c, pp. 235–6, 1921b, pp. 205–6). The 'master planning and scheduling' was the most significant, meaning the plan and schedule regarding new and old products:

> Sales engineering should become the coordinating function of the entire business. In this field it can relieve the administrative and managerial executives of many of their most troublesome and time-consuming problems. In this activity sales engineering should strive to be months ahead of any of the operating divisions. Only thus can the purchasing, financial, personnel and production divisions have adequate time to plan for their respective activities (Taylor Society 1920c, p. 236, 1921b, p. 206).

The comment showed that the 'engineering' or planning function of marketing began to embrace consciously the coordination between production and marketing, pivoting on the plan and schedule of the products. Figure 4.1 shows the role of sales engineering as a coordinator between production and sales operation, as illustrated by the Taylor Society (1920d), although the figure in itself was mainly to illustrate 'sales operation'.

It should be noted that this idea did not emerge as a logical development in thought, but was based on specific experience after the First World War at the Winchester Repeating Arms Co.

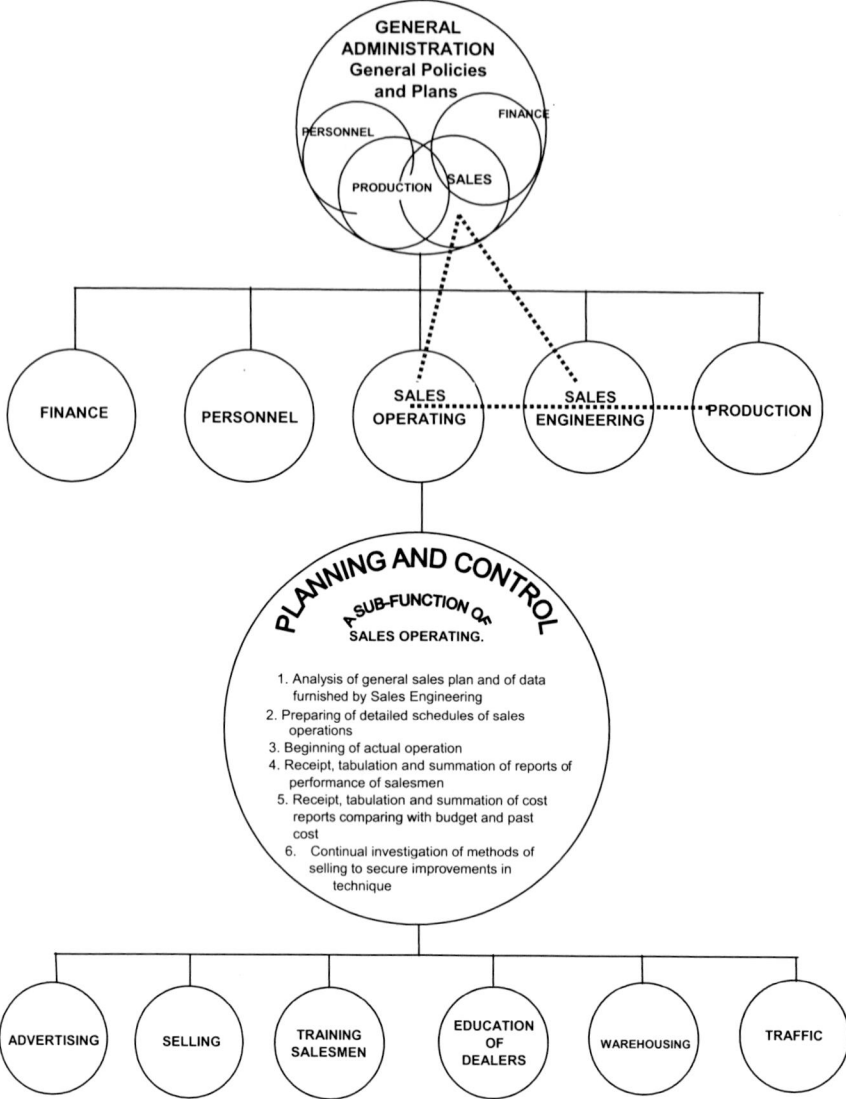

Source: Taylor Society 1920d, p. 239, 1921c, p. 209.
Note: The figure omits some explanatory text in the largest circle to show the sub-functions of sales operating.

Figure 4.1   The relationship between sales engineering, sales operating and production as charted by the Taylor Society in 1920

Diversification of Product Lines by the Winchester

The Winchester, a famous manufacturer of weaponry, started its business in the 1850s. As Chandler (1977, p. 314) indicated, it integrated activities vertically by organizing its own wholesale branches in the 1890s. During the First World War, the company hugely expanded the plants and plant facilities, according to Freeland four times beyond the stage of 1914, so that it faced a serious problem of the overcapacity of production after the armistice. 'That plant must be filled with new production', reported Freeland (1920, p. 202). Confronted by the pressing task of occupying the partially vacant factory with new production, John E. Otterson, the President of the company, instituted the organization which the company called the Sales Engineering Department (Freeland 1920, p. 203).

The activities of this department were as follows (see Williamson 1952, pp. 286–8). In the latter part of 1919 and continuing through 1920 various departments of the company made surveys of a large number of products. The 'sales engineers' occupied a strategic position for these activities. They passed on the advisability of adopting new product lines and items after marketing and production analysis. If the decision was favourable, they also suggested output quotas and sales prices. Then the 'manufacturing engineers' estimated the cost of manufacture based on the output quota and the method of manufacture. If the estimated manufacturing cost was within the limits of the sales prices set by the sales engineers, the products under consideration were adopted. The company thereafter flowed two ways to build up its production facilities; one was to begin the production of items that seemed adapted to the methods and equipment already being used in gun and ammunition manufacture, and the other was to acquire the companies from which any advantages could be gained in terms of existing manufacturing equipment that could be immediately used for the new lines, technical or manufacturing experience including the employment of key personnel, patents, trade marks and/or access to marketing channels. Following this method, the company bought nine companies between June 1919 and May 1920. Based on these procedures, Winchester added about 750 new items such as cutlery, including kitchen knives, scissors, shears and pocket knives, tools including screw drivers, chisels, punches, hammers, hatchets and pliers, batteries, flashlights, fishing rods and reels, fishing lines and bait, roller skates and ice skates (Williamson 1952, pp. 288–95).

These moves were the basis of Freeland's discussion. Defining sales engineering as the 'master planning' that will guide a whole organization, Freeland set the duties of sales engineers in his speech at the Conference in June 1920. 'In the first place, the master planner must have close contact with all parts of the organisation' and must make intensive study of 'consumer demands', 'economic trends' and 'factory facilities'. 'After these preliminary studies, it becomes the sales engineers' duties to select the items and lines to be manufactured. Having done this it is up to him to present this matter in such a way that the operating parts of the organization can go to work in some coordinated manner' (Freeland 1920, p. 203).

Thus, the explanation in the Preliminary Report of the Taylor Society was dominated by Freeland's idea based on actual activities at the Winchester. The tense situation at Winchester after the First World War had produced the discussion on the coordination between production and marketing pivoting on adopting or diversifying to new products. But the idea of sales engineering had two weak features as well.

The first was that the idea was not purely limited to the coordination function, but included many other factors, as already shown in the discussion on three major phases of sales engineering. Again, this feature reflected various activities at Winchester, particularly regarding marketing channel. Although the Winchester had originally sold its products through jobbers or wholesalers to retail dealers, the company decided to change this method because some new products the company had adopted would be competing with established brands that the jobbers owned, and because it would take a long time to reach the desirable volume of distribution (Williamson 1952, p. 275). Therefore, the Winchester adopted the 'dealer-agency plan', at which the company bypassed the jobber and sold directly to a selected group of exclusive retailers in the towns throughout the USA with 50,000 population or less.

The company also tried to establish its own retail stores, in cities with 50,000 population or more, whereas it decided to adhere to the traditional channel through the jobber in terms of trade in guns and ammunition (Otterson 1924, p. 329, Williamson 1952, pp. 227–9). The dealer-agency plan started in October 1919 and was rapidly expanded; by February 1920 almost 2,400 dealers, by the end of 1920 close to 3,400, and by the end of 1921 almost 4,000 dealers had signed the contract (Williamson 1952, pp. 295, 301 and 303). These dealers were organized into district associations or clubs, which met periodically to discuss topics of mutual interest. The National Association of Winchester Clubs was also organized. Winchester supplied advertising display for each dealer at an average cost of five dollars per month, put national advertisements in some periodicals, published a monthly house journal, *Winchester Herald*, and sent it to each dealer, provided plans for modernizing the store layouts at a nominal cost and dispatched a representative to supervise the installation, and furnished some advice on the matters of proper store accounting, methods of finance, and analysis of credit risk (Williamson 1952, pp. 301–2).

According to Freeland (1920, pp. 204–5), the sales engineering staff committed themselves to convention and club work, as well as furnishing technical information for advertising and publications and reports to organize the marketing channel. Reflecting these miscellaneous activities, the discussion of sales engineering included various factors rather than limiting itself to product planning. In this sense the concept was not so clearly defined, but the activities of Winchester were an eminent example in marketing history.

The second, but perhaps more fatal, weak point was that the terminology of 'sales engineering' carried the wrong implications. The editor of the *Bulletin of the Taylor Society*, which carried the Preliminary Reports for the first time, commented, 'The use of the term "sales engineering" in these reports is largely an accident, and the question of terminology is an open one' (Taylor Society 1920a, p. 229). Also, an early management handbook published in 1924 indicated,

> **Sales engineering** is a term sometimes incorrectly used as descriptive of market analysis, based on idea that engineering principles are being applied to selling. This use of the term should not be confused with another sense in which sales engineering is correctly used,

namely, that of engineering or technical service rendered to customer by the salesman, who is an engineer and is able to help customer solve technical problems arising in connection with use of product under consideration (Bradford 1924, p. 1433, bold is original).

In fact, sales engineering at the Winchester involved more or less 'field research'; it was only natural to infer at the time that the word represented market research. Although the term 'sales engineer' indicating a knowledgeable salesman has survived until now, as exemplified by the AMA dictionary, 'A salesperson who has extensive product knowledge and uses this knowledge as a focal aspect of the sales presentation' (Bennett 1995, p. 250), the concept of sales engineering as product or marketing planning did not survive even until the 1930s. Instead, the concept of merchandising gradually became the focus.

The Concept of 'Merchandising' and Marketing by Dennison Manufacturing Company

The Idea of Merchandising and the Activities at the Dennison Mfg. Co.

At the same Conference of Sales Executives at which Freeland introduced the concept of sales engineering, Henry S. Dennison (1877–1952), the President of Dennison Manufacturing Company and also the President of the Taylor Society at the time, gave a keynote speech before Freeland's report giving an essence of the idea of 'merchandising'. Although the concept of sales engineering happened to be predominant at first in the Taylor Society, it was not easily accepted in general. In contrast, Dennison's concept of 'merchandising' was becoming more and more popular in this decade and exerted a strong influence on contemporary marketing people even outside the Taylor Society.

As the keynote speech of the Conference of Sales Executives, Dennison mentioned 'a very notable discovery' – 'none of us knows much about the very necessary process of selling' and 'every one of us is extremely anxious to know something of it' – that was found by the small group which decided to call the conference. 'The point is about this, I think', Dennison (1920, p. 200) explained, 'that as we develop efficiency in production, as we go along the road of more scientific management of production process, we begin to come up against the difficulties which arise out of unscientific selling or which arise out of an absence of coordination between selling and manufacturing.' The speech would echo the awareness of the pioneers in the 1910s, explored in Chapter 2. However, the idea of 'coordination between selling and manufacturing' deserves attention in historical research.

This idea derived from the experience of the Dennison Manufacturing Company. According to Dennison, in addition to the manufacturing department and the selling department that managed the salesmen, there was a third department equal to each of them, that is, what his company called the merchandising department. 'The merchandising department controls the goods, their quality, their character, their price, their put-up, and at the present time it has the largest control of the scheduling of their manufacture – that is, the quantity of those goods that must be made in any given period in the future' (Dennison 1920, p. 200).

This comment at the keynote speech drew a rough sketch of the concept of merchandising. In due course Dennison (1926, 1927a, 1927b) introduced the idea in more detail. He admitted that there was 'a complete lack of an accepted definition of the term "merchandising"' (Dennison 1927a, p. 526); however, he underlined his company's definition, 'a co-ordinating force between the job of selling goods and the job of manufacturing the goods to be sold' (Dennison 1927a, p. 526). According to this, the task of merchandising was made up of the following four elements:

1. The study of the merchandise relative to:
    a. Creating new merchandise
    b. Finding new uses for standard merchandise and
    c. Watching the trends of the market, particularly to avoid the retention of items that give indication of becoming obsolete.
2. The study of the merchandise relative to estimating the amount of production necessary, most importantly – in cooperation – to meet the market requirements at different seasons and periods.
3. The study of the merchandise relative to making price estimates on special merchandise and to making changes in list prices of stock merchandise.
4. To make lines of merchandise of continuing interest to the selling organization (Dennison 1927a, p. 526; see Dennison 1927b, p. 109).

It can be concluded that the definition was successful in co-ordinating production and sales pivoting on the products. Dennison (1927a, 529) emphasized: 'Merchandising, as described above, is truly a catalytic agent. It not only makes co-ordination possible, but is a positive force towards leadership and progress. It recognizes consumer's demands as the origin of economic impulse and as dynamic and changing. Production must discover these changing demands and adapt itself to them.' The comment was far-sighted because he initiated the philosophy of consumer orientation through identifying the coordinator named merchandising between production and selling.

The Dennison Manufacturing Company that introduced such a definition was 'one of the best-known medium-sized companies in American industry' (Urwick and Brech 1951, p. 112). The company was founded in 1844 to manufacture jewellers' boxes, and expanded to include tags, crepe paper, and many other stationery supplies (Hayes and Heath 1929). In 1906 when an energetic, autocratic executive controlling product policy retired, the company began to develop merchandising as a separate function. Merchandising committees comprising from eight to 15 members were formed for each of the six major lines at the time, that is, tags, crepe, jewellers' items, adhesives, Christmas items and the so-called consumers' items (goods not for resale, but for use in the retailer's own business, such as printed shipping tags, marking tags and gummed labels). At first, however, the committees were to meet only once a year and their chairmen were to give only part of their time to this work (Hayes and Heath 1929, pp. 498 and 167; see Dennison 1926, p. 81). It was said that the committee system was too new to have much effect on product policy at the time (Hayes and Heath 1929, p. 498). It was in 1917, when H.S. Dennison was inaugurated President of the company, that a 'general merchandising committee', which it is supposed that Dennison introduced as the 'merchandising department', was formed, including the other chairmen of the committees. Thus, Dennison's use of the term merchandising that determined the products which were to be dealt in, and was composed of four elements, that is, creation of new merchandise, scheduling production, pricing and market interpretation, was established (Hayes and Heath 1929, pp. 167 and 184–5).

When considering this situation, it is evident that the idea of merchandising was derived from the experience of such a company that a diversification strategy in products, including adding, modifying and eliminating a lot of items, was the lifeline. The historical evaluation was twofold, both negative and positive. A contemporary researcher in the 1920s investigating the company's history raised a question about centralized merchandising. When the company organized the general merchandising committee in 1917, an urgent task was to eliminate the less important items, rather than add new ones under wartime conditions, resulting in dropping 1,500 items (Hayes and Heath 1929, pp. 185–6). The researcher questioned if with the actual organization of the company, the most important element of the merchandising function – that of creation of new merchandise – might be neglected for the other elements, pricing, scheduling, and servicing, because acquaintance with factory facilities and their limitations might easily be overemphasized, so that new ideas were to be judged more according to the ease with which the factory could comply mechanically than according to their sales appeal. The researcher indicated the necessity of separating the 'creative side of merchandising' from its other elements, although she admitted that progress was just beginning (Hayes and Heath 1929, pp. 198–9). This indication struck home. The issue of creative work for developing saleable products became the main theme in product planning in the 1930s, even though the historical concept of merchandising was widely accepted, as will be seen in the next chapter.

Influences of Dennison's Concept of Merchandising

The influence of Dennison's definition was immense, although it sometimes raised questions (see *Printers' Ink* 1928, 1932a, 1932d, 1936). When the Taylor Society compiled a book on the 1920s version of scientific management, a chapter on 'merchandising standards' was included, where the definition of merchandising was very similar to Dennison's (Keir and Dennison 1929, p. 163). Even W.E. Freeland, who had advocated the concept of sales engineering, admitted in 1926 – he left Winchester and became Assistant Professor of Marketing at the Massachusetts Institute of Technology at the time – that the concept of merchandising was beginning to be accepted as an advance in marketing organization: 'Most recently of all, a function has emerged which usually bears the name of merchandising. As yet no standardization of this function is visible but in general it takes over those problems of marketing which have to do specifically with the product and the coordination of the sales and production programs' (Freeland 1926, p. 208).

The most remarkable influence was on M.T. Copeland, who was to define with Learned in 1933 the term merchandising as product planning, as shown in the early part of this chapter. In 1924 when Copeland ([1924] 1978, pp. 3–4) published a book entitled *Principles of Merchandising*, his definition was totally different from that of the 1930s: 'Merchandising is the term applied to the active solicitation of patronage – by stimulating consumers to purchase a specific product, by encouraging wholesale and retail merchants to aid in promoting the sales of the product, and by formulating and executing comprehensive and consistent plans for distributing the product, effectively and economically, from producer to consumers.' As Copeland himself (1927, p. 21) admitted later, this contrasted completely with his later definition: 'In fact, in my book "Principles of Merchandising," published in 1924, I used the term "merchandising" broadly to cover all the marketing functions.'

Nevertheless, after only a few years, Copeland realized the altered usage of the term. 'As conditions change in an industry', he wrote, 'companies add new products to their lines, revamp some of the old products and discard others. Even Mr. Ford has changed his hardy perennial model' (Copeland 1927, p. 21). As is well known, in 1927 Henry Ford unwillingly changed his famous Model T, which had been supposed to require no model change. Copeland continued,

> Changes in the needs and fancies of consumers, changes in manufacturing technique, new inventions and changes in the arts, all are working to bring about more or less frequent alterations in many types of products.
>
> The problems of determining what to add to a line, what to discard and what to revamp, have become more and more pressing and complex with the increase in the sizes of industrial units and with the diversification of industry.
>
> The function of dealing with these problems relating to the determination of what to make, is merchandising. Clear-cut recognition is a recent development (Copeland 1927, p. 21).

In the final year of the 1920s, Copeland explicitly defined merchandising as 'product planning', substantially in the same way as his 1933 definition, which was cited in the opening of this chapter.

> A characteristic of many American industries during the nineteenth century and the early twentieth century was mass production of more or less standardized articles, a system which reached its zenith in the Ford plant. ... Since 1920, however, a different set of conditions has been apparent, as indicated by the new tempo of demand, the rapidity of style changes, and the receptivity of consumers to new varieties and types of products. ... This tendency toward greater variety may be regretted, but it is a fact that cannot be disregarded by alert business executives. These conditions have placed a premium on keen foresight in product planning, that is, on constructive merchandising.
>
> Merchandising includes the determination of what goods to produce in order to meet actual or potential demands, what changes to make in existing products, what style or finishes to provide for, what methods of packing to adopt, what products to discard, and what quantities to make (Copeland 1929, p. 329).

Soon after this explanation, Copeland cited Dennison's definition of merchandising (Dennison 1927b, p. 109) and described it as a significant development produced in the 1920s:

Until recently, in most manufacturing companies this merchandising function has been assigned to various executives or shared jointly by numerous members of a manufacturing and sales organization. But within the last ten years, several companies have recognized the importance of this function and have set up in their organizations the office of merchandising manager, or its equivalent, to centralize the control of the merchandising function and to insure its proper performance. This probably has been one of the most noteworthy marketing developments during this period (Copeland 1929, p. 330).

Clearly the groundwork of the historical concept of merchandising that was recognized as a feature of the 1930s had been already laid in the previous decade.

Conclusion

The two historical concepts of 'sales engineering' and of 'merchandising' were the products of discussions mainly at the Taylor Society in the 1920s. The discussions were made to develop the idea of marketing management, based on the developing experiences of manufacturers at the time.

The concept of 'sales engineering' could not survive or influence the development of the marketing management idea. A reason was that the word 'engineering' could not evoke any proper images of planning in product policy and/or marketing, having been influenced directly by mechanical engineers, among whose field the idea of Taylor's scientific management arose. In addition, the concept of 'sales engineering' was too broadly defined. It included not only product planning, but also channel selection and channel promotion. In this respect, the concept of 'sales engineering' was almost equivalent to the concept of marketing management rather than product policy. Although the efforts to generalize the 'sales engineering' concept failed to develop the idea of product planning, it can be evaluated as one of the serious efforts to define marketing management itself during the period when the concepts of marketing and marketing management were not yet clearly recognized.

In the meantime, the concept of 'merchandising' proposed by Dennison was successful in defining the function of product planning for the manufacturer more clearly. As the recognition spread of the importance of coordination between manufacturing and sales, so this concept became accepted in the business world. The sluggish business conditions in the 1930s especially promoted this recognition connected with the concept of 'merchandising'.

An essential question was already raised regarding this concept even at the time. Recognition of the importance of an independent 'merchandising' function could not automatically teach how to create an attractive product for the consumer. The 'creative side of merchandising' (Hayes and Heath 1929, p. 198) or how to create a saleable product, still remained as an important and unsolved issue.

An ongoing problem is how the manufacturer can make the product marketable. The next chapter explores how manufacturers developed this idea, focusing on the design issue of products.

Chapter 5

The Redesign Movement and Development of Product Policy: A Meeting of Marketers and Industrial Designers

'Merchandising' as product policy was so widely supported in the 1930s that the genuine reasons for this may be obscured by the textbooks. This chapter considers a remarkable contemporary event in marketing practice, and looks at the way that event related to 'merchandising' and how the idea of product policy gained ground as a result.

The significant event is the boom in industrial design. It is clear of course that in the long history of commercial trade, design was often the decisive element that influenced the saleability of products, as exemplified by Wedgwood pottery in the eighteenth century (McKendrick, et al. 1982, ch. 3; see also Fullerton 1988). Nevertheless, during the two decades between the world wars, and in the 1930s in particular, the design issue assumed a new significance. As many kinds of consumer durables and mechanical products became increasingly widespread, so their design became more and more important in marketing strategy. This chapter looks at the relationship between the boom in design and redesign at the time, which is called the 'redesign movement' (Meikel 1979, p. 68), and the idea of merchandising or product policy.

The first section will analyse the concept of 'design', because this term is very often equivocal. The next section will explore the conditions in which design exponents began to take an active part in marketing, citing some outstanding cases: marketing of a gas cooker, an automobile, a radio set and a refrigerator. Some features of these cases were directly influential, while others were not. This process is inevitable because in contrast to the primitive stage, when the idea emerged directly from the background, as seen in Butler's case, its development brought the concept a greater currency but lost sight of its origin. The cases considered here will illustrate this. The latter part of the chapter tries to trace the concept of product policy back to the contexts in the redesign movement that fostered its development.

Design – Engineering or Aesthetics: An Analytical Point of View

The history of design is almost as long as the history of humanity. The origin of design can be discovered in the distinction between humankind and other animals. A bee, for instance, constructs its cell as well as, or perhaps even better than, a human architect does, but it is only the human that can visualize the form, structure and functions in the imagination before actually constructing it. Nagata (1983, p. 224), a Japanese philosopher on design, calls this activity, unique to humankind, the 'conception of a shape'. So designing is an essential attribute that distinguishes humanity from other animals (Kawazoe 1979, p. 27).

Supposing an object hand-made by a single person, the 'conception of a shape' in the mind and the actual process of making it by hand must be inseparable, and the interactive process between mind and hands must progress more or less by trial and error. Through this experimental process, the artisan accumulates knowledge and skills of how to design the object. This process in craftsmanship has survived until now, especially in the field of craft design. In contrast, where the process of making the object needs many workers' co-operation based on a division of labour, the 'conception of a shape' must be shown objectively via drawing, blueprint or pattern book for the workers to recognize it before starting their work. In this case, what is called the 'separation of design from the processes of production' (Heskett 1987, p. 20, see Bradley 1946, p. 27) would be inevitable. Heskett (1987, p. 11) indicated that this separation appeared even in the early capitalist industrial organizations that were based on craft methods of production; for instance, pattern books illustrating decorative forms, patterns and motifs for ribbon-making or cabinet-making were utilized by nascent designers as early as the sixteenth century in Italy and Germany.

However, another separation became remarkable and problematic especially after the Industrial Revolution. In the case of machine products and those made of new materials like cast iron, the shape of products was generally decided by engineering requirements, without reference to aesthetic codes. This is called the 'divorce between art and industry' (Heskett 1987, p. 27). Not all traditional designers were separated from the industrial world, but they tended to evolve in what *Fortune* (1934, p. 98) called the 'art industries,' such as ceramics, enamels, furniture, leatherwork, plasterwork, rugs, carpets, silverware, textiles, wallpaper, jewellery and so forth, and work for wealthy patrons. In contrast, it was generally engineers who decided the shape of machine-related products.

According to Nagata (1983, pp. 225–8), the 'conception of a shape' is originally composed of two essential moments (the 'moment' here is a philosophical term, meaning a constituent element of a complex entity): that is, the 'moment of function and engineering' and the 'moment of sensation and aesthetics'. The former moment is symbolized by an engineer and the latter by a designer, even though in fact an eminent engineer is often sensitive to the latter moment, and an eminent designer to function and engineering. The gulf between art and industry can be interpreted as a contradiction between these two moments. As is well known (see for example Pevsner 1949), modern design movements such as the Arts and Crafts movement, the Bauhaus and the Art Deco movement appeared from the late nineteenth century onwards in an effort to reverse the division between art and industry. Nagata (1982, 1983) explains that these movements attempted to allow the 'moment of sensation and aesthetics' to be dominant in deciding the whole shape of products. This chapter focuses on the design issue in this narrower sense; that is, the struggle to let the 'conception of a shape' based on the 'moment of sensation and aesthetics' gain the dominant position in decision making on the whole shape of machine-related products.

The event which occurred in the 1930s in the USA can be recognized as a development of this modern design movement. At the time, industrial design was established as a new profession, and began to be directly committed to the industries. Apparently, the USA was not the only country that invented industrial design and designers; for instance, some historians (Forty 1986, ch. 2, also see Heskett 1987, pp. 15–18, McKendrick, et al. 1982, ch. 3) indicate that a prototype of industrial design is found in the manufacturing process of pottery by Josiah Wedgwood in the eighteenth century, and Carrington (1976) narrates the history of industrial design in Britain. However, the movement in the USA was on a massive scale, so that art and industry were more firmly united than ever before.

An important point is that it was 'merchandising' or product policy in marketing management that actually arranged the strong marriage between art and industry. The next section analyses how industrial designers obtained a dominant position in the conception of the shape of machine-related products, and how the practice of marketing management and its thought were advanced by this unity between designers and marketers.

The Redesign Movement and Marketing: Product Design as a Basis of Consumer Orientation

The Consultant Industrial Designer as a Newcomer

Industrial design has been called the 'depression baby' (Meikel 1979, p. 68). It began to appear in the latter half of the 1920s, and became a boom in the American business world within a few years after the Wall Street Crash.

In the USA, the term 'industrial design' was first used as early as 1913 (Lorentz 1986, p. 10), and the title of 'industrial designer' was taken by Joseph Seinel in 1919 (*Business Week* 1936, p. 17, Meikel 1979, p. 19). Nevertheless, designers retained a traditional image at the time because many designers engaged in the so-called 'art industries'. It is true that mass marketing which was launched from the late nineteenth century exploited many design-related factors such as packages and trademarks as a means of product differentiation. The 1920s also saw the colour movement in industry, when many kinds of artificially coloured products, such as beds painted in red, yellow, blue, green, purple and mauve, for instance, became widespread in everyday life (*Fortune* 1930a, p. 85, see also Keppel 1933). Ornament appeared even in such unexpected settings as a locomotive covered with roses. Nevertheless, this trend did not directly lead to the dominance of industrial design in the 1930s. Rather, it showed that the 'moment of sensation and aesthetics' had not yet taken control in deciding the whole shape of products, but was still playing a minor role in product design. Those specializing in surface ornament were condemned as 'misguided decalcomaniacs' (Streichler 1963, p. 36) by emerging industrial designers.

Table 5.1   Leading industrial designers as of 1934

Industrial Designer	Age	Years as Industrial Designer	Previous Career	Staff Members	Typical Achievements	Clients
Dohner, Donald	41	7	University design teacher, Freelance designer	8	Vacuum cleaner Mechanical water cooler Air-conditioning	Westinghouse
Dreyfuss, Henry*	29	5	Theatre sets	5	Washing machine Alarm clock Check protector	Sears, Roebuck Western Clock Co. Todd Co.
Geddes, Norman Bel*	40	7	Theatre sets and costumes	30	Gas range Telephone index Radio	Standard Gas Equip. Co. Bates Mfg. Co. Philco
Guild, Lurelle	35	10	Art director, Furniture expert	4	Refrigerator Cooking utensils Stoves to roller skates	Norge Corp. Wear-Ever Aluminium Co. Montgomery Ward
Jensen, Gustav	35	6	Artist	3	Telephone Metal kitchen sink Water heater	AT&T International Nickel Co. L.O. Koven & Bro.
Loewy, Raymond*	40	6	Electrical engineer, Free-lance advertising	1	Motor car Duplicator Kitchen sink and bathroom units	Hupp Motor Car Corp. Gestetner Co. (British) Sears, Roebuck
Sakier, George	36	11	Mechanical engineer, Art director	11	Bathtubs, Wash basins, etc. Bathroom units Vacuum equipment	American Radiator & Standard Sanitary The Accessories Co. Schellwood-Johnson Co.
Teague, Walter D.*	48	6	Advertising designer	4	Cameras Furnace Mimeograph	Eastman Kodak National Radiator A.B. Dick Co.
Van Doren, Harold	38	4	Painter, Ghost writer	8	Scales Kitchen grill Paint gun	Toledo Scale Co. Swartzbaugh Mfg. Co. DeVilbiss
Vassos, John	35	7	Advertising agency, Illustrator	3	Drink dispenser Turnstile Radios	Coca-cola Perey Mfg. Co. RCA

Source: Fortune 1934, p. 43. Some parts are omitted and revised.
* Those known as the 'big four' in New York in the 1930s (Meikel 1979, pp. 42–3).

Table 5.1 details the ten leading industrial designers as listed by *Fortune* in 1934. Several features stand out. First of all, apart from Donald Dohner, who was hired by Westinghouse as an in-house designer from 1930 (Meikel 1979, p. 40), these were independent freelance consultants, generally on a contract basis (Streichler 1963, p. 3). Heskett (1987, p. 111) indicated that in Europe, such consultant designers hardly existed until after the Second World War. Second, the American industrial designers had set up in business only in the 1920s, and had not yet achieved prominence. In the case of Geddes's office, a relatively big one, it hired engineers, draftsmen, artists, material experts, marketing experts and architects, in addition to part-time staff depending on the contracts with clients (*Fortune* 1934, p. 94, Streichler 1963, p. 45). Third, the individuals had relatively recent experience, and their backgrounds were varied, showing that they did not come from traditional, legitimate decorative art. Finally, these designers were involved mainly in the so-called 'artless industries' (*Fortune* 1934, p. 98), where designers and artists had rarely been involved. All these four features show that the industrial designers were different from the traditional designers.

These industrial designers worked to their clients' specification. For instance, as of 1939 Loewy's office estimated that 20 per cent of its total design work was in packaging, 40 per cent in products, 30 per cent in transport and 10 per cent in interiors (Meikel 1979, pp. 100–101). Package design gained more and more significance even in the boom in industrial design in the 1930s (see for example *Fortune* 1931, *Printers' Ink* 1932b, 1932c, Nash 1934, Larrabee 1936). Nevertheless, the essential feature of industrial design, which should be distinguished from traditional design, was deciding the fundamental shape of machine-related products or products made of new materials. The following case studies will focus on this issue.

Redesign of a Gas Cooker: a 'Magic Wand' for Marketing

As Meikel (1979, p. 39) indicated, 'Industrial design was born of a lucky conjunction of a saturated market, which forced manufacturers to distinguish their products from others, and a new machine style, which provided motifs easily applied by designers and recognized by a sensitized public as "modern".' In other words, it was marketing that mediated between the saturated market and the new machine style. The story of a cooking stove became famous both in the business world at the time (*Printers' Ink* 1933a, pp. 51–2, *Fortune* 1934, p. 42) and in design history (Meikel 1979, pp. 101–2, Heskett 1987, pp. 145–6) as a typical success in industrial design.

Gas cooking became popular in the 1920s based on the expansion of supply of gas to the home. The increase in households with gas supply from 1920 to 1930 was 41 per cent, which was bigger than the increase in the number of households itself, 23 per cent (Ogburn 1933, p. 668). Production of gas cookers increased 108.1 per cent in 1927 and 108.6 per cent in 1929 on the 1925 figures (Lynd 1933, p. 899). By the end of 1920s the gas cooker was fully developed in terms of its functions, so that functional differentiation of the product was difficult (*Printers' Ink* 1933a, p. 51).

The Standard Gas Equipment Corporation of New York, which was originally established as the Baltimore Gas Appliance & Manufacturing Company in 1911 and bought and renamed as the SGE by the William M. Crane Company of New York in

1924, fell into deficit in 1930 due to the impact of the Great Depression (Moody's Manual 1932, p. 639). The company decided to engage Norman Bel Geddes, an independent consultant designer, to redesign their kitchen stove, which had been designed by in-house engineers thus far. At first the company offered $1,500 for rough sketches, but Geddes refused it and instead demanded $25,000 plus costs and royalties for developing a new design in depth (Meikel 1979, p. 101).

First, Geddes launched market research on 12,000 housewives and domestics. The research revealed that ease of cleaning was the main consideration in judging stoves, along with Geddes's design. He gave the stove a skirt that extended to the floor, instead of four legs that provided a dust-harbouring space beneath the stove, and panels for covering burners and controls when not in use. He also provided a finish in white, psychologically the most sanitary colour, instead of the dignified black of cast iron or marbleized sheet metal that had been widely used (*Fortune* 1934, p. 42, Meikel 1979, p. 101). His design improved the overall appearance, with clean lines punctuated by large heat-resistant handles, and rounded edges (Heskett 1987, p. 145).

Furthermore, Geddes improved the production method that led to cost reduction. He adopted enamel sheets with stove panels that hooked onto a tabular frame flexible enough to absorb transportation stress, instead of cast iron jointed rigidly by bolts. In addition, he introduced a 'system of modular construction', which enabled the company to make sixteen different models by combining twelve standardized component units (*Fortune* 1934, p. 42, Meikel 1979, pp. 101–2, Heskett 1987, pp. 145–6). The selling campaign also had a distinguishing feature. Each stove bore Geddes's monograph and the statement that he designed it. Successive mail campaigns to dealers and advertising agencies introduced Geddes's name as a great designer first, and then sold the stove to the public on the strength of it. Thus the product had an image of a 'signed appliance' by Geddes (Meikel 1979, p. 102).

In retrospect, it is very doubtful whether this redesign strategy could have been decisive in the recovery of this company because, referring to *Moody's Manual* (1936, p. 2940), the company's deficit could not be overlooked even after Geddes' design was introduced to the market in 1933. Nevertheless, this case was typical in terms of the relationship between marketers and industrial designers, in that: (1) the industrial design contract resulted from a direct meeting of a designer with the top-level officers, usually including the president, of a client firm, (2) the industrial design team first studied the product to be redesigned and conducted market research so as to analyse consumer wants, competing products and others, and (3) the design team actually intervened in the production process of the factory and took a lead in redesigning the existing product so as to enhance its saleability.

For the actual process of intervening in production, the design team usually arranged a factory tour to assess a client's manufacturing capabilities, decide what factors could be changed without prohibitive expense, and cooperate with people such as engineers and sales managers, who would otherwise jeopardize association with the design team (see Teague 1932, Meikel 1979, pp. 89–91). Thus, significantly, redesign strategy fostered increased contact between the design side (effectively meaning the marketing side, even though in-house sales managers sometimes opposed out-of-house designers) and the production side, often leading to control of the design side by top management.

Many other successful cases were featured in business journals (e.g. *Fortune* 1930b, 1934, *Business Review* 1930, *Forbes* 1930, *Printers' Ink* 1933a, *Business Week* 1936), such as D.R. Dohner's design of Westinghouse's electric range which increased sales 600 per cent while lowering tool cost and production cost; and Harold Van Doren's design for Toledo's scales which increased sales 900 per cent with a lowering in factory costs. The lesson rapidly spread in the business world that well-redesigned products could increase sales and often reduce costs, despite the sluggish business conditions in the 1930s. In addition, a favourable change in the macroenvironment supported the design strategy. During the Depression, the NIRA (National Industrial Recovery Act) was inaugurated in 1933 and promoted to set the codes of fair competition, which allowed trade organizations to stabilize resale prices. As a business journal (*Forbes* 1934, also see Streichler 1963, pp. 43–44) indicated, this condition had the effect of turning consumer attention to non-price aspects such as design rather than the price itself.

In the end, industrial design became a boom among American industries. According to a survey of the manufacturers of mechanical and metal products by the journal *Product Engineering* (1936, p. 406, 1937, p. 423), 87 per cent of 363 companies in 1936 and 59 per cent of 506 companies in 1937 reported having redesigned existing products or developed new products, and the majority of these were redesign. By the mid-1930s, the services of industrial designers were recognized as essential for product policy in the American business world (see Streichler 1963, p. 97, Meikel 1979, p. 68).

However, the significance of this new practice varied among industries. The following three cases will show that redesign strategy contributed differently to competition in different industries, and that not only manufacturers adopted it. Managerial thinking about marketing did not fully recognize these differences, but was generally developing based on the new practice of industrial design.

Redesign of Cars: Temptation to Buy a New Car with Trade-in

In US marketing history, the story of Harley J. Earl is renowned. While Henry Ford reluctantly agreed to change the famous 'Model T,' which had been supposed to require no model change, General Motors established the 'Art and Color Section' as a part of the corporation's staff organization and in 1927 appointed Earl, a car body designer of Hollywood, as its head, soon after his initial success with a new styled car, 'LaSalle' (*Fortune* 1939, Sloan, 1963, pp. 269–70, also see Chandler 1964, pp. 154–5). From 1927 to the Second World War, GM enjoyed the top market share, whereas Ford competed for second position with a newcomer, the Chrysler Corporation (Federal Trade Commission [1939] 1983, p. 29). Since then the automobile industry has been a major battlefield for industrial designers.

From the aesthetic point of view, the car industry was one of the main stages on which the streamlined design, often called the 'teardrop' form, was eagerly tried. The 1930s is called the 'streamlined decade' (Bush 1975): this shape dominated the design world in the USA. Streamlining was rooted in hydrodynamics and aerodynamics in the nineteenth century. It pointed out the distinction between laminar flow and turbulent flow, and when a body that was immersed in the flow did not induce turbulence, this was called 'streamlined' (Bush 1975, pp. 4–5). Under the Great Depression, streamlining was eagerly introduced as a motif signifying speed and efficiency and saving time and energy (Bush 1975, p. 1), and became synonymous with American industrial design (Heskett 1987, p. 120). Whilst this shape had been introduced in the 1910s and 20s or even earlier (Bush 1975, pp. 7–8 and 98–9), it was the book *Horizons* by Geddes ([1932] 1977) that was a driving force in extending streamlining throughout American society in the 1930s (Syllas 1969, Plummer 1974, Greif 1975).

The 'Airflow', marketed by Chrysler, was a remarkable case in design history (see Bush 1975, pp. 118–22, Meikel 1979, pp. 148–151, Heskett 1987, pp. 122–3). After the publication of *Horizons*, Walter P. Chrysler, the company founder, utilized the book to persuade in-house marketing experts who were reluctant to adopt the streamlined shape devised by the engineers, and made a contract with Geddes both for improving design of the car and coordinating publicity. The case of Airflow is known as a marketing failure (despite a good reception at the automobile show), resulting in withdrawal from the market in 1937. It is reported that Geddes himself recognized the cause of failure as halfway streamlining due to the forward-placed engine (despite his publicized admiration of the first authentic streamlined car) (Meikel 1979, pp. 149–51), whereas many commentators believed the Airflow went too far too fast with design, beyond public taste and acceptance (Bush 1975, p. 121). The latter idea led to a famous axiom of industrial design, MAYA (most advanced yet acceptable). Whatever the real cause, Airflow had a strong impact on automobile design, resulting in moderately streamlined cars in all price ranges before the end of the 1930s (Bush 1975, p. 127).

It is significant that from a managerial point of view on marketing, streamlining was eagerly utilized as a measure in the annual model change strategy for cars, which aimed at tempting the consumer to buy a new design to replace an existing car. This policy is recognized as originating with General Motors, but the company did not intentionally formalize the strategy at first. According to Sloan (1963, p. 167), GM had changed the models virtually every year since 1923, but it was some time in the 1930s when the company officially defined this thinking. From the macro point of view, this strategy never did change the structure of the automobile market. In the depression decade, some manufacturers of luxury cars appealed on lower prices (Bernstein 1987, pp. 59–60), but without success. In the 1930s, these independents decisively lost their market (Rae 1965, p. 124), whereas the market share of the 'big three' – GM, Ford, Chrysler – reached nearly 90 per cent in 1937 in terms of number of passenger cars (Federal Trade Commission [1939] 1983, p. 29). Thus, the strategy that tempted consumers into buying a newly redesigned car by trading in an obsolete one never played a role in changing the oligopolistic market structure; it tended rather to strengthen oligopoly in the industry. While the strategy itself was generalized as part of product policy, as will be seen below, the industry-wide effect of design marketing on competition was never considered in managerial thinking.

Redesign of the Radio Set: Damage to Patent Monopoly by Independents

The arena for redesign strategy was essentially different in the radio set industry. Here, redesign of products by independent manufacturers using industrial designers was an effective weapon for marketing competition.

After KDKA began radio broadcasting in November 1920, the number of radio stations rapidly increased from 30 in 1921 to 556 in 1922 (Department of Commerce 1975, p. 999). The Radio Corporation of America (RCA) was organized in 1919 when General Electric (GE) bought the American Marconi Company. By 1921, major patents for manufacturing radio sets, originally held by RCA, GE, Westinghouse and the American Telephone & Telegraph Co. (AT&T) were pooled to RCA (Archer [1939] 1971, pp. 4–8; Maclaurin 1949, pp. 111–12; Uchida 1974, pp. 253–4). Thus a monopolistic company was established.

In the early 1920s, there existed many small-sized manufacturers of the crystal set. As superiority of the vacuum-tube set became apparent, however, so the patent issue became more and more important. RCA aggressively obtained almost all the patents for the circuit design, the tube, loudspeakers and others. The company often raised lawsuits to get them. It was said that by 1928, new radio sets could not be made without infringing the patents of RCA (Maclaurin 1949, pp. 117–31), so that *Fortune* reported that during the four years to 1933, 90 per cent of radio sets were made under licence using RCA patents (*Fortune* 1933a, p. 102). The monopoly looked impregnable.

Nevertheless, some independents challenged RCA. Because the assembling of radio sets did not require either much capital or highly technological knowledge (Maclaurin 1949, p.133), it was relatively easy for independents to enter this market except for the patent issues. Therefore, many independents rushed to RCA to get the licences to use the patents. The Federal Trade Commission ran an anti-trust investigation, and an anti-trust suit was instituted by the Department of Justice (Archer [1939] 1971, pp. 133–6, 353 and 365–86); the royalties were reduced from 7.5 per cent of the net selling price in 1927 to 2.5 per cent by the end of the 1930s, thanks to successful lawsuits by independents (*Fortune* 1933a, pp. 102 and 104, Maclaurin 1949, pp. 133–9). As a result of these reductions, some independents such as Philco, Zenith, and Emerson grew rapidly to be almost a match for RCA's market share. The major weapon was product design, in two principal areas.

The first is small-sized radio sets. Soon after the crash of 1929, a major trend in radio sets became to reduce the size, accompanied by a reduction in retail prices. In 1930, several small manufacturers on the West coast had begun to introduce a small-sized radio, called 'Jalopy' (*Fortune* 1935, pp. 164 and 166), but it was Emerson that had a great impact on the radio market by introducing the 'baby radio' in August 1932 (*Fortune* 1933b, p. 64). It weighed only five pounds and was as small as eight and a half inches long, six and a quarter high, and three and three quarters deep. The list price was $25, but the actual retail price was said to be 10 dollars or less in the market. This radio made a big impact because the average price of radio sets in 1929 was $133, by 1930 when 'Jalopy' started it was $87, and 'Jalopy' itself was $59.50 (*Fortune* 1933b, pp. 64–5). Other manufacturers rapidly followed. As of May 1933, 24 companies, including not only independents but also RCA and GE, produced 'baby' radios, so that it was said 40–60 per cent of the radio market in volume of sales was captured by the 'baby' (*Fortune* 1933b, p. 65). After the early stage of price reduction by size reduction, design competition came in.

Reducing the size of radio sets in itself was an engineering issue. However, the manufacturers who competed in selling the smaller-sized radios hired or contracted with industrial designers in order to ensure differentiation of products from the 'sensation and aesthetic' point of view. The fundamental technologies of manufacturing the sets were developed in the 1930s (*Fortune* 1935, p. 118, Maclaurin [1949] 1971, p. 666). A few minor technological advances were made, such as installing a short wave band and a tone control, but the short-wave technology was easily followed by competitors and the tone control was almost meaningless for cheaper models (*Fortune* 1935, p. 118). So functional differentiation became increasingly difficult, and differentiation of cabinet design became the key for marketing competition. Introducing plastic, which was entirely suitable for making the streamlined or rounded shape of the cabinets, further encouraged design competition (Meikel 1979, pp. 181–2). Thus, design and redesign of small-sized radios was keenly pursued. Air-King Products was just one example, which hired industrial designers Harold Van Doren and John Gordon Rideout, not only to design the cabinet but also to reduce the costs by using plastic.

The other field was larger-sized radio sets, where the design issue was even more essential. For instance, Philco, a powerful independent company, made a contract with Geddes through its manufacturing subsidiary, Philadelphia Storage Battery Company, to mark all the radio cabinets with the 'NBG' monograph and the words, 'This Cabinet Designed by Norman Bel Geddes' (Meikel 1979, p. 85). Philco was keen to gather information through distributors to ascertain consumer taste and realize it in their products. The 'console radio', equipped with a record player and a large-sized speaker system, was popular as designed furniture that considered the tastes of housewives (*Fortune* 1944, p. 118). Zenith, another independent, also became popular by producing the 'arm chair model', a large-sized radio set designed as a side table of an armchair, with which a listener could easily tune the channel and control the volume by merely extending an arm (*Fortune* 1938, p. 118, 1945, p. 141; see Maclaurin [1949] 1971, p. 777).

In short, the radio industry was another major battlefield for industrial design which served as a model for writers on product policy. However the industry-wide effect was different from that in the automobile industry, and this was not absorbed into managerial thinking. In the radio industry, design strategy served as a driving force for the independents to undermine RCA's monopolistic dominance by pooling patents, resulting in a big market share for a few independents. According to estimates by Maclaurin ([1949] 1971, p. 888), as of 1940 RCA's market share was 14.4 per cent, whilst Philco's was 14.2 per cent and Zenith and Emerson had 8.9 per cent respectively on a sales unit basis including both domestic sales and export. *Fortune* (1938, p. 120) indicated that for the domestic market in 1937, unit sales by Philco were the largest at 1,550,000 units, compared with RCA's 725,000.

In due time, another feature of design marketing became increasingly apparent. Despite the serious depression, the penetration ratio of radio sets increased steadily, estimated to have risen from 34.6 per cent in 1929 to 81.1 per cent in

1940 (Department of Commerce 1975, pp. 43 and 796). In this saturated market, frequent redesign of radio cabinets increasingly served to tempt trade-in. *Fortune* reported, '[R]adio now depends enormously on its replacements. Last year home-set replacements in fact account for some 3,000,000 units, or nearly three-fifths of total U.S. home-set sales. The answer is that radio, like the automobile industry, is doing a good job of making its past-sold products look obsolete' (*Fortune* 1938, p. 118). This new role, similar to that in the car industry, became the basis of a new discussion of product policy.

Redesign of the Refrigerator: Marketing a Retailer's Brand

In the electric refrigerator industry, a large-sized retailer increased the market share of its private brand by utilizing redesign strategy, resulting in a match with the market share of many other manufacturers' brands. This suggested that retailer-led marketing, in contrast to manufacturer-led, had begun to develop, although the growing managerial idea of 'merchandising' tended to obscure the source of the redesign strategy.

The spread of the refrigerator came relatively late compared with the electric vacuum cleaner and washing machine. The diffusion ratios among electrified households from 1925 via 1929 to 1938 are estimated from 21 per cent via 33 per cent to 58 per cent in the case of washing machines, and 31 per cent, 44 per cent and 49 per cent in the case of vacuum cleaners. In contrast, the popularity of electric refrigerators was limited in the 1920s, being 2 per cent in 1926 and 9 per cent in 1929, whereas it rapidly rose in the 1930s, reaching 52 per cent in 1938 (TNEC 1941, p. 118). The main reason was a technological problem of refrigerant. Although the safe and effective material for refrigerant was not yet discovered in the 1920s (Ichiba 1977, Kato and Kurata 1978, Tedlow 1990, pp. 310–11), the innovation of 'Freon' by the laboratory of GM in 1930 gave momentum to the spread of refrigerators.

As described by Tedlow (1990, pp. 315–28), Sears, Roebuck & Company, a leading retailer originally developed from mail order business and adapting to a dual policy of non-store and store retailing in the 1920s, was committed to providing its own private brands of refrigerators from 1922, but was not successful. Contracting with a non-refrigerator company to produce the fridges, Sears introduced the private brand, 'Coldspot', in 1931, but this was again a failure. This business was restored by a combination of low price policy with redesign strategy.

The investigation by the Senate committee, the TNEC (Temporary National Economic Committee), indicated that after the more severe price war during 1931–32, the refrigerator industry paid less attention to prices and placed more stress on the 'development of efficiency' and the 'modern-style equipment' (TNEC, 1941, p. 131). Table 5.2 shows how prices of refrigerators were uniform at the time: only the prices of 'Coldspot' by Sears, nevertheless, were set clearly lower than others. This pricing policy was effective just because other manufacturers were pursuing non-price competition.

Table 5.2   List prices of electric refrigerators 1938, principal companies

Size, cubic feet	Frigidaire (GE)	General Electric	Westinghouse	Kelvinator	Crosley	Leonard	Norge	Stewart Warner	Universal Cooler	Coldspot
3.0–3.9:										
Size ...	3.1	-------	3.2	3.16	3.16	3.14	3.12	-------	-------	-------
Model ...	D3	-------	HDS-32	K3-38	KB5-31	L3-38	R32-8	-------	-------	-------
Price ...	$119.50	-------	$118.95	$118.95	$117.50	$118.95	$117.50	-------	-------	-------
4.0–4.9:										
Size ...	4.1	4	4.2	4.15	4.3	4.1	4.14	4.5	-------	4.2
Model ...	N4-38	B-4	HDS-42	K4-38	KB5-43	L4-38	R41-8	458	-------	3804
Price ...	$144.50	$144.50	$144.50	$142.95	$142.50	$142.95	$142.50	$144.75	-------	$114.50
5.0–5.9:										
Size ...	5.1	5	5.2	5.16	5.07	5.12	5.15	5.64	5.25	-------
Model ...	Sp.5-38	JB-6	HS-52	KS5-28	KB5-50	LS5-38	S52-8	770	AD-658	-------
Price ...	$164.50	$164.95	$162.95	$162.95	$162.50	$162.95	$162.50	$164.75	$164.95	-------
6.0–6.9:										
Size ...	6.1	6.1	6.2	6.13	6.0	6.09	6.15	6.3	6.51	6.3
Model ...	Sp.6-38	JB-6	HS-62	KS6-38	KB5-60	LS6-38	S62-8	770	AD-658	3816
Price ...	$184.50	$184.50	$189.50	$182.95	$182.50	$182.95	$182.50	$179.75	$184.95	$169.50
7.0–7.9:										
Size ...	7.2	7.1	7.2	7.19	7.1	7.3	7.14	-------	7.45	-------
Model ...	Sp.7-38	JB-7	HS-72	KS7-38	KB5-71	LS7-38	S62-8	-------	AD-758	-------
Price ...	$204.75	$204.75	$209.50	$202.95	$202.00	$182.50	$182.50	-------	$204.95	-------
8.0–8.9:										
Size ...	8.25	8.1	-------	-------	-------	-------	8.11	-------	-------	8.6
Model ...	M8-38	B-8	-------	-------	-------	-------	R81-8	-------	-------	3838
Price ...	$264.50	$264.50	-------	-------	-------	-------	$259.50	-------	-------	$179.50

Source: TNEC 1941, p. 162.

Note: Prices are on lowest price comparable model in each size group.

However, success was due not only to low pricing, because Sears' private brands had failed thus far; cheap prices may have given an impression of bad quality. Sears asked an industrial designer, Raymond Loewy, to redesign the existing model in 1932, and a newly-designed Coldspot was introduced to the market in 1935. It became remarkably famous in design history (see Bush 1975, pp. 145–6, Meikel 1979, p. 104, Heskett 1987, pp. 106–7; also Kato and Kurata 1978, pp. 106–7). The combination of low prices and good redesign restored Coldspot and increased Sears' market share from only 1.4 per cent in 1931 to 14.1 per cent in 1938 at a peak, which compared with refrigerator manufacturers such as GM (18.2 per cent), GE (13.5 per cent), Kelvinator/Leonard (6.7 per cent), Westinghouse (6.6 per cent) and others. Thus, marketing by large-sized retailer was becoming established, although not fully recognized by managerial product policy at the time.

In the meantime, Sears encouraged an arguable idea. The company continuously required Loewy to introduce minor changes in design, resulting in the appearance of successive annual models of Coldspot in the 1930s (Meikel 1979, pp. 104–7). In contrast to the car and radio industries, not all manufacturers followed Sears' way. There was a serious doubt whether 'the desire to own the latest model of refrigerator can ever be quite as impelling as the wish to display the newest style of automobile' (TNEC 1941, p. 150). Nevertheless, as the market for refrigerators (and washing machines and vacuum cleaners too) was becoming increasingly saturated, so replacement sales became undeniably important. The TNEC estimated that about 20 per cent of sales of household refrigerators in 1938 involved the replacement of a unit previously used by the same family – and in the case of washing machines 46 per cent, and vacuum cleaners 35–40 per cent (TNEC 1941, p. 149). Persuasion increased for regular replacement of existing products. As a commentator indicated,

> The refrigerator industry debates with itself how long a refrigerator should last, how soon it becomes obsolete. In some cases the useful life of a mechanical refrigerator may be 15 years or more, although refrigerator sales executives would be ineffably shocked were you to voice such an opinion to them. The goal of the industry is to get the public thinking more in terms of obsolescence which may come in 5 or 7 years after the mechanical refrigerator has been put into use in the home. ... Apparently, therefore, refrigerator men are going to be up against the same problem that the auto industry faces, that of getting people to replace outmoded products (Hirose 1936, pp. 60 and 62).

This practice, combined with many similar practices in other industries, encouraged the establishment of an idea of obsolescence in product policy.

Development of Product Policy Based on the Redesign Movement

The Redesign Issue in 'Merchandising' Thought and Consumer Orientation

Based on the redesign movement described above, the managerial idea of product policy, called 'merchandising' at the time, incorporated the design issue into its discussion. Nevertheless, the approach to it naturally depended on each author's interest.

In some cases, it is hard to identify how much importance they gave to it because their textbooks simply enumerated various components in merchandising. For instance, Pyle mentioned in his textbook entitled *Marketing Management*: 'design as an element of merchandising' and even the 'effect of re-designing industrial products' (pp. 135–7), but he also listed many other factors in parallel with them. Richmond (1931), a contributor of a chapter on 'merchandising' to a business management handbook (Donald 1931), also stated, 'Style movements tend to spread over all lines of merchandise, exerting a parallel influence on lines quite unrelated. The modernistic movement, for example, has influenced architecture, silverware, furniture, floor coverings, watches, and numerous other products. There are, in fact, few lines which have escaped its influences' (p. 73). Nevertheless, he enumerated fifteen components of merchandising, so that it was not so clear how important this issue was.

In other cases, the authors' emphasis can be uncovered by comparing the different versions of textbooks and/or by referring also to specialized papers that concentrated on their chosen issues. An example is Tosdal, an eminent writer of marketing casebooks as shown in the conclusion of Chapter 3. On the textbook level, he indicated a design element as a part of 'policies relating to product' (product policy) even before he used the term 'merchandising' in the 1930s. The 'style policy' in his 1921 book (pp. 228–30) dealt with the cases of shoes and men's clothing marketing, which typically corresponded to marketing in the so-called 'art industry'. The 1925 book (pp. 243 and 254–61) focused on the reduction of the number of styles as 'policy regarding change of style and products', which apparently reflected the movement toward simplification in the 1920s. In contrast, the books in the 1930s began to discuss the redesign issue in the 'artless industries', in addition to the traditional design issue. In a 1933 book, for instance, noting that 'design and redesign' could give 'additional selling points for products' (1933a, p. 26), Tosdal took up the design of electric clocks and radio cabinets by a famous designer of '"modernistic" creation' (1933a, pp. 29–32), which are related to the issue of the redesign movement. His 1939 book (pp. 74–5) discussed design for radio cabinets, and his 1940 book (pp. 116–19) design for electric clocks. This transition suggests that progress in product policy resulted from the redesign movement.

In addition, Tosdal's academic article published in 1933, entitled 'Some recent changes in the marketing of consumer goods', indicated directly (1933b, p. 156) that the 'increasing emphasis upon the consumer and his needs and wants' was one of the general changes in marketing after 1929. According to him, 'Superficially, at least, the idea that consumer needs and wants should be the starting point for business thinking is certainly not revolutionary,' because for a century or more economists had made assertions that the aim of economic activities was the 'satisfaction of consumer needs' (p. 157). However, Tosdal recognized that translating the theory into practice had been long delayed, so that the 'students of marketing' had to agree with the criticism brought at the time that the 'manufacturers as a whole have been giving only lip service to the consideration of consumer wants and needs' (p. 157). Conditions were changing after 1929. '[W]e are just beginning to realize that provision must be made for furnishing the manufacturer in advance of production with knowledge of what the consumer wants if we are to avoid recurrence of such catastrophic events as have characterized the past three years' (p. 157), and 'today to study consumer wants appears to be the basis for a permanent merchandising policy' (pp. 157–8).

Tosdal emphasized the actual changes in marketing practice with regard to merchandising or product policy, as follows:

> Although students of marketing have continuously advocated the necessity for planning products so that they satisfy the demand of consumers, it is only in recent years that one can notice a decline in the respect paid to high-pressure selling and a concomitant increase in the emphasis upon designing and planning of products so as to meet the needs and wants of consumers … The growth of merchandising departments, the increased emphasis upon style research, the art-in-industry movement, the redesigning of packages, the notable success of certain well designed products when in a period of depression – all of these bear testimony to this growth in emphasis upon product planning (pp. 161–2).

Amazingly, here it was clearly recognized that merchandising was centred on design-related activities, and the general idea of satisfying consumers' needs and wants was becoming operational and practical based on this merchandising concept. This idea is fundamentally the same as what is usually called 'consumer orientation' and the core element of the marketing philosophy called 'marketing concept'. As explored in Chapter 3, White (1929, p. 97) had already declared that 'Marketing centers in all cases around the needs of the consumer', requiring standardization of marketing activities based on optimism in forecasting consumer demands. In a totally different context, Tosdal here insisted on the same philosophy of consumer orientation; this suggests that the consumer-centred philosophy had been advocated in a generalized form from time to time based on different historical contexts, and did not emerge for the first time in the 1950s, as many marketing-related people believe even now.

Another outstanding advocate is Elder, who contributed a 'merchandising' chapter to a marketing textbook (Alexander 1940) in which he placed 'redesigning the old product', obviously evoked by the redesign movement, as a measure for 'diversification' (Elder 1940, p. 123). Elder had already published a practical paper titled 'Product design for the market' (1933) and indicated,

> In fact, it has of recent years become quite proper to render lip service to the dogma that "the Consumer is King." Yet as a practical matter of fact it is fairly obvious that the average concern today neither designs its product, nor manufactures it, nor distributes it on the basis of consumer requirement (p. 543).

Here again the philosophy of consumer orientation is identifiable with relation to the redesign issue. In Elder's view, 'the real problem involved is twofold … to develop means for ascertaining with some degree of precision what consumers' real wants are, in order that they may be correctly anticipated by manufacturers', and that 'the organization should be so set up as to be able to translate them into production in an economic fashion' (p. 544). Elder insisted that the latter was solved by the organization of 'product control' or 'merchandising,' whereas the former was by designers.

The problem of finding out what the consumer wants enough to pay for is a perplexing one, but without its solution, changing the organization set-up avails nothing. The consumer is an inarticulate creature. His criticism of the goods put before him is passive, not active. If you ask him what he is going to want six months from now, he cannot tell you, for he does not know. If you ask him how to redesign your product to meet his requirements, he may offer a few minor suggestions, but following those suggestions will not insure his continued patronage. The designer of a product must go beyond the consumer's expressions on the subject and anticipate wants that are still latent (p. 545).

This comment by Elder is accurate even today for creating a product that consumers really want, still the most difficult dimension in product planning.

One expert's opinion had attracted attention in the late Thirties: Ben Nash neither contributed to textbooks, nor focused on the concept of 'merchandising'. Instead, he published a specialized paper entitled 'Product development' (Nash 1937). Elder (1940, p. 115, fn. 1) indicated that Nash's concept of product development was the same as the concept of merchandising widely discussed at the time.

Nash advocated what is now called competitive advantages. 'You can price the product right, you can advertise it to pre-sell consumers, and you can display it well at the point of sales, but the *product* must be "competitively right" or there will be costly, wasted effort' (1937, p. 254, italic is original). In order to make the product 'competitively right', Nash enumerated (p. 254) four steps in product development; that is, (1) laboratory research (to find new processes, new materials, new efficient utilization of waste and by-products, and new products), (2) product research (to disclose the effect of consumer and trade habits on product acceptability), (3) industrial styling (to be accurately keyed to market needs, ensuring greater product saleability), and (4) coordinated planning (to relate the result of product development to promotional and selling strategy).

Of these four, Nash's focus was on the styling or design issue: 'product development' was 'frequently more concerned with improving present products than creating new products', to make them 'more efficient, more useful, and certainly more attractive in relation to current consumer demands' (p. 254). Referring to a case of cabinet development by Philco in the radio industry (pp. 258–9) and emphasizing the 'importance of appearance' (p. 255; see also Nash's discussion in Wilder 1932, p. 37), he concluded, 'The point for all of us to remember is that the consumer is the final boss – and the consumer is a fickle boss, quick to change from the old to the new when better and more suitable products are offered' (p. 262). Here in design marketing, as in consumer orientation, 'the consumer is the final boss'.

Thus, the redesign movement not only encouraged the development of merchandising or product policy, but also provided a key answer to the question about the 'creative side of merchandising' (Hays and Heath 1929, p. 198), which had been raised concerning the origin of the idea of merchandising initiated by the Dennison Manufacturing Company. Making the product 'competitively right' through redesigning products, by hiring or contracting industrial designers – this was the actual way to respect consumer wants and needs at the time. The philosophy of consumer orientation became an operational concept in marketing management.

Relationship between the Designer and the Engineer

The redesign movement encouraged the actual intervention of industrial designers in the in-house production process. This raised a new organizational and personnel issue – what the relationship should be between the designer and the engineer, between those who embodied the 'moment of sensation and aesthetics' and those embodying the 'moment of function and engineering'. This problem became apparent in the process of overcoming the 'divorce between art and industry'. The discussions took place not in textbooks dealing with the merchandising concept, but in specialized books and papers stimulated by them.

The two significant moments in design activities were already recognized by Nystrom ([1932] 1986) as the transformation from 'engineering designing' to 'style designing'. As the size of manufacturers grew larger, the design function became separated, but still remained as the function of 'mechanics' or 'engineering', so that many design departments in leading manufacturers were still 'mechanical design departments' (pp. 52–3). Nevertheless, Nystrom emphasized that as consumers often required an aesthetic quality in products, many engineers had recently begun to pay attention to 'style'.

G.S. Brady, editor of the journal *Product Engineering*, which was central to the redesign movement, had made the same point.

> Product design, or product engineering, is a new function which has come into being only just recently. There has always existed the function of design relating to the product, but product design as a complete function in itself that not only sees the technical design of a product but also visualises it in its entire scope from inception to its place in the hands of the customer, is so new that many designers have not yet grasped its significance (1931, p. 675).

At the same time, discussion was progressing beyond the dual nature of design to improving the relationship between industrial designers and engineers which had sometimes caused tension (see Meikel 1979, p. 77). This harmonization was essential to the progress of any redesign projects. The designers felt this practical necessity particularly, so a call for the 'sympathetic cooperation of artist and engineer' (Teague 1932, p. 246) emerged from the designers' side. One significant issue was the relationship within management: at the 'inception of the association of engineer and artist in American industry' (*Iron Age* 1933, p. 25), new ideas arose.

For instance, Kimball (1931) proposed a new managerial position called 'design engineer'. 'He must have,' insisted Kimball, 'the artist's feeling for beauty – artist's appreciation of color, line, rhythm, and he must have the engineer's sense of construction, the engineer's instinct for practical, workable value.' 'It is his job to see that every physical element expressing his company to the outside world should have beauty, unity, authority – style, as well as utility' (p. 105). The idea seemed to be sensitive, but it reflected the actual problem of the relationship between engineering department and designers.

One extreme opinion was 'advocating and suggesting to management that engineering departments be placed under the jurisdiction of sales departments' (Brady 1931, p. 676). 'To us engineers,' Brady wrote, 'such an arrangement may seem ridiculous, but we had better wake up to the fact that there is reason behind it' (1931, p. 676). This was because 'Sales value is the ultimate end to be sought in any product' (1931, p. 675). Brady recognized, 'It is only recently that any considerable attention was centered on appearance in design' (1932, p. 648), but many chief engineers did not yet realize it. The goal was for the 'chief engineer' to be in harmony with the sales manager and to 'increase saleability through appearance in the product'; Brady applauded some examples that promoted the 'chief engineer' from the engineering department to the same rank with the sales manager and others (1931, p. 676; see also Meikel 1979, p. 79).

Elder's (1932) opinion arose from the designer's side. He believed that engineering education had not been capable of creating a multidimensional person who could cope with the demands of both engineering and market (pp. 544–5). Elder advocated putting designers into a superior position. His idea paved the way for inverting the traditional production-centric thought in favour of a market-centred mindset.

> Design is fundamentally an engineering function. It cannot, if maximum efficiency is desired, be delegated to persons unacquainted with production machinery and processes. Still less, however, can it be left to those who fail to realize the problems and needs of the consumers, from whom profits must in the last analysis come. The ideal solution is the development of a type of engineer who can visualize and correlate problems of both consumption and production. We have all too few such men. The answer is simple. Train your designers in production methods, but make them understand that methods and processes are their servants, not their masters. Keep them in touch, as directly as possible, with your ultimate customers. Let them realize the importance of the product in the selling scheme. Then revamp your organization so as to bridge the gap between the requirements of the market and those of the factory. In no other direction do there exist better possibilities for reducing selling costs and increasing profits (pp. 546 and 565).

Brady and Elder agreed that the integration of engineering and aesthetics was essential, but they saw different management routes to integration. There was no consensus at the time on the best solution, and present-day solutions are still widely different. However, it is evident that the market-centred idea, which was the inverse of the traditional production-centred one, was emerging not simply as an abstract and impractical vision, but based on practical operational necessity at the time. In the end, the discussions came very close to the 1952 idea of GE, now celebrated as the very first announcement of the 'marketing concept' (see King 1965, pp. 76–8, Barksdale and Darden 1971, p. 29); that is, 'This ['an advanced concept of marketing'], in simple terms, would introduce the marketing man at the beginning rather than the end of the production cycle and would integrate marketing into each phase of the business' (General Electric 1952, p. 21).

Birth of Planned Obsolescence and its Critics

Frequent redesign of existing products gave birth to another managerial idea – obsolescence. It emerged in parallel with increasing recognition of the importance of the replacement market for consumer durable goods and mechanical products, rather than traditionally fashionable products in the so-called 'art industries', and it was accompanied by a society-wide controversy.

While discussing merchandising, Elder (1940) indicated 'diversification with respect to the dimension of time, involving the modification of products or their designs to adapt them to minor and probably fugitive changes in market requirements' (p. 121). What he called a kind of 'diversification' here had been termed 'obsolescence' elsewhere (Elder 1932, p. 545); so he recognized obsolescence as a marketing policy. Again the main body of this discussion appeared not in textbooks of merchandising, but rather in an associated field.

An early advocate was J.G. Frederick, the well-known writer of a sales management textbook ([1919] 1978), soon after the change in the Model T Ford.

> I refer to a principle which, for want of a simpler term, I name *progressive obsolescence*. This means simply the more intensive spreading – among those people who now have buying surplus – of the belief in and practice of buying more goods on the basis of obsolescence in efficiency, economy, style or taste. We must induce people who can afford it to buy a greater variety of goods on the same principle that they now buy automobiles, radio and clothes, namely: *buying goods not to wear out, but to trade in or discard after a short time, when new and more attractive goods or models come out* (Frederick 1928, pp. 19–20, italics are original).

The background to this advocacy was apparently the emerging redesign movement at that time, as Frederick applauded the rapid introduction of new models in the automobile and radio industries as 'brilliant examples' (p. 20): 'Even Ford has been forced to bow before the god of obsolescence' (p. 44).

Frederick trusted the principle of 'progressive obsolescence' completely, and that adopting the principle could ensure not only the success of individual marketers, but also great progress for America. He emphasized,

> We no longer buy a house to live in until we die, a refrigerator to last until it falls apart, an automobile until it refuses to go, a radio that simply brings in a station. We are able to indulge in our own individual ideas, and in constant new offerings, promptly discarding the old. If this spirit of progressive obsolescence is encouraged and developed we will see a great new advance in American industry, and many of our most difficult problems will be solved (p. 44).

Such a straightforward encomium of obsolescence would rather surprise many current readers. Interestingly, however, despite Frederick's strong belief, his idea was harshly attacked as a 'path to industrial suicide' soon after his paper was published. A commentator criticized his idea on both economic and moral grounds.

> A glimpse through the microscope of economics at modern industry reveals that progressive obsolescence leads *beyond* increased production to *de*creased production. For as rapidly as Mr. Frederick would increase the number of styles and models of his product, so would his cost of production increase (Cardinal 1928, p. 25, italics are original).

Mr. Frederick is blind to economics, and blinder still to the disastrous effects his scheme would have on the moral backbone of our nation – yes, even on the destiny of all modern civilization. For his progressive obsolescence will be successful only in so far as it plays upon the selfish pride of men and women, tempting them with old things in new and more flattering forms into an era of ludicrous, selfish and wasteful spending, an endless orgy of extravagance (Cardinal 1928, p. 89).

Thus, social controversy about planned obsolescence appeared as early as the late 1920s. As is known, it was after the Second World War that the controversy was renewed, from the economic point of view (see Gregory 1947, Stewart 1959). Much later, Packard (1960), a famous social critic, would condemn this marketing strategy, including Frederick's proposal (p. 63), on moral grounds. But criticism had arisen of planned obsolescence before the Second World War as a background to marketing management.

It is interesting to note that almost simultaneously with Frederick, A.W. Shaw (1928), a pioneer described in Chapter 3, proposed the same idea. Describing contemporary society as 'moving at a new, high speed – transportation, communication, money, inventories', Shaw advocated 'high-speed obsolescence' as a key solution to the problem of over-production. 'No longer is the question involved one of "wearing out". Instead, it is a question of always using the newest and best' (p. 263).

In the 1930s, based on the Great Depression and the boom in redesign strategy utilizing industrial designers, pro-obsoletism increased. While Frederick (1930) himself maintained his advocacy of obsolescence as the 'fine edge of the axe which is laying about with great stocks and cutting the pathway for our great new engines of production' (p. 227), a businessman admired the 'progressive obsolescence basis of consumption' as a substitute for the 'old high-pressure personal salesmanship doctrine' (Abbott 1930, p. 155), and another executive insisted durability of products was not important (Kelly 1936; see also Packard 1960, pp. 63–4). Freeland (1934), the originator of the idea of sales engineering, identified good responses by consumers against new product designs that made existing ones obsolete, although he admitted this strategy risked economic and social disputes (p. 278).

An earnest supporter in the 1930s was E.E. Calkins, who had been one of the pioneering writers on advertising thought (Calkins 1915). He ran an advertising agency, at which Walter D. Teague, a leading industrial designer in the 1930s, had worked as a freelance illustrator (Meikel 1979, p. 11). Calkins (1930, p. 120) advocated 'consumer engineering' or 'consumption engineering,' which he believed to be the 'new business science'. The concept was defined as 'shaping a product to fit more exactly consumers' needs or tastes', while he insisted, 'in its widest sense it includes any plan which stimulates the consumption of goods' ([1932] 1976, p. 1). In any case, a core of this idea was what he called 'obsoletism' ([1932] 1976, p. 7) or 'artificial obsolescence' (1930, p. 120). 'Goods fall into two classes, those we *use* such as motor cars or safety razors, and those we *use up* such as toothpaste or soda biscuit. Consumption engineering must help us use up the kind of goods we now merely use' (1930, p. 120, italics are original). The following remark was therefore quite natural.

Clothes go out of style and are replaced long before they are worn out. That principle extended to other products – motor-cars, bathrooms, radios, foods, refrigerators, furniture. People are persuaded to abandon the old and buy the new to be up-to-date, to have the right and correct thing. Does there seem to be a sad waste in the process? Not at all. Wearing things out does not produce prosperity, but buying things does. Thrift in the industrial society in which we now live consists of keeping all the factories busy. Any plan which increases the consumption of goods is justifiable if we believe that prosperity is a desirable thing ([1932] 1976, p. 7).

This straightforward confession merely extended the proposals by Frederick and Shaw late in the 1920s.

In the meantime, anti-obsoletism continued. Robert S. Lind, a scholar of sociology and a member of the Consumers' Advisory Board of the NRA, pointed out,

Deliberate obsolescence, the speeding up of styling in all kinds of goods from automobiles to clothing and furniture, advertising devices calculated to put "allure" into silk stockings or snob prestige behind a product – all these things reveal the long and adroit fingers of the producer tampering with what the consumer "wants" (Brainerd with Lind 1934, p. xi, this part written by Lind).

Referring to Veblen's (1923) critical point of view – 'The production of customers by sales-publicity is evidently the same thing as a production of systematized illusions' (pp. 306–7, fn. 12) – Lind accused marketing and the redesign movement: 'What actually happens is that the producer, bent on "making" sales, has sedulously connived with susceptible human nature in building up folkways called "style", "this year's model", "modern", and similar terms' (Brainerd with Lind 1934, p. xii).

Another commentator, Dameron (1939), discussed the consumer movement at the time and stated, 'the introduction of the annual or seasonal model, induced by the dictum of progressive obsolescence, reflects the force of business competition and a commercially controlled standard of consumer buying' (p. 272). As is well known, from the late 1920s to the 1930s a second wave of the consumer movement arose. The feature of this movement was to provide consumers with relevant information about products, derived from tests and comparisons, through the magazines of consumers' organizations. This system was adaptable to the frequent redesign and model changes in existing products.

From a practical point of view, an executive posed a question about the tendency in industries to bring a 'high factor of obsolescence' to products and insisted that a 'low factor of obsolescence' would make a stronger selling point (Weston 1933). The question, 'Have manufacturers over-styled?' was also discussed in the business world (*Printers' Ink* 1937).

Thus, the strategy of obsoletism ('planned obsolescence' became a popular term after the Second World War) was formulated, based on marketing practice to promote redesign by industrial designers. This strategy led to societal or macro-level debate after the Second World War. Generally speaking, speeding-up of obsolescence was not a natural result of aesthetic creativeness, but rather of commercial marketing and business. This was a controversial aspect produced by the marriage of art and industry.

Conclusion

This chapter has focused on the redesign movement as an important event that occurred in the progressive process of marketing management practice. The encounter of mass marketers and emergent industrial designers was a driving force to overcome the 'divorce of art and industry' dating from the latter half of the nineteenth century. The result was the promotion of designers to a dominant position in deciding the shapes of products in the industrial world, and this event was not limited to design history: it also exerted major influences on the idea of marketing management.

First, the historical concept of 'merchandising' as product policy, which had been evolving since the 1920s, recognized the design and redesign issue as a component. In contrasting responses, Tosdal and Elder recognized it as central to their merchandising concept, while Nash's 'product development', which was recognized as equivalent to the concept of merchandising, was also centred on the redesign movement. Based on this actual movement, their thoughts also embraced the philosophical idea of consumer orientation although the same philosophy had been advocated based on the idea of standardization in the 1920s. This fact suggests that the philosophy of consumer orientation is old-yet-new; it has been preached from time to time in different historical contexts.

Secondly, overcoming the 'divorce of art and industry' by the intervention of designers in the production process stimulated organizational and personnel discussions on the relationship between engineers and designers, leading to the dominance of designers, who could reflect market requirements in products more than engineers. The discussion led to the idea that marketing should come at the beginning, not at the end of business, which is often thought to have been formalized as a marketing concept as late as the 1950s.

Finally, the redesign movement fostered a new idea, a forerunner to what is known as planned obsolescence. This idea was controversial from the start with regard to consumer welfare in the face of manipulation. Opinions continued to differ after the Second World War.

It should be noted that the idea of marketing management did not articulate all the dimensions of the redesign movement. Redesign strategy had different effects on the actual marketing scene, whether strengthening an oligopolistic market structure like car marketing, or undermining monopolistic dominance and fostering the growth of independents in areas like radio manufacture. Redesign strategy was also utilized by the innovative retailer who employed a private brand or own brand strategy. However, the managerial idea of product policy at the time did not necessarily identify these features. These omissions show in themselves that the progress from a primitive to a mature managerial idea was on one hand the process of generalization of the idea that was applicable in any situation, and on the other hand decontextualization of the idea that had lost sight of its historical context.

Chapter 6

Development of the Idea of Channel Selection and Distribution Structure between the Two World Wars

The idea of channel selection has been an essential part of the 4Ps type of managerial idea from the beginning. As was explored in Chapter 1, the new type of manufacturers, who had integrated mass production with mass marketing, set up their own sales offices or branches and often eliminated some intermediate steps, from late in the nineteenth century onwards. These activities, and the conflicts between manufacturers and merchants that they caused, encouraged the articulation of the idea of channel selection as an indispensable part of marketing management. Chapters 1 and 3 explored the progress of the ideas in the 1910s. This chapter is to explore how the idea developed during the two decades between the world wars.

When analysing the historical background of channel thought, it is clear that the USA was in an advanced position: it started census investigation on distribution from 1929. The census data are helpful in understanding the structure of wholesale and retail distribution, the framework on which the ideas of marketing channels were built. This chapter begins by analysing census data to identify some characteristics of the structure of distribution. It also sheds light on two historical factors – one is the development of retail formats, which arose autonomously from manufacturers' channel policy and provided a different point of view on channels from the manufacturers' one, and the other is the political and judicial movement of anti-trust policy as a macroenvironment of the channel idea. After considering this background, this chapter explores the channel idea, introducing books written from the managerial point of view on marketing. The three major criteria on channel selection, the long-or-short, the wide-or-narrow, and the open-or-closed criteria, which were referred to in Chapter 1, are utilized again as a measure for analysis.

Factors Underlying the Managerial Idea on Marketing Channels in the Interwar Period

Some Features of the Structure of Wholesale Distribution

'[T]he American business man has been playing the game alone. … We have not even a census of wholesale and retail merchants' (Shaw 1914a, pp. 445 and 447). More than ten years later, the Department of Commerce (1927, p. 77) took an 'experimental "census of distribution"' in eleven cities, including Baltimore, Chicago, Fargo,

Seattle, Denver, San Francisco, Kansas City, Springfield, Providence, Syracuse and Atlanta. In 1929 it started the nationwide census survey of distribution as a part of the Fifteenth Decennial Census. Before the next decennial census of distribution in 1939, two other censuses were taken as 'emergency projects' (Department of Commerce 1942a, p. 1) in 1933 and 1935. As a result, material from four censuses was available between the two world wars. Enumerators visited each 'establishment' (the place of business). The method was changed to a mail canvass in 1954.

Tables 6.1–6.3 show what kind of wholesale organizations the manufacturers were able to select as the members of their marketing channels, although as will be seen below, some data reflected a feature of retail distribution. Table 6.1 represents the component ratios of the number of wholesale establishments and of their sales volume according to the 'types of operation' (the character of establishment and functions performed). In terms of manufacturer's marketing, the most outstanding feature of this table is the importance of 'manufacturers' sales branches', which included 'wholesale outlets owned and operated by manufacturers' which did not include their plants primarily for the purpose of carrying stocks, selling and delivering their products, and 'sales offices' without facilities for the physical storage, handling, and delivery of merchandise.

Table 6.1   Component ratios of wholesale establishments according to the types of operation (1929, 1933, 1935, 1939)   (Unit: %)

Type of operation	Number of establishments				Sales			
	1929	1933	1935	1939	1929	1933	1935	1939
Full-service and limited-function wholesaler	47.0	50.5	50.2	50.4	42.5	40.4	39.5	40.9
Voluntary group wholesalers [1]	–	–	(0.1)	(0.3)	–	–	(0.2)	(1.3)
Retailer-cooperative warehouses [1]	–	–	(0.1)	(0.1)	–	–	(0.5)	(0.1)
Manufacturers' sales branches	10.1	10.3	8.9	9.0	23.7	23.5	24.8	23.4
Outlets with stocks [1]	–	(7.6)	(6.6)	(6.4)	–	(16.0)	(16.7)	(15.3)
Offices without stocks [1]	–	(2.7)	(2.4)	(2.5)	–	(7.5)	(8.1)	(8.1)
Petroleum bulk stations and terminals	11.6	16.0	15.4	15.3	3.5	5.9	6.1	6.6
Chain store warehouses [2]	0.3	0.3	0.3	0.6	2.8	4.5	4.2	4.4
Agents and brokers	10.8	8.4	10.2	10.4	20.7	20.2	19.9	19.4
Assemblers (mainly farm products)	20.2	14.6	15.0	14.4	6.9	5.5	5.5	5.3
Total	100.0	100.0	100.0	100.0	100.0	100.0	100.0	100.0

Source: Calculated from Department of Commerce 1935, 1937, 1942a. Data of 1929 adopted from the 1933 census because some original data were revised by the 1933 census.

Notes: 1. '–' represents no data. '( )' shows breakdown detail figures from the major categories.
2. 'Chain store warehouse' was eliminated from the wholesale census in 1935 and 1939. In order to be comparable with the data of previous years, the data concerned were picked up from the retail census and used to calculate the component ratios.

The period shown in the table was one of upheaval due to the Great Depression, as exemplified by the fact that total sales of wholesale establishments fell dramatically by more than half from 68,950 million dollars in 1929 to 32,151 million dollars in 1933 on a nominal basis (Department of Commerce 1935). Despite such a wild fluctuation, the ratio of sales volume by manufacturers' sales branches maintained stability, nearly one fourth of the total sales. This means that manufacturers' sales branches were firmly established as part of the structure of wholesale distribution, which was not largely influenced by business fluctuations. The establishment of manufacturers' sales branches was a feature of the structure of wholesale distribution at the time. This was recognized not only by scholars after the Second World War, such as Engle (1954, p. 70), Barger (1955, p. 72) and Porter and Livesay (1971), but also by a contemporary commentator between the two world wars. 'If business census figures were available for 1909 and 1919, it is likely that the growth of manufacturers' sales branches and offices ... would be found to have been largely at the expense of full-service and limited service wholesalers' (Haring 1940, p. 40).

Manufacturers' sales branches had been organized originally late in the nineteenth century as an intervention in wholesale distribution, and took a firm hold in the interwar period. However, this development does not mean traditional wholesalers were always bypassed. On the contrary, the majority who assumed the functions of wholesale distribution were still the traditional wholesalers. As Table 6.1 shows, 'full-service and limited function wholesalers', who engaged primarily in the buying and selling of goods on their own account and were largely independent in ownership, were always the main forces of wholesaling.

The main body of 'full service wholesalers' were 'wholesale merchants' (often called jobbers), who bought and sold in the domestic market and performed all of the principal wholesale functions. Although the classification was changed in each investigation year, in 1939 wholesale merchants' establishments accounted for 45.3 per cent and their sales for 32.3 per cent of the total wholesale establishments and sales. Traditional wholesalers also included some types of 'limited-function wholesalers', such as 'cash-and-carry' outlets (the census defined as those who bought and sold merchandise in their own name, carried stocks, usually in large quantity, and sold in small amounts to retailers or other dealers who called for the goods at the wholesalers' place of business and paid cash for them), 'drop shoppers or desk jobbers' (who took title to the goods they sold but did not perform warehouse or storage function as they did not handle the goods), and 'wagon distributors' (who combined the function of salesmen with those of deliverymen), although their sales accounted for only small ratios: 0.2 per cent, 0.8 per cent, and 0.1 per cent respectively in 1939. The existence of these traditional wholesalers provided manufacturers with options in their channel selection.

In the same table, 'agents and brokers' (defined as individuals or concerns who were in business for themselves, negotiated purchases and/or sales in domestic or foreign trade, but did not take title to the goods) were included as sub-categories, in addition to many other types of merchants, traditional representatives for manufacturers. The category of 'manufacturer's agents' accounted for 2.4 per cent of the total wholesale in the year 1939. Other such categories included 'commodity and merchandise agents' and 'selling agents'. The first were wholesale middlemen who negotiate transactions between buyers and sellers without having direct physical control of the goods and without taking title, or assuming the risk of price fluctuations; the second were independent business entrepreneurs on a commission basis, principally to sell the output of a given line of goods for one or more manufacturers. Both categories may also often have committed to mediate sales by manufacturers to others, but 'commodity and merchandise agents' were not continuous with any particular manufacturers, and the authority of the manufacturers' selling agents was limited (Department of Commerce 1942, pp. 33–4). Their sales accounted for 5.9 per cent, 1.0 per cent respectively in 1939. Selling to agents at hand was an old way of selling for manufacturers. Thus, selecting these traditional agents meant establishing narrow, and sometimes closed, ties with merchants.

Table 6.2   Component ratios of sales to classes of customers by each type of wholesale establishment (1939)[1]   (Unit: %)

	Total	Sales to retailers for resale	Sales to household consumers	Sales to industrial users	Sales to wholesalers	Sales to export intermediaries	Export sales to buyers in foreign countries
Full-service and limited function wholesalers	100.0	58.9	1.9	23.6	11.1	0.5	4.0
Manufacturers' sales branches with stocks	100.0	39.4	0.5	34.6	24.2	0.3	1.0
Manufacturers' sales branches without stocks	100.0	13.0	0.2	64.9	19.6	0.3	2.0
Petroleum bulk stations and terminals	100.0	74.0 [3]	– [2]	26.0 [2]	– [3]	– [3]	– [3]
Agents and brokers	100.0	16.8	0.7	35.8	39.5	1.1	6.1
Assemblers (mainly farm products)	100.0	13.5	6.2	21.3	54.2	1.6	3.2

Source: Abstracted from Department of Commerce 1942a.

Notes: 1. The data were obtained not from all the wholesale establishments surveyed, but from those which replied to the questionnaires (84%).
2. Data for 'sales to household consumers' included in 'sales to industrial users'.
3. Data for 'sales to wholesalers', 'sales to export intermediaries', and 'export sales to buyers in foreign countries' included in 'sales to retailers for resale'.

Table 6.2 represents the ratios of wholesale business according to the type of customers in the year 1939. The table reveals that while manufacturers' sales branches without stocks (sales offices) referred to marketing channels of industrial products, manufacturers' sales branches with stocks (wholesale outlets) were both channels for industrial and consumer products. Selling from manufacturers' sales branches to retailers for resale (39.4 per cent) refers to manufacturers which sold their products via their branches directly to retailers and entirely bypassed independent wholesalers, although the branches were also selling to independent wholesalers (24 per cent). Thus, manufacturers had the option to select wholesale channels according to the long-or-short criterion.

It should be noted that the wholesale census excludes the data on selling at the manufacturing establishments (i.e. factories or plants) to merchants and customers because manufacturing establishments never fall naturally into the wholesale establishment category. The census (Department of Commerce 1942a, p. 2) explained, 'Establishments engaged in both manufacturing and merchandising goods are included only in the Census of Manufactures if the major portion of the goods they sell is of their own make', although 'Sales branches operated, apart from plants, primarily for disposal at wholesale of the manufacturers' products are included in the Wholesale Census.'

In order to compensate for the lack of this kind of data, the Department of Commerce provided a 'special schedule' of statistics for distribution of sales by manufacturing establishments. Table 6.3 represents the component ratios of the distributed sales by manufacturers' establishments according to the type of customers.

Table 6.3   Component ratios of distributed sales[1] from manufacturers' plants according to the class of customers (1929, 1935, 1939)   (Unit: %)

Class of customer	1929	1935	1939
Sales to or through own wholesale branches or offices	17.5	21.7	23.8
Sales to or through own retail stores	2.4	2.3	2.8
Sales to wholesalers and jobbers	32.8	26.2	26.5
Sales to retailers for resale	18.0	21.1	19.9
Sales to industrial, and other large users	27.5	26.4	25.2
Sales to consumers at retail	1.8	2.3	1.8
Total	100.0	100.0	100.0

Source: Department of Commerce 1942b.

Note: 1. 'Distributed sales' represent the total sales of plants. For the most part it was based on the F.O.B. but in a few instances sales were reported on the basis of 'delivery' value rather than the F.O.B. factory. The data was provided by the 1939 Census that adjusted information in each year to be comparable; as a result, the data did not include all the figures reported in each year. Distributed sales for the three years amounted to 69%, 70% and 67% of the total distributed sales respectively.

Although the data cannot be connected directly with that in the previous tables, the table shows again that there was an option of selecting marketing channels in terms of the long-or-short criterion, from bypassing independent wholesalers completely to utilizing various kinds of traditional wholesalers. It is interesting to read the comment by the census, 'The sales direct from plants to retailers for resale and sales to or through own retail outlets are increased. In contrast, sales to wholesalers decreased' (Department of Commerce 1942b, p. 7).

In short, these three tables suggest that the structure of wholesale distribution allowed manufacturers to choose a longer or shorter method when they considered establishing new marketing channels or modifying their existing ones. The structure was a result of manufacturers' marketing activities from late in the nineteenth century and was reinforced during the two world wars. It established a situation that provided manufacturers with affordable options.

Some wholesale activities by retailers can be also recognized at the time, as Table 6.1 shows. For instance, 'chain store warehouses' were maintained by retail chains as distributing stations used to supply their stores with merchandise. Although Beckman and Nolen ([1938] 1976, p. 8) indicated that these warehouses sold some volume of products to retail organizations outside their own chain organizations, the census transformed it from a main category of wholesale establishments to a sub-category of retail establishments after 1935; therefore, both figures in Table 6.1 are calculated picking up from the retail census in years 1935 and 1939. The figures represent buying activities by corporate chain stores. The following section will explore in more detail the backward activities by chain stores.

Some Features of the Structure of Retail Distribution

In contrast with the wholesale field, the structure of retail distribution was not directly eroded by manufacturers' channel policy. Although Table 6.3 suggested some manufacturers engaged in retail activities, normally retail was governed by the retailers themselves. Furthermore, the autonomy of retailers gave manufacturers crucial opportunities to consider the issue of wide-or-narrow selection in their channels, rather than the long-or-short issue.

A characteristic of the retail structure shown by the census was polarization of retailers; that is, there existed many traditional, small-sized or petty retailers on one hand, alongside a small number of strongly influential, large-sized retailers. Table 6.4 represents the component ratios by the size of retailers, 'size' being measured by the number of employees hired by each establishment or store. The table shows that even in the year 1939 the retailers hiring one or no employees (the term 'employee' included both full-time and part-time paid employees, but excluded proprietors-owners and unpaid members of the retailer's family) accounted for more than two thirds of the total number of stores, and the shops with not more than five employees accounted for more than 90 per cent in terms of the number of stores and nearly half of retail sales. These small-sized retailers provided the possibility of wide retail distribution for manufacturers.

Table 6.4   Component ratios of retail establishments by size of establishment based on the number employed (1939)   (Unit: %)

Number of employees per store	Stores	Sales	Employees
100 or more	0.1	11.0	15.0
20 to 99	1.6	17.8	21.2
10 to 19	2.9	12.9	14.5
8 or 9	1.6	4.8	5.2
6 or 7	3.4	7.7	8.4
4 or 5	6.9	10.6	11.6
3	6.9	7.5	7.9
2	11.4	8.7	8.7
1 or fraction on monthly basis average	22.6	9.8	7.5
No paid employees	42.6	9.2	–
Total	100.0	100.0	100.0

Source: Department of Commerce 1943. The data on 'eating place' and 'drinking place' were included as data of retailing.

In contrast, Table 6.4 also shows that stores hiring one hundred or more employees, although only 0.1 per cent in terms of the number of stores, captured more than 10 per cent market share of retail sales, and those with 20 or more employees, although less than 2 per cent in the number of stores, dominated nearly 30 per cent in total sales. However, these large-scale stores must include a few different types of retail formats because the classification system in the census was not necessarily a one-to-one correspondence with each retail format.

For instance, the census defined 'department stores' as general merchandise stores selling a number of lines of merchandise with sales in excess of $100,000. The census revealed that these stores numbered 4,221 (0.3 per cent in the total number of retail stores) in 1929, 4,201 (0.3 per cent) in 1935, and 4,074 (0.2 per cent) in 1939 respectively, and that they captured 9.0 per cent in 1929, 10.1 per cent in 1935, and 9.5 per cent in 1939 of the total retail sales (calculated from Department of Commerce 1943). Nevertheless, these 'department stores' included not only the usual type of department stores but also lower-priced 'basement department stores', which were estimated to be more than one sixth of the 1939 total sales (Department of Commerce, 1943, p. 44), and 'leased department stores' (department stores operated not by an owner of the store, but by an outside independent operator or a lessee who owned the merchandise and directed its price), which accounted for 0.3 per cent in 1929 and 0.7 per cent in 1939 total sales (calculated from Department of Commerce 1943, including both independents and chains). More importantly, the category of 'department stores' also included 'mail-order houses in general merchandise stores' (Department of

Commerce, 1943, p. 839), such as Montgomery Ward and Sears, Roebuck and Co. that, as is well known, began to make major investments in stores in the 1920s (e.g. Tedlow 1990, p. 284). Manufacturers could not be unaware of this option.

However, from the manufacturers' point of view regarding their marketing channels, the most problematic retail format had been the chain store ever since the 1910s, as was seen in Chapter 1. The census defined 'chains' as retail establishments operating with 'four or more' unit stores, although, especially in its early days, a unit store in a chain organization was often so small that not all the unit stores were covered in the large-sized establishments included in Table 6.4. According to the census, the market share of chain stores with four or more units grew from more than one fifth to around one fourth; that is, 22.2 per cent in 1929, 25.8 per cent in 1935 and 24.1 per cent in 1939 respectively (calculated from Department of Commerce 1943). These figures embraced a few different types of chain. They included 'local chains' (substantially all units located in and around a city), which accounted for 6.7 per cent in 1929, 3.1 per cent in 1935 and 3.8 per cent in 1939 of total retail sales, whereas they also included 'department store chains', which operated four or more large-sized department stores, which market share rose from 1.5 per cent in 1929 to 2.8 per cent in 1939 of total retail sales (calculated from Department of Commerce 1943, p. 15).

Table 6.5 shows the component ratios of chain stores by size in terms of the number of unit stores as of 1939. Amazingly, the very large-sized chain stores with more than 100 units, although only 3.4 per cent of the total number of retail stores, dominated 13.4 per cent of the total retail sales. Furthermore, according to the major commodity classification, the market shares of large-sized chains with more than 100 units were tremendously high especially in the food group and in the liquor stores; 22.4 per cent and 29.9 per cent in the total sales of each commodity group respectively (calculated from Department of Commerce 1943).

Table 6.5   Stores and sales of chain stores according to the number of unit stores (1939)

Size of chains	Number of organizations	Number of store units	Percentage of the number of stores [1]	Percentage of sales [2]
Chains with 4 to 10 units	5,105	28,584	1.6%	4.5%
Chains with 11 to 25 units	1,191	18,926	1.1%	2.9%
Chains with 26 to 100 units	542	24,252	1.4%	3.3%
Chains with more than 100 units	131	61,021	3.4%	13.4%

Source: Calculated from Department of Commerce 1943. 'Eating places' and 'drinking places' were included in retail establishments.

Notes: 1. Percentage of the number of store units to the total number of retail stores.
         2. Percentage of sales volume of chains to the total retail sales.

Clearly, at the opposite pole from the petty and traditional retailers, large-sized retailers, in terms of the number of hired employees and/or the number of unit stores in an organization, captured the dominant position in retailing, and in turn exerted strong influences on manufacturers' selection of their channels. This tendency was clearly recognized by a contemporary commentator. Discussing the 'trends in the manufacturer's choice of marketing channels,' Tosdal (1930, p. 3) recognized the 'growth of large scale buying' by such organizations as chain stores, large department stores and voluntary associations of retail merchants (organized to combat the threat by cooperative chains to traditional retailers), and pointed out that due to the concentration of buying power, there was a growing probability of direct dealing between these large-scale purchasers and manufacturers. Thus the growth of large-sized retailers accompanied by organizational buying encouraged the bypassing of wholesale merchants and established short channels direct between manufacturers and retailers.

The feature of retail structure shown as the polarization of retailers established the basis of wider, dense distribution, and also the basis of short-cut, direct distribution between manufacturers and retailers.

The Role of Innovative Retailers

A feature of retail distribution in the USA was the successive emergence of innovative retail formats or institutions. The famous model of the 'wheel of retailing' by M.P. McNair (1931b; see also Hollander 1960, Goldman 1978, Brown 1988, 1990, 1991) showed that at the first stage, new and innovative retail formats start off on a price basis by distributing merchandise at low prices with low overheads; the second stage is 'the "trading up" of the quality of merchandising handled'; and at the third stage, they compete with each other by providing services of all kinds with high costs, competitive advertising, and a high ratio of fixed investment. When a large number of retailers reach this third stage, 'someone else starts all over again on the low overhead, low price basis' (McNair 1931b, p. 39). Although some doubts have been cast as to the general applicability of this model, the USA was an example at least at the time.

As was considered in Chapter 1, manufacturers tended to have an ambiguous attitude to emergent chain stores in the 1900s–1910s; that is, they were in favour of the chains' potential for large-scale sales on one hand, but they hated their aggressive price cutting of manufacturers' national brands on the other hand, with the result that some manufacturers refused to sell their products. Nevertheless, as chain stores became more and more popular in the retail industry in the 1920s, so the decision to refuse chain stores became generally more and more ineffective. Under this circumstance, the indication by Lebher, who was the editor of *Chain Store Age*, hit the mark.

> So far as the manufacturer who either cannot or will not sell to the chains is concerned, their growth is certainly not going to make his problem any easier. To the extent that the chains increase their proportion of the entire retail volume, such manufacturers will indeed find their market diminished (Lebher 1930, p. 5).

As regards the situation of chain stores, their strategy of aggressively low price appeals, very common in their early days, was gradually disappearing in the 1920s (Nakano 1965a, p. 236, 1993, pp. 8–9). As a result, in the 1930s it was recognized that the price spread between independent retail stores and chain stores was narrowing (Tedlow 1990, pp. 198–9). Lebher indicated, taking an example of the grocery field:

> Slowly at first, but with increasing rapidity as the chains revealed their fundamental soundness and gave signs of inevitable growth, manufacturers receded from their original position with the result that today the chains are regarded as a most desirable channel of distribution by most grocery manufacturers (Lebher 1933, p. 23).

Even the variety store chains, which always had to appeal on lower prices, 'abandoned their former 5 and 10 cent limitation on prices, have added more lines of merchandise and have developed a fountain and lunch business equal to 10 cent or more of total sales', as the census described (Department of Commerce 1943, p. 15). These changes in pricing strategy by chain stores were equivalent to the concept of 'trading up' in the model of the 'wheel of retailing'.

Nevertheless, while chain stores 'traded up', some new retail formats emerged that advertised aggressively low prices. The keenest interest at the time focused on pine-board stores and supermarkets. Pine-board stores were the historic format of druggists who used cheap pine-board for the sales counters and shelves for stocks and aggressively discounted the national brands of products (Palamountain 1955, p. 104, fn. 52). In contrast, supermarkets are recognized as the innovation in retail format in the 1930s, and their definition by the Super Market Institute is well known: 'A Super Market is a highly departmentalized retail establishment, dealing in foods and other merchandise, either wholly owned or concession operated, with adequate parking space, doing a minimum of $250,000 annually. The grocery department, however, must be on a self-service basis' (Zimmerman 1955, p. 18, see also Charvat 1961, p. 7, Appel 1972, p. 39, Mayo 1993, p. 117). The retail census in 1939 indicated:

> Although no precise definition is yet recognized by the trade, it is generally accepted that a supermarket is a large cash-carry combination food store ($100,000 per year of sales is the usual minimum) with its merchandise arranged in open displays permitting individual selection without the assistance of salespeople, whereby operating expense is kept to a minimum by restricting sales service, delivery, and other customer services including credit (Department of Commerce 1943, p. 5).

The census defined 'combination stores' as those engaged primarily in selling the same line of merchandise as 'grocery stores' – that is, all sorts of canned foods such as soups, vegetables, fruit and meats, dry groceries, either packed or in bulk, such as tea, coffee, cocoa, dried fruits, spices, sugar, flour, and crackers, as well as smoked and prepared meats, fresh fish and poultry in limited quantities, and usually fresh vegetables and fruits – in combination with fresh meats. In addition, the census pointed out the principal part of this 'combination stores' classification was constituted by 'supermarket,' which increased from 36.0 per cent in 1929 to 54.0 per cent in 1939 of total food store sales (Department of Commerce 1943, p. 16).

The supermarkets at the time are also well known to have been aggressive price cutters on national brands of manufacturers.

From the manufacturers' standpoint, the emergence of these new retail formats was provoking the same type of problem as the chain stores had caused in their early days. Lebher (1933, p. 22) commented, 'A parallel to the situation which has arisen since the development of these pine-boards and super-markets is to be found in the history of the early days of the chain stores.' Suggesting that price cutting by these new retailers was not 'legitimate price competition' but 'unfair price cutting', Lebher explained what he defined as a problem of 'too many channels of distribution' for manufacturers:

> I want to point out that even though a particular type of distribution may violate neither law nor ethics, it still remains for each manufacturer to decide whether or not it is to his own interest to use it. If he believes that unfair price cutting is undermining his channel of distribution, he might be well-advised to refuse to sell those factors who are responsible for it (Lebher 1933, p. 25).

Thus, when selecting retail channels, manufacturers faced a problem in the context of the 'wheel of retailing' model: retail formats or institutions that had appeared with attractive low prices gradually 'traded up' the quality of lines handled and finally abandoned their low-price appeal, while other new retail formats entered the field in their turn with low prices, low status and low margins and filled the vacant slots. In this case, the problem manufacturers confronted was not the selection of long-or-short channels, but of wide-or-narrow channels: retailing is the last link in the chain, defined as one selling to the final consumer and the point was whether or not manufacturers should allow some particular retail formats to resale their national brands.

Another important implication for channel thought was the maturing retail format, chain stores, rather than emerging new formats. As was already recognized in the 1910s, chain stores had aggressively introduced private brands. This practice steadily developed during the two world wars. According to the investigations by the Federal Trade Commission, in 1929–30, the chains that owned private brands were 412 companies. This accounted for about one-fourth of the 1,660 that answered the enquiry about brands, but their influence was huge; these companies operated 77 per cent of the stores, and their sales accounted for 75 per cent of the total business all reporting chains transacted. Similarly in 1931, 351 chains, or 28 per cent of the 1,247 chains, owned private brands. Their stores accounted for over 81 per cent and their transactions for nearly 81 per cent of 1,247 chains reporting to the investigation (FTC [1933b] 1985b, p. xiv).

These chain stores selling private brands tended to commit to manufacturing products themselves. In the year 1930, the chains that manufactured part of the goods they went on to sell were 162 companies or 15 per cent of the total 1,068 reporting chains, and the stores operated by them comprised 60 per cent of total stores and their sales were 58 per cent of the total sales. Approximately 80 per cent of the manufacturing chains owned private brands, while only 20 per cent of the non-manufacturing chains owned such brands (FTC [1933a] 1985a, pp. ix and xi).

The activities of backward integration by chain stores, symbolically exemplified by A&P (see Tedlow 1990, pp. 206–13), gave a new stimulus to develop the channel idea, as will be considered below.

Politics and Judicial Environments of Manufacturers' Channels

The macro environment in terms of politics and laws surrounding manufacturers' marketing channels was also changing during the decades between the two world wars, resulting in twofold effects on channel policy.

As was well described by Palamountain (1955), the anti-chain store movement by traditional retailers flourished at the time. As a result of this 'politics of distribution', many States introduced taxation targeted at chain stores in order to reduce their ability to discount sales. In addition, the Robinson–Patman Act came into force in 1936. This federal law reinforced the prohibition of price discrimination that was generally defined in the Clayton Act in 1914 (Neale 1960, Matsushita 1982). From the manufacturers' standpoint, because they hated 'a differed discount' and 'price concessions' to large buyers (Copeland 1931, pp. 305–6), local and federal governments' antagonism towards chains was welcome. The Robinson–Patman Act made it possible for them to maintain their sales prices to chain stores and other large-scale buyers (Nakano 1965b, pp. 29–30, Teraoka 1984, p. 31).

In addition, the movement of 'fair trade' – the term always used for resale price maintenance by its supporters (essentially associations of small retailers) – made a great hit under the extremely sluggish business conditions in the 1930s. Opponents spoke of 'price rings' (Nealt 1960, p. 346, fn. 1). After California made resale price contracts lawful by establishing the 'fair trade' law for the first time in 1931, and especially after the Supreme Court upheld the constitutionality of the State laws in 1936, the 'fair trade' movement spread like wildfire, so that forty-five States enacted the 'fair trade' laws by 1941 (Neale 1960, p. 347). And finally, the Miller–Tidings Act, a federal 'fair trade' law, amended the Sherman Act and legalized resale price maintenance in interstate trades in 1937 (Neale 1960, pp. 348–9; see Palamountain 1955, chapter 8). These legislations of 'fair trade' laws both on the state and federal levels meant that the severe environment of law regarding vertical price maintenance before the First World War was fundamentally changed and became much more favourable to manufacturers.

Thus, powerful political movements developed by traditional retailers as a main force produced favourable environments for manufacturers' channels policy because these situations kept keep prices vertical and avoided price competition. Although this does not mean the price-cutting problem completely disappeared, as mentioned above, the legal situations which allowed manufacturers to maintain prices would have made new price-cutters very obvious.

In contrast with such a favourable macro environment for pricing, the limit on establishing a closed relationship with merchants in manufacturers' marketing channels became much stricter due to the enforcement of anti-trust laws. As early as 1914, the conflicts in marketing channels between suppliers and merchants led to the establishment of the Clayton Act, in which Section 3 defined exclusive dealing as unlawful when it 'may be to substantially lessen competition or tend to create a monopoly in any line of commerce'. The judicial decisions in this area were stiff in its early days. It was known that the Supreme Court's decision on *Standard Fashion Company* vs. *Magrane Houston Company* in 1922 introduced the principle of 'quantitative substantiality', which decided there had been an infringement of the Clayton Act when the company controlled the market to a certain extent (see Neale 1960, pp. 189–90, Stelzer 1976, pp. 316–17, Matsushita 1982, pp. 158–9). In this case, Standard Fashion Co., already controlling almost 40 per cent of all the agencies of paper patterns of women's clothing in the USA, had contracts with retailers under which the retailers undertook not to sell or permit to be sold on their premises any other make of patterns, and Standard Fashion Co. sued Magrane Houston Co., a retailer, for breaking the contract of exclusive dealing; but Standard Fashion lost their suit. This was because the effect of exclusive-dealing arrangements that controlled almost 40 per cent agencies classed them as contracts that 'may substantially lessen competition or tend to create a monopoly' defined by Section 3, and infringed the Act. Although the principle of whether or not the Clayton Act was infringed was made more flexible by introducing the principle of 'qualitative substantiality' after the Second World War, strict judicial attitudes exerted influence on the discussions of channel selection at the time.

On the actual business scene, merchants with a spirit of independence often opposed the exclusive dealing and other restricted requirements laid down by their suppliers. The automobile retailers were one case. In this industry, while the old marketing channel of 'manufacturer – to distributor – to dealer' generally changed to the direct-to-dealer channel in the 1920s (Davisson 1954), manufacturers began to exercise an increasing degree of control over retail outlets to increase sales quotas and insist on 'exclusive representation' from their dealers, in addition to retail price maintenance and territorial protection for dealers already in existence under franchise agreements (Hewitt 1956, p. 65). However, car dealers rebelled against the rigid control of manufacturers, as Palamountain (1955, chapter 5) relates concerning the resistance movement against manufacturers by the National Automobile Dealers Association (NADA) in the 1930s. The Federal Trade Commission, although generally concluding that consumer benefits from competition in this industry 'have probably been more substantial than in any other large industry studied by the Commission', recommended that 'present unfair practices be abated to the end' (FTC [1939] 1983, pp. 1074 and 1076). While the Motor Vehicle Act of 1940 drafted by NADA was shelved, the political movement by dealers led to the enactment of the Good Faith Act in 1956, which fundamentally supported the dealers' standpoint against manufacturers (see Hewitt 1956, chapters 8–9). Thus, those retailers who were trapped in closed marketing channels often struggled for greater independence. These attitudes of retailers, in addition to the judicial background regarding closed linkages in marketing channels, tended to make discussions about the open-or-closed criterion very delicate.

Development of Managerial Ideas on Marketing Channels during the Two World Wars

Development of Ideas on Long-or-Short Selection

During the period between the two world wars, several managerial books on marketing were published in the USA, all of which naturally included the idea of channel selection. The features of the distribution structure and environments surrounding manufacturers' channel selection, shown above, affected academic opinion. There were naturally many differences in these ideas, perhaps due to differences in individual business experiments, standpoints in terms of business and society, theory, individual preferences and so forth. The traditional type of marketing literature, although it embraced many aspects of macro issues in marketing, often included micro-oriented or managerial thinking on channel selection, as exemplified by Duncan's book (1922, pp. 327–32). Nevertheless, this chapter focuses on the writings that intentionally took the managerial point of view and that set the precedents for today's mainstream marketing thought.

As seen above, the idea of channel selection was, first of all, developed based on the criterion of long-or-short. This discussion was the core of marketing books in the 1910s and during the interwar period; even in the Second World War, any authors who contributed to the development of the 4Ps idea, as shown in Chapter 3, discussed channel selection according to this criterion. A pure, but very simple, version was provided by Reed (1929), who suggested in his discussion of distribution the 'usual type of distribution open to the manufacturer':

1. Producer to special distributors, such as brokers, equipment or supply houses, agents, commission houses and commission men, specialty houses and exclusive agencies.
2. Producer to wholesaler or jobber.
3. Producer to retailer.
4. Producer to consumer direct (Reed 1929, p. 75).

Hayward (1926) took the same standpoint and advocated fundamentally the same options as Reed for a 'producer' who might use 'either one method alone or combining several methods into one system' (pp. 150–51).

Tosdal also gave the same explanation. As was already shown, he published various versions of his book on sales management that was synonymous with marketing management. The only difference in Tosdal's options of 'distribution policies' (Tosdal 1931, pp. 252–4, 1933, p. 106, 1939, pp. 197–9, 1940, p. 144) was that he added a 'combination of two or more of the above' as his fifth element.

The paper by James (1931) contributed a part of the marketing section in a handbook of business administration (Donald 1931), and presented a variant of the long-or-short list by adding the consignment system to the basic options regarding the length of channels (James 1931, p. 117).

Finally, Pyle (1942) enumerated not only the same four options as Reed for the 'possibilities that a producer might follow in distributing his merchandise', but added also two other options for manufacturers of industrial products: the manufacturer sells to 'industrial distributor – to industrial user' and also to 'broker, manufacturer's agent, sales agent, or other similar intermediary – to wholesaler or industrial distributor – to final user' (Pyle 1942, p. 309).

Thus, all these contributors devoted attention to the idea of selecting long-or-short channels. It should be noted that although the census of distribution recognized manufacturers' sales branches as a distinct 'establishment', these contributors did not mention them as the first step in channels because these were organizations inside a 'company' from a strategic point of view.

In the meantime, these writers naturally discussed determinant factors when manufacturers selected their channels. Reed (1929, pp. 80–83) pointed out six considerations, that is, 'distribution costs' or 'prices, discounts, terms and profit margins' that were 'inextricably bound together', technical or repair 'service' the product requires, availability of storage and transportation facilities, cooperation of distributors, sales management and its organization, and company policy. Hayward (1926, pp. 155–7) enumerated eight factors; that is, type of product, capital availability, volume of business, range of distribution (limited or broader territories), service requirements, relative costs, closed channels of distribution, and company policies. He also discussed the timing when manufacturers should 'change' marketing channels (Hayward 1926, p. 158). Five years later Tosdal (1931, pp. 254–5; 1939, pp. 199–200; see 1940, pp. 144–5) discussed four factors – the type of product, existing trade organizations, policies and circumstances of an individual manufacturer, and personal preferences and prejudices of executives – which played a part in manufacturers' choice. In his later book Tosdal indicated (1940, p. 145) that three major factors should be considered when selecting channels of distribution: volume of sales, margins of profit to be secured, and costs necessary to implement the policy. A famous paper by Duncan (1954, pp. 368–9) summarized development of channel selection after the Second World War, indicating these three 'general factors' affected choice of the channel of distribution. Thus, discussions in channel after the war had been already prepared in the interwar period.

An evocative issue in discussions was the direct relationship between manufacturers and retailers. The shorter channel, direct to retailers, was manufacturers' strategy to gain control in marketing channels. In this respect, discussing a few examples of 'the struggle for great control of wholesale and retail outlets', Reed (1929, pp. 78–9) described 'evidence of a struggle for a great degree of control over distribution by manufacturers and more direct contact with the consumer .... Mass production cannot survive and grow without mass distribution'. At the same time, however, as retailers' practices of backward integration were progressing as mentioned above, a shorter channel was also becoming an option for retailers. Tosdal's textbook explained this tendency:

> The choice of selling direct to retailer will involve in some trades selling direct to voluntary associates or buying syndicates. When powerful enough, these groups demand the right to purchase directly from the manufacturer, even where he customarily sells through wholesalers. Again, sale to retailers may involve sales to chains of retail establishments which sell either a single line, or many lines, as in chain department stores, mail-order houses with accompanying chains of stores, chains of leased departments, and the like (Tosdal 1931, p. 253).

Thus, the channel idea of 'long-or-short' selection, which originally started as an issue for manufacturers, was embracing the retailers' point of view, resulting in generalization and greater acceptance of the managerial idea of channel selection.

Determinants for Wide-or-Narrow Selection

From the manufacturers' point of view, the channels of large-scale retailers held both attractions and risks for manufacturers. This ambiguity was recognized by Butler, as shown in Chapter 1. In the interwar period, Hayward raised substantially the same view.

> If he [the large-scale retailer] cannot secure this discount, he will purchase a competing brand or even manufacture the goods himself. Furthermore, he feels at perfect liberty to cut the price if he cares to do so and finds it a profitable merchandise expedient.
>
> The manufacturer is placed between two fires. On the one hand, he dislikes to lose the sales outlet offered by the large-scale retailing systems, yet on the other hand he does not care to offend the jobbers or independent retailers who are compelled to sell at higher prices than the department or chain-store systems (Hayward 1926, p. 191).

The formats or institutions of large-scale retailers, therefore, were the factors for consideration by manufacturers when selecting their marketing channels. This decision naturally leads to a wide-or-short, rather than long-or-short, selection of channels. Reed (1929, p. 75) raised sub-options for several types of retailers such as independent stores, chain stores and others when manufacturers selected 'selling to retail outlets,' but Surface (1940) gave a more straightforward explanation. He contributed to *Marketing* (Alexander et al. eds., 1940), a traditional type of textbook which became more management-oriented in its second edition (Alexander et. al., eds., 1949). His 1940 list of channel options was as follows:

1. Manufacturer → wholesaler → retailer → consumer
2. Manufacturer → retailer → consumer
3. Manufacturer → consumer
4. Manufacturer → chain stores → consumer
5. Manufacturer → voluntary chain → consumer (Surface 1940, p. 377).

Clearly the list was a mixture of long-or-short and wide-or-narrow criteria; options 2, 4 and 5 were the same in terms of length but different in width, and showed selective channels at the retail level. The list shows historical evidence that obvious growth of large-scale retail buyers encouraged the discussion of selective channels or the criterion of wide-or-narrow.

On the theoretical level, the classification of products was commonly recognized at the time as the determinant for selection of wide-or-narrow channels. The major figure in this field was Copeland (Furo 1968, p. 199; see also Ishihara 1969, p. 121, Kometani 1974, p. 78, Ozaki 1990, pp. 14–15). Inheriting the idea from C.C. Parlin (see Copeland 1923, p. 282, fn. 2), Copeland modified the method of classification and placed it at the centre for deciding marketing and channel policy.

This classification of merchandise that is sold for retail distribution into convenience goods, shopping goods, and specialty goods serves as a guide for the formulation of the general plans of distribution. The determination of the class into which a particular commodity falls is one of the first tasks to be undertaken in laying out a systematic plan of distribution (Copeland [1924] 1978, p. 129).

An essential feature is that the classification of products was based on 'consumers' buying habits' and 'patronage motives', not simply on the physical features of products themselves, so that the distinction among them was not automatic; policy and strategy by marketers played an important role. Advocating the concept of 'density of distribution', Copeland discussed the wide-or-narrow selection of channels in each type of products. Copeland's general conclusion was as follows:

> For convenience goods a manufacturer seeks to obtain distribution of his product through as many stores as possible in each community. A manufacturer of shopping goods undertakes to have his wares sold to as many shopping institutions as possible in each shopping district. A manufacturer of specialty goods, however, utilizes selected retail distribution by choosing one or at most a few stores in each city to which to sell his product (Copeland [1924] 1987, pp. 117–18).

Copeland's discussions were accompanied by his reflections on which retail formats would be suitable for each category of products: an idea of channel selection was shaped by the same conditions producing the appearance of autonomous retailers at the time.

The great influence of Copeland's work can be recognized in Hayward's (1926, p. 155) statement, '[T]he distribution of necessities or convenience goods demands a maximum number of retail outlets', or Tosdal's (1931, p. 254), 'The number of outlets necessary to reach consumers will be relatively smaller in the case of so-called speciality products than in the case of convenience goods', and Surface's (1940, p. 392) insistence, 'Convenience goods are especially likely to need complete retail coverage; specialty goods should be sold to consumers through a few selected outlets.'

From the Closed Channel to the Vertical Distribution System

Finally, while discussions of open-or-closed selection also developed, an embryonic idea of the vertical marketing system was emerging even in the interwar period.

Copeland again was early in discussing the exclusive channel: 'Frequently, exclusive agencies are granted to retailers for the distribution of specialty goods. An exclusive agency is seldom, if ever, justified for any line which is not a specialty line' (Copeland 1923, p. 285). At the same time, however, he noted the judicial decision of *Standard Fashion Company* v. *Magrane-Houston Company* mentioned in the previous section, and cast doubt about it: 'If the same rule were generally to be applied to all exclusive agency agreements in which a retailer undertakes to restrict his purchases of competing brands of specialty goods, it would conflict seriously with sound business policy … and not to the advantage of consumers' (Copeland [1924] 1987, pp. 118–19).

It should be noted that the judicial decision did not mean that all agreements which precluded handling competing products were immediately unlawful: in several industries they survived. For instance, in the automobile industry, 'took on a competing line' was listed as the principle cause for dealer cancellations by leading manufacturers in the 1920s, and this survived until 1949 when the Department of Law guided manufacturers to eliminate it from their agreements (Hewitt 1956, pp. 65 and 232).

In the meantime, however, discussions on exclusive or closed channels became more deliberate in managerial textbooks on marketing. For instance, Converse's *Sales Policy* (1927), which also covered substantially all the fields of marketing management, discussed the case of retail exclusive agencies or dealers selected by manufacturers:

> He [the manufacturer] may require the dealer to give up the sale of competing products and put all his efforts behind the one product. He cannot legally require this, under the Clayton Act, if the contract substantially lessens competition. This law should not be forgotten. He may, however, refuse to sell the dealer [sic] if he handles a competing product, so that the dealer may have to decide which product he prefers to handle. A wrong choice, under such circumstances, means a loss of business.
>
> If the manufacturer does not make unreasonable requirements, and if he does not require the dealer to give up the sales of competing products, the dealer generally has more to gain than to lose from an exclusive agency (Converse 1927, p. 353).

This suggests that the contract for what was called 'exclusive agency' did not necessarily prohibit handling competing products or brands, although it may have included the clause that the manufacturer would sell to no other dealer in the territory specified, or that the manufacturer would definitely limit the number of dealers in a city or town, or others (see Converse 1927, p. 348). Similar indications are found in Hayward (1926, pp. 193–5) and Pyle (1942, pp. 318–19), as well as the book by Agnew and Houghton (1941, p. 69) entitled *Marketing Policy* that is described in Chapter 3.

Therefore, Duncan (1954, p. 376) indicated in his post-war summary that there were two types of 'exclusive agency agreements' – one required agents not to handle competing products, and the other granted certain retailers 'the sole right to sell their products in specified area' but did not require that the retailers refrain from handling competing lines. In the meantime, development of chain stores that integrated backwards toward production encouraged recognition of a different type of vertical system from the manufacturer's channels.

While Edwards (1937) pointed out the 'struggle for the control of distribution' among manufacturers, wholesalers and retailers, Craig and Gabler (1940) made a significant contribution to the discussion. They recognized that the collapse of the economic system in 1929 was a turning point that intensified 'the struggle between the older and the newer forms of distribution'. According to them, 'the manufacturer-guided distribution system' was the older one, and especially after 1929, the system of manufacturer-guided distribution was no longer so smooth and inexpensive: instead, the 'retailer-guided distribution system' developed. They believed that this retailer-guided system was much more suitable than the manufacturer-guided one. Although they admitted (Craig and Gabler 1940, p. 94) the manufacturer-guided system could be effective if manufacturer's brands built up consumer demand by adding 'enough intangible value' and made them not interchangeable with other brands, they focused on a problem of 'discrepancy between manufacturer and consumer assortments': 'Vertical integration in distribution, especially when it starts from the manufacturer, may be unsuccessful because of the difference between merchandise assortments at the manufacturer's level and merchandise assortments at the consumer's level' (Craig and Gabler 1940, p. 91).

> Theoretically, since buying starts with the consumer, the ideal system would begin with the ultimate consumer, organize his wants and needs, and express them in terms of merchandise ... Consumer buying ... is hardly ever rational. Since the majority of the consumer's wants are emotional his buying is accordingly, and he is unwilling to go to the trouble of organizing his wants. ... For that reason the selling function between retailers and consumers must remain, and the task of analyzing and synthesizing consumer wants falls logically on the part of the business system which is closest to the consumer. That is the retailer (Craig and Gabler 1940, pp. 86–7).

Therefore, their conclusion was as follows.

> We have shown the origin, the development, the causes, the advantages and disadvantages under different market situations of the two types of major distribution systems, which make up the competitive struggle for market control.
>   The change from one system to the other will probably continue, because the retailer-guided system, judged by the existing evidence, seems better adapted to the situation of a buyer's market, and because it does not now seem likely that this situation will again be reversed in the calculable future (Craig and Gabler 1940, p. 106).

It can be evaluated that their recognition of the 'discrepancy between manufacturer and consumer assortments' stands out as a precedent of the concepts of 'sorting' and 'assortment' developed by Alderson (1957, chapter 7, 1965, chapter 3; on the historical contribution of Alderson, see Bartels 1976, p. 158, Reekie 2006, p. 358) after the Second World War. Furthermore, their recognition of the vertical system as a competitive unit was also a precedent of the discussion on the 'vertical marketing system' popular in current textbooks of marketing management.

Their emphasis on the retailer-guide rather than the manufacturer-guide channels was essentially a transition of channel thought from the primitive idea discussed purely from the manufacturer's point of view to the developed idea that did not confine the thought but covered all standpoints of business organizations. This feature was produced by development of marketing activities, that is, chain stores and other retail formats actually integrating backwards, as Craig and Gabler clearly recognized:

> The principle examples of integration at the retail level are the chain stores and the mail-order houses. Beginning as individual retail stores, they have added wholesale units and have integrated vertically to the extent of manufacturing a number of their own products. ... These three types of integration [centrally owned chains, buying groups and retailer co-operatives] spring from the retailer-guided idea and present the major economic

development in the field of distribution during the last twenty decades. The centrally owned group took the lead. The co-operative groups came later in self-dense. Both have made considerable inroads on the manufacturer-guided system (Craig and Gabler 1940, p. 95).

Thus, the managerial idea of marketing channels was advancing, based on progress by innovative retailers – towards a mature, generalized system.

Conclusion

The idea of channel selection, begun from the standpoint of the newly emerged manufacturers who integrated mass production with mass distribution, steadily developed in the interwar period. On the level of wholesale distribution, the manufacturers' activities had themselves created the distribution structure late in the nineteenth century, providing some affordable options for long-or-short that manufacturers could establish as their marketing policies or strategies in the interwar period. In the retail field, development of new retail formats had produced a polarized structure, providing manufacturers with an option of wide distribution by petty retailers on one hand, and encouraging short, direct contacts between manufacturers and large-sized retailers on the other hand. In addition, aggressive price policies by retailers in newly emerging formats often forced manufacturers to decide whether or not to choose a narrow channel. The political and judicial environments created by traditional independent retailers brought favourable conditions for manufacturers to maintain prices vertically, but sometimes also difficulty in establishing a closed relationship with merchants. All these factors exerted strong influences on the managerial idea of marketing channels.

Between the two world wars, a succession of managerial books on marketing appeared which included channel thought and long-or-short selection, and some contributors discussed the wide-or-narrow or open-or-closed options. Theoretical development was especially clear on the issue of wide-or-narrow selection, utilizing the idea of trinomial classification of products, while discussions on closed channels reflected the movement of judicial decisions regarding anti-trust laws.

Important progress was made based on the vertical activities of corporate chains and other retail formats or institutions. The primitive idea of marketing channels that had arisen directly from the manufacturer's point of view was now maturing and no longer confined to that standpoint. The concepts of discrepancy of assortments, the vertical competitive unit, and the advantages of retailer-guided channels were outstanding constructs that embodied this progress. The process of creating these new concepts enriched knowledge on channels, so that it broadened the original, restricted standpoint from the manufacturer and generalized the idea that was applicable for any kind of marketer.

After the Second World War, D.J. Duncan (1954) advocated a popular typology of channel selection (the extensive or widespread distribution, selective selling and exclusive agencies), inheriting the pre-war discussions. In the meantime, further theoretical endeavours started by adopting the so-called systems approach to marketing channels (see McCammon and Little 1965, pp. 327–31), including the ideas of channel administration by Ridgeway (1957), dynamism of conflict and cooperation among channel members by Mallen (1963), and the 'organized behavior system' by Alderson (1950, 1957, 1963, see also Wooliscroft, Tamilia and Shapiro 2006). While the systems view more or less referred to the general systems theory by Ludwig von Bertalanffy that was rapidly gaining ground among marketing and business scholars (Lazer and Kelley 1962, Kelley and Lazer 1967), the reason why this view was effectively introduced was the maturity of channel behaviours that had already produced the perception on the vertical competitive unit before the war. Then the power/conflict paradigm, which referred to the idea in political science, sociology and social psychology (see e.g. French and Raven [1959] 1966, Dhal 1959, Emerson 1962), became popular especially from the end of the 1960s (see e.g. Assael 1968, 1969, Beier and Stern 1969, Stern and Gorman 1969, Little 1970, Rosenberg and Stern 1971, El-Ansary and Stern 1972, Stern, Sternthal and Craig 1973). This development was an extension to the systems approach that saw channel relationships as a system, through which the basis of power and the settlement of conflicts could be explored.

In the early days, channel conflicts only led to the idea of channel selection as shown in the case of Butler in Chapter 1. Meanwhile, the development in both channel behaviours and ideas between the two world wars provided the groundwork that introduced the systems approach and the power/conflict paradigm after the Second World War.

Concluding Remarks

As indicated in the introductory chapter, the traditional functional approach in marketing combines two different streams of thought: functions in distribution or marketing channels and functions of management. Figure CR.1 distinguishes between these two genealogical lines.

Although previous research in the functional approach focused mainly on channel functions, this book has explored the birth and development of managerial functions in marketing along with their historical context. The discussion of managerial functions emerged at the same time as the traditional functional approach in marketing channels. Arch W. Shaw, the originator of the functional approach, also embraced the discussion of managerial functions (discussed in Chapter 3). Much simpler but clearer was Butler's idea (Chapter 1). This can be considered the first step in articulating explicit knowledge on managerial functions in marketing in that the planning function, which included a prototype of the 4Ps idea, was separated from the implementation function. Genealogically, a circular form of the idea of managerial functions was promoted by P. White in the 1920s (Chapter 3) and became merged with the management process school. In the meantime, the content of the planning function of marketing was developed by several scholars such as H.R. Tosdal, W.D. Hayward, P.D. Converse, V.D. Reed, W.J. Donald, J.F. Pyle, H.E. Agnew and D. Houghton between the two world wars (Chapter 3), who contributed to the 4Ps idea.

After the Second World War, McGarry (1950, p. 269) proposed 'a new list of functions of marketing' that was composed of: (1) contractual [sic], (2) merchandising, (3) pricing, (4) propaganda, (5) physical distribution, and (6) termination. Here, McGarry utilized the historical terminology of 'merchandising' (shown in Chapters 4 and 5), and other factors are also managerial functions in marketing rather than traditional 'marketing functions' dedicated to marketing channel. Then, Howard (1957, pp. 4–9) advocated the famous distinction between 'the controllable' and 'the uncontrollable' in the process of decision making in marketing, in which the controllable features were product variation, marketing channels, price, promotion (advertising and personal selling) and location, whereas the uncontrollable features, from the viewpoint of marketing managers, were competition, demand, non-marketing cost, the structure of distribution and marketing law. Finally, McCarthy (1960, pp. 45–52) offered what became the renowned definition of the 4Ps. Although Hunt and Gloosby (1988, p. 40) indicated that McGarry was presaging the rise of managerial approach to the study of marketing and the demise of the functional approach, it should be added that the 4Ps type of managerial idea had a different pedigree from the functional approach in market distribution, and was a legitimate child of the development of the functional approach in management at least from the 1910s.

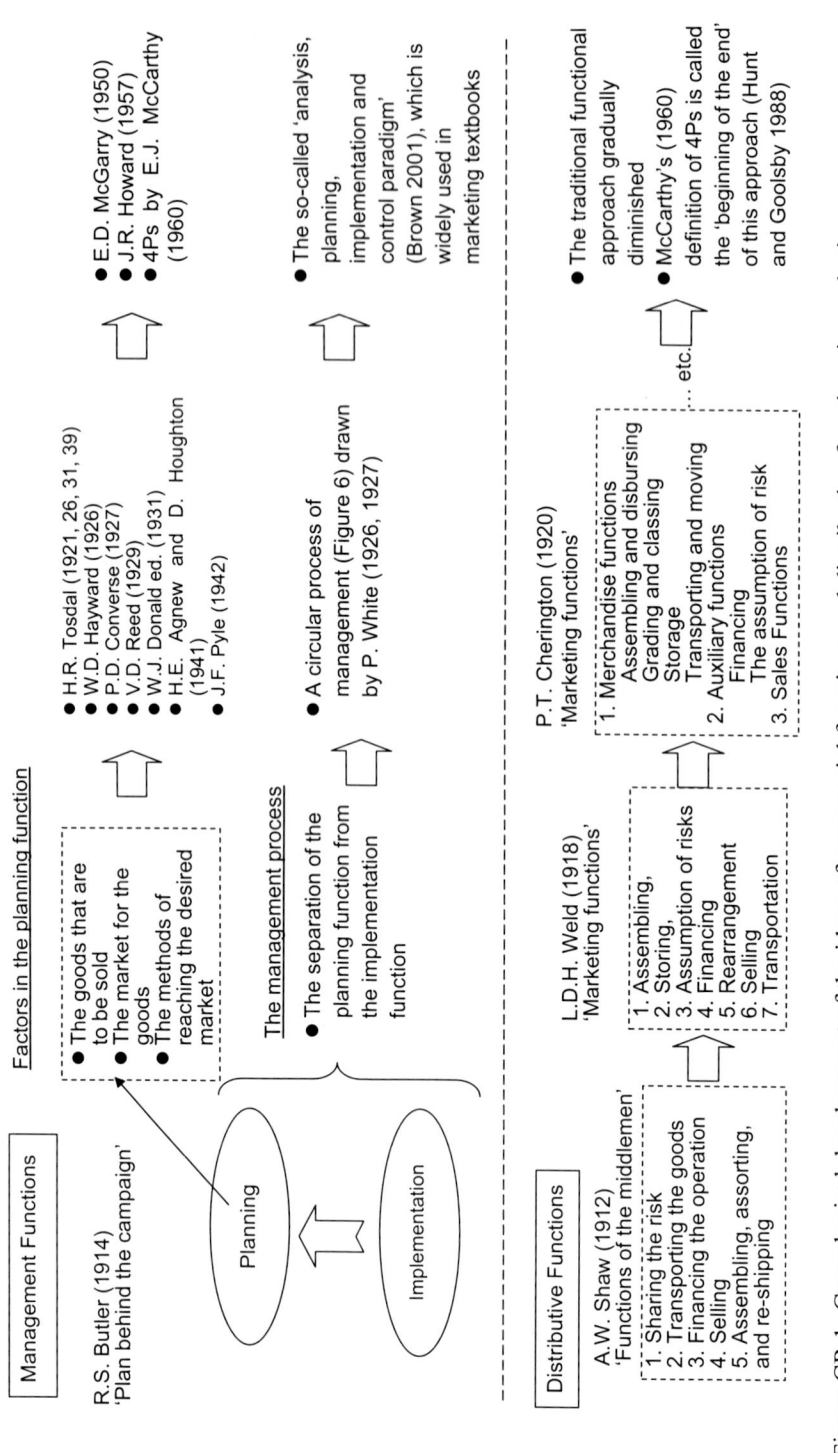

Figure CR.1 Genealogical development of the ideas of managerial functions and distributive functions in marketing

Such progress was achieved by making explicit the hitherto tacit knowledge which entrepreneurs had derived by experience. In addition to the general driving forces of this articulation such as the progress of managerial capitalism accompanied by the development of higher business education, this book suggests that a direct precursor of the 4Ps idea was marketing by manufacturers, rather than just merchants. As emphasized by R.S. Butler (Chapter 1), the primitive version was generated from the standpoint of manufacturers, the main body of whom could be considered the new type of manufacturer emerging from the late nineteenth century, who integrated the process of mass production with that of mass distribution within a firm. It was this narrow standpoint that made it possible for Butler to articulate product policy and channel policy in particular, which are essential factors in the 4Ps model. In Butler's primitive version, the introduction of a new product to market, such as Crisco by P&G, and the selection of channel members among merchants, which often led to conflicts with manufacturers, were viewed from the manufacturers' standpoint. Butler's discussion gives us a suggestion of an analytical perspective on the original form of the 4Ps concept. Although other scholars in the same period as Butler did not necessarily limit their point of view to that of manufacturers, they embraced the manufacturers' issues at least as an essential component, as exemplified by the concept of 'merchant producer' by A.W. Shaw.

The maturing of marketing management was a two-fold process – generalization of the idea to make it applicable in numerous situations and decontextualization of the original. The endeavour to combine explicit knowledge of both marketing management and scientific management (Chapters 2 and 3) was a process of theoretical development through generalization and decontextualization. As such, the discussions on this depart from the direct background of manufacturers' marketing, although these sometimes played an important role, as shown by the work of Taylor's immediate disciples (Tabor Manufacturing Company), C.W. Hoyt's idea of 'scientific sales management' (e.g. the sales talk standardization in the cases of NCR and P&G), and A.W. Shaw's concept of 'merchant-manufacturers'. In these endeavours, the concept of standardization was the key, which was applied to the idea of sales force management (Chapter 2) and the basic framework of marketing management (Chapter 3).

In the meantime, along with the progress of marketing practices between the two world wars, a different type of marketing was mixing with the managerial idea, while manufacturers' marketing continued to provide a stimulus to progress. A result of this was the further development of generalization and decontextualization.

The concepts of 'sales engineer' and 'merchandising' (Chapter 4), which were attempts to clarify planning functions, especially product planning functions, were basically the manufacturers' marketing activities. The redesign movement (Chapter 5), in which marketers redesigned their existing products by employing the emergent profession of industrial designers, added new issues to the idea of 'merchandising' and product policy, and the drivers of this movement were primarily the manufacturers. The idea of channel selection was maturing during the two world wars based on manufacturers' activities (Chapter 6).

At the same time, the innovative retailers, especially those who integrated backward towards the wholesaling and the manufacturing processes, came in as another important factor to advance the idea of marketing management. Several factors promoted the definition of the idea of channel selection from the manufacturer's standpoint (Chapter 1). These included early problems caused by the relationship with old- and new-type of merchants (such as private brands and resale price maintenance by emergent chain stores and other merchants, and traditional merchants' nostalgia, describing themselves as 'real merchants' competing against manufacturers' national brands). In contrast, in the process of development from primitive to mature knowledge, the progress of backward channel activities by chain stores encouraged the idea of the 'retailer-guided system' of marketing channel, which was different from the manufacturer's point of view (Chapter 6). Even within the redesign movement, the case of Sears' private brand (Chapter 5) was an example of product development by retailers. Thus, the managerial idea was becoming applicable to any situation and enriched.

Research for this book also indicated that there existed many different contexts that produced the consumer-focus philosophy. Parlin's advocacy for being 'a student of human wants' connoted a recommendation that the traditional merchants should deal willingly with the manufacturers' national brands (Chapter 1). Shaw's insistence on shaping the products 'more closely to the needs and uses of consumers' often implied the scientific approach to marketing (Chapter 3). White's emphasis that 'marketing centers in all cases around the needs of the consumer' implied the idea of standardization (Chapter 3). The historical concept of 'merchandising' included the philosophy of consumer-focus as a coordination of production with consumers' demands (Chapter 4). In the redesign movement in the 1930s, the philosophy of 'satisfaction of consumer needs' or that the 'consumer is the final boss' was recognized as not merely lip service, but a reality of business in the face of frequent changes in designs by industrial designers. Even the idea of planned obsolescence was proposed in the name of consumers' wants (Chapter 5). The idea of retailer-guided distribution systems was also advocated because it seemed suitable for consumers' buying (Chapter 6). Thus, in spite of the famous myth that the philosophy of consumer orientation was invented in the 1950s, marketing management was already well aware of a consumer-oriented philosophy. The philosophy, however, was raised in many different contexts so that each one embraced a different implication.

Regarding the promotion of this philosophy in the 1950s, it has been indicated (King 1965, pp. 76–8, Barksdale and Darden 1971, p. 29) that the first declaration introducing the new marketing concept was made by the annual report of General Electric: 'In 1952 your Company's operating managers were presented with an advanced concept of marketing, formulated by the Marketing Service Division. This, in simple terms, would introduce the marketing man at the beginning rather than the end of the production cycle and would integrate marketing into each phase of the business' (General Electric 1952, p. 21). The background of this concept was that the company was just in the process of introducing a multidivisional organization (Chandler [1962] 1969). Each division was required to run with the focus of consumers as profit centres. The situation also applied in the Westinghouse Electric Corporation (*Printers' Ink* 1958). This context was forgotten again, when the generalized consumer-focus philosophy became prevalent.

Along with the promotion of marketing concepts, a crucial change took place within the discipline of marketing – the managerial approach signified by the 4Ps model became predominant, as the three traditional approaches diminished. As a result, marketing became substantially synonymous with marketing management. The mature idea of marketing management was well articulated and free to spread globally after the Second World War, and similarly expanded to nonprofit organizations and even individuals from the end of the 1960s onwards.

This mature knowledge of marketing management does not cancel out the need for innovative, creative, risk-taking entrepreneurship. On the contrary, professional managers who learn the idea of marketing management have to challenge new opportunities under changing and uncertain circumstances. Explicit knowledge about marketing provides 'a solid operational basis' to entrepreneurial decision making. As Cole (1946) once put it, 'innovation without a solid basis' tends to be ineffective, while 'management without innovation' gives a poor prognosis. In this sense, the 'marketing/entrepreneurship interface' (Hills and LaForge 1992, Gardner 1994) or the so-called 'entrepreneurial management' (Drucker [1985] 1993, see also Kaplan 1987) is inherently required.

Furthermore, even in the case of routine management practice, each manager has to recognize the unique tacit knowledge embedded in each unique context. According to the perspective of 'distributed cognition' (Salmon 1993, see also Engeström 1987, 1999), human cognition or human intelligence is distributed among the environments in which the human lives, so that each practitioner has to recognize situation-specific knowledge embedded in each unique context. This is also very true in the ethnic context because much cultural knowledge is tacitly embedded in each ethnic situation. In this regard, both microcosmic analysis of human behaviour (see e.g. Lave and Wenger 1991, Wenger 1998) and international comparative study are necessary.

Bibliography

Abbott, Charles F. (1930), 'Obsolescence and the passing of high-pressure salesmanship', in Frederick 1930, pp. 155–73.

Agnew, Hugh E. and Houghton, Donald (1941), *Marketing Policy*, New York and London: McGraw-Hill Book Company, Inc.

Alderson, Wroe (1950), 'Survival and adjustment of organized behavior systems', in Cox, R., and Alderson, W. (eds), *Theory in Marketing: Selected Essays*, Chicago, Illinois: Richard D. Irwin, Inc., pp. 65–87.

—— (1956), 'Charles Coolidge Parlin', *Journal of Marketing*, 21 (1), July, 1–2. (Also, in Wring and Dimsdale 1974, pp. 103–5.)

—— (1957), *Marketing Behavior and Executive Actions*, Homewood, Illinois: Richard D. Irwin, Inc.

—— (1965), *Dynamic Marketing Behavior*, Homewood, Illinois: Richard D. Irwin, Inc.

Alexander, David (1970), *Retailing in England during the Industrial Revolution*, London: The Athlone Press, University of London.

Alexander, Ralph S. et al. (eds), (1940), *Marketing*, Boston: Ginn and Company.

—— et al. (eds), (1949), *Marketing*, 2nd ed., Boston: Ginn and Company.

Alford, W.E. (1981), 'New industries for old? British industry between the wars', in Floud, Roderick and McCloskey, Donald (eds), *The Economic History of Britain since 1700, Volume 2: 1860 to the 1970s*, Cambridge: Cambridge University Press, pp. 308–46.

Allen, Frederick Lewis (1931), *Only Yesterday: An Informal History of the Nineteen-Twenties*, New York and London: Harper and Brothers Publishers.

AMA: American Marketing Association (1948), 'Report of the definitions committee', *Journal of Marketing* 8 (2), October, 202–17.

—— ([1960] 1963), *Marketing Definitions: A Glossary of Marketing Terms*, Chicago: American Marketing Association (Reprint, AMA).

Anderson, Adam (1764), *An Historical and Chronological Deduction of the Origin of Commerce, From the Earliest Account to the Present Time*, London: Printed for A. Millar et al.

Anderson, Arthur D. (1917), 'The dealer's right to push private brands', *Printers' Ink*, April 5, 37–8.

Anderson, Paul F. (1983), 'Marketing, scientific progress, and scientific method', *Journal of Marketing*, 47(4), Fall, 18–31.

Appel, David (1972), 'The supermarket: early development of an institutional innovation', *Journal of Retailing*, 48 (1), Spring, 39–53.

Arakawa, Yuhkichi (1960), *Modern Theory of Haikyu*, Tokyo: Chikura-shobo (in Japanese).

—— (1978), *A Pedigree of Marketing Science*, Tokyo: Chikura-shobo (in Japanese).

Archer, Gleason L. ([1939] 1971), *Big Business and Radio*, New York: The American History Co., Inc. (Reprint, New York: Arno Press.)

[Armour & Co.] (1916), 'Armour's campaign against "cost of living" censure', *Printers' Ink*, 12 December, 57–8.

Arndt, Johan (1982), 'The conceptual domain of marketing: an evaluation of Shelby Hunt's three dichotomy model', *European Journal of Marketing*, 16 (1), 27–35.

Arnold, A. (1974), 'Einige Gedanken zum Begriff "Marketing"', *Zeitschrift für Betriebswirtschaft*, 44 (5), May, 367–74.

Ashley, W.J. (1908), 'The enlargement of economics', *The Economic Journal*, 18 (70), June, 181–204.

—— (1926), *Business Economics*, London: Longmans, Green, and Co. Ltd.

Aspley, J.C. (1929), *Intensive Sales Management*, Chicago and New York: The Dartnell Corporation.

Assael, Henry (1968), 'The political role of trade associations in distributive conflict resolution', *Journal of Marketing*, 32, April, 21–8.

—— (1969), 'Constructive role of interorganizational conflict', *Administrative Science Quarterly*, 14, December, 573–82.

Baba, Keiji (1924), *Function in Industrial Business and Its Specialisation*, Tokyo: Daitetsu-kaku (in Japanese).

Bagozzi, Richard (1975), 'Marketing as exchange', *Journal of Marketing* 39 (4), October, pp. 32–9.

Baker, Michael J. (1976), *Marketing: Theory and Practice*, London and Basingstoke: The Macmillan Press Ltd.

Barger, Harold (1955), *Distribution's Place in the American Economy since 1869*, Princeton: Princeton University Press.

Barksdale, Hiram C. and Darden, Bill (1971), 'Marketer's attitudes toward the marketing concept', *Journal of Marketing*, 35 (4), October, 29–36.

Barney, P.R. (1910), 'The private brand pitfall', *Printers' Ink*, 4 August, 8–10.

Bartels, Robert (1951), 'Influences on the development of marketing thought, 1900–1923', *Journal of Marketing*, 16 (1), July, 1–17.

—— (1962), *The History of Marketing Thought*, Homewood, Illinois: Richard D. Irwin, Inc.

—— (1976), *The History of Marketing Thought*, 2nd ed., Columbus, Ohio: Grid Inc.

—— (1988), *The History of Marketing Thought*, 3rd ed., Columbus, Ohio: Grid Inc.

Barton, Bruce (1929), 'Introduction', in Charles W. Hoyt, *Scientific Sales Management Today*, New York: The Ronald Press Company, 1929, pp. iii–iv.

Beckman, Theodore N. and Nolen, Herman C. ([1938] 1976), *The Chain Store Problem: A Critical Analysis*, New York and London: McGraw-Hill Book Company, Inc. (Reprint, New York: Arno Press.)

Beem, Eugene R. (1973), 'The beginning of the consumer movement', in Kelley, W.T. (ed.), *New Consumerism: Selected Reading*, Columbus, Ohio: Grid Inc., pp. 15–21.

Beier, F.J. and Stern, L.W. (1969), 'Power in the channel of distribution', in Stern L.W. (ed.), *Distribution Channels: Behavioral Dimensions*, Boston: Houghton Mifflin Company, pp. 92–116.

Bell, Daniel ([1976] 1996), *The Cultural Contradictions of Capitalism*, New York; Basic Books, Paperback edition.

Bell, Martin L. and Emory, C. William (1971), 'The flattering marketing concept', *Journal of Marketing*, 35 (4), October, 37–42.

Bennett, Peter D. (ed.) (1988), *Dictionary of Marketing Terms*, 2nd ed., Chicago: American Marketing Association.

Bernstein, Michael A. (1987), *The Great Depression: Delayed Recovery and Economic Change in America, 1929–1939*, New York: Cambridge University Press.

Borch, Fred J. (1957), 'The marketing philosophy as a way of business life', in *Marketing Series*, *99, The Marketing Concept: Its Meaning to Management*, New York: American Management Association, Inc., pp. 3–16.

Borsodi, Ralph ([1927] 1976), *The Distribution Age: A Study of the Economy of Modern Distribution*, New York and London: D. Appleton and Company. (Reprint, New York: Arno Press.)

Bradford, E.S. (1924), 'Market analysis', in Alford, L P. (ed.), *Management's Handbook*, New York: The Ronald Press Company, pp. 1432–55.

Bradley, C.B. (1946), *Design in the Industrial Arts*, Peoria, Illinois: The Manual Arts Press.

Brady, George S. (1931), 'Product design for increased utility and improved marketability', *Mechanical Engineering*, 53 (9), September, 675–6.

—— (1932), 'Appearance as a sales factor in design', *The Iron Age*, October 27, 648–9.

Brainerd, J.G. with Lind, Robert S. (1934), 'Introduction', *The Annals of The American Academy of Political and Social Science, 173, The Ultimate Consumer: A Study in Economic Illiteracy*, May, ix–xiv.

Brennan, E.J.T. (1975), *Education for National Efficiency: the Contribution of Sidney and Beatrice Webb*, London: The Athlone Press of the University of London.

Breyer, Ralph F. (1931), *Commodity Marketing: The Marketing of a Number of Selected Non-Agriculture Products and Public Utility Services*, N.Y. and London: McGraw-Hill Book Co. Ltd.

Brisco, Norris. Arthur (1916), *Fundamental Salesmanship*, New York: D. Appleton-Century Co., Inc.

Brown, H.W. (1914), 'Scientific management in the sales department', *Bulletin of the Society to Promote the Science of Management*, 1 (1), December. [pp. 3–4.]

Brown, Stephen (1988), 'The wheel of the wheel of retailing', *International Journal of Retailing*, 3 (1), 16–37.

—— (1990), 'The wheel of retailing textbooks', *Journal of Retailing*, 66 (3), 337–2.

—— (1991), 'Variations on a marketing enigma: the wheel of retailing theory', *Journal of Marketing Management*, 7, 131–55.

—— (2001), 'Marketing for muggles: Harry Potter and the retro revolution', *Journal of Marketing Management*, 17 (5–6), July, 463–79.

——, Hirschman, Elizabeth C. and Maclaran, Pauline, 'Always historicize! Researching marketing history in a post-historical epoch', *Marketing Theory*, 1 (1), March, 49–89.

Brown, V.B. (1910), 'A "private brand" manufacturer hits back', *Printers' Ink*, September 15, pp. 17–19.

[BTS: Bulletin of the Taylor Society] (1920), 'Membership of the Taylor Society as of June 20, 1920', *Bulletin of the Taylor Society*, 5 (3), Supplement 1, July, 9–14.

Bucklin, Luis P. (1966), *A Theory of Distribution Channel Structure*, Berkeley, California: Institute of Business and Economic Research, University of California.

Bush, Donald J. (1975), *The Streamlined Decade*, New York: George Braziller, Inc.

[Business Review] (1930), 'The eyes have it', *The Business Review*, 29 January, 30–32.

[Business Week] (1936), 'Industrial design comes of age', *Business Week*, 23 May, 16–18.

[Butler, Ralph Starr] (1911a), *Sales, Purchase, and Shipping Methods*, Madison, Wisconsin: The University of Wisconsin, University Extension Division, Course 153 (Microfilm).

Butler, Ralph Starr (1911b), 'Part II: Selling and buying', in Galloway, Lee and Butler, Ralph Starr, *Advertising, Selling and Credit*, New York: Alexander Hamilton Institute, Modern Business, Vol. 9, 1911.

—— (1914), 'Part I: Marketing Methods', in Butler, Ralph Starr, DeBower, Herbert F., and Jones, John G., *Marketing Methods and Salesmanship*, New York: Alexander Hamilton Institute, Modern Business, Vol. 3, 1914.

—— (1917), *Marketing Methods*, Modern Business, Vol. 5, New York: Alexander Hamilton Institute.

—— (1918), 'Investigating the market: factors to be considered', *Printers' Ink*, 2 December, 10, 12 and 16–17.

—— and Swinney, John B. (1918), *Marketing and Merchandising*, Modern Business Vol. 5, New York: Alexander Hamilton Institute.

Calkins, Ernest Elmo (1915), *The Business of Advertising*, New York and London: D. Appleton and Company.

—— (1930), 'The new consumption engineer, and the artist', in Frederick 1930, pp. 107–29.

—— ([1932] 1976), 'What consumer engineering really is', in Sheldon and Arnest [1932] 1976, pp. 1–14.

—— and Holden, R. ([1905] 1985), *Modern Advertising*, New York: D. Appleton-Century Company, Inc. (Reprint, New York and London: Garland Publishing, Inc.)

Cammelgaard, Soren (1958), *Resale Price Maintenance, Project No. 238*, Paris: The European Productivity Agency of the Organisation for European Economic Co-operation.

Cantillon, Richard ([1755] 1959), *Essai sur la Nature du Commerce en Général*. Edited with an English translation and other materials by Henry Higgs, *Essay on the Nature of Trade in General*, London: Frank Cass and Company Ltd.

Cardinal, Paul J. (1928), 'Progressive obsolescence is the path to industrial suicide!' *Advertising & Selling*, 3 October, 25 and 88–9.

Carrington, Noel (1976), *Industrial Design in Britain*, London: Allen and Unwin Publisher.

Carter, J.W. (1917), 'The method of making route charts and route sheets', *Bulletin of the Taylor Society*, 3 (4), August, 19–27.

Casson, Herbert N. ([1914] 2002), *Ads and Sales: A Study of Advertising and Selling from the Standpoint of the New Principles of Scientific Management*, Chicago: A.C. McClurg & Co. (Reprint, Bristol, UK: Thoemmes Press [London: Sir Isaac Pitman & Sons, Ltd. Publishers, 1914 Version].)

CEWI: Committee in the Elimination of the Waste in Industry (1921), *Waste in Industry*, Washington, DC: Federated American Engineering Societies.

Chandler Jr., Alfred D. ([1962] 1969), *Strategy and Structure: Chapters in the History of the Industrial Enterprise*, Paperback Edition, Cambridge, Massachusetts: The MIT Press.

—— (comp. & ed.) (1964), *Giant Enterprise: Ford, General Motors, and the Automobile Industry; Sources and Readings*, New York: Harcourt Brace & World, Inc.

—— (1969), 'The structure of American industry in the twentieth century: a history of overview', with 'Appendix: oligopolists in American manufacturing and their products, 1909–1963', by Porter, G. and Livesay, H.C., *Business History Review*, 43 (3), Autumn, 255–98.

—— (1977), *The Visible Hand: The Managerial Revolution in American Business*, Cambridge, Massachusetts and London: The Belknap Press of Harvard University Press.

—— (1990), *Scale and Scope: The Dynamics of Industrial Capitalism*, Cambridge, Massachusetts: The Belknap Press of Harvard University Press.

—— and Daems, Herman (1974), 'Introduction – the rise of managerial capitalism and its impact on investment strategy in the Western World and Japan', in Daems, H. and Wee, Herman van der (eds), *The Rise of Managerial Capitalism*, Louvain: Leuven University Press.

—— and Tedlow (1985), *The Coming of Managerial Capitalism: A Casebook on the History of American Economic Institutions*, Homewood, Illinois: Richard D. Irwin, Inc.

Charvat, Frank J. (1961), *Supermarketing*, New York: The Macmillan Company.

Cherington, Paul. T. ([1913] 2002), *Advertising as a Business Force*, New York: Doubleday, Page & Company (Reprint, Bristol, UK: Thoemmes Press.)

—— (1920), *The Elements of Marketing*, New York: Macmillan Company.

Chisholm, Cecil (1927), *Simplified Practice*, London: Chapman and Hall, Inc.

Church, Alexander Hamilton (1911), 'Has "scientific management" science?' *American Machinist*, 35, 108–12.

——([1914] 1977), *The Science and Practice of Management*, New York: Engineering Magazine. (Reprint, Easton, Pennsylvania: Hive Publishing Company.)

Church, Roy (1999), 'New perspectives on the history of products, firms, marketing, and consumers in Britain and the United States since the mid-nineteenth century', *Economic History Review*, 52 (3), pp. 405–35.

Churchill, Neil C. and Muzyka, Daniel F. (1994), 'Defining and conceptualizing entrepreneurship: a process approach', in Hills, Gerald E. (ed.), *Marketing and entrepreneurship: Research Ideas and Opportunities*, Westport, Connecticut: Greenwood Press, pp. 11–23.

Clerk, Fred E. (chairman) (1926), 'Reducing costs of marketing', *The American Economic Review*, 16 (1), *Supplement, Papers and Proceedings of the Thirty-eighth Meeting of the American Economic Association*, March, 250–65.

Coats, A.W. (1961), 'The Political Economy Club: a neglected episode in American economic thought', *The American Economic Review*, 51 (4), September, 624–37.

Cole, Arthur H. (1946), 'An approach to the study of entrepreneurship: a tribute to Edwin F. Gay', *The Journal of Economic History*, 6, Supplement, May, pp. 1–15.

Cole, Michael and Engeström, Yrjö (1993), 'A cultural-historical approach', in Salmon, Gavriel (ed.), Distributed Cognition: Physiological and Educational Considerations, Cambridge: Cambridge University Press, pp. 1–46.

Colgate, Samuel (1969), 'American soap factories', in Depew, Chauncey M. (ed.), *One Hundred Years of American Commerce*, New York: Greenwood Press, Publisher, 422–32.

Collins, James H. (1910), 'Price maintenance – the biggest issue of the mercantile world', *Printers' Ink*, 6 April, 3–6.

Converse, Paul D. (1927), *Selling Policy*, New York: Prentice-Hall Inc.

—— (1930), *The Elements of Marketing*, New York: Prentice-Hall, Inc.

—— (1959a), *The Beginning of Marketing Thought in the United States: With Reminiscences of the Pioneer Marketing Scholars*, Austin: Bureau of Business Research, The University of Texas. (Reprint, New York: Arno Press, 1978.)

—— (1959b), *Fifty Years of Marketing in Retrospect*, Austin: Bureau of Business Research, the University of Texas. (Reprint, New York: Arno Press, 1978.)

Coolsen, Frank Gordon (1947), 'Pioneers in the development of advertising', *Journal of Marketing*, 12 (1), July, 80–86.

—— (1958), 'Marketing ideas of selected empirical liberal economics 1870 to 1900', unpublished PhD thesis, University of Illinois.

—— (1960), *Marketing Thought in the United States in the Late Nineteenth Century*, Texas: Texas Technical Press.

—— (1962), 'Marketing and economic development', in Decker, William S. (ed.), *Proceedings of the Winter Conference of the American Marketing Association, December 27, 28, 29, 1962, Pittsburgh: Emerging Concepts in Marketing*, Chicago: American Marketing Association, pp. 26–37.

Copeland, Melvin T. et al. (1921), 'Standardization of products', Bulletin of the Taylor Society, 6 (2), April, 55–76.

—— (1923), 'Relation of consumers' buying habits to marketing', *Harvard Business Review*, 1 (3), April, 282–9.

—— ([1924] 1978), *Principles of Merchandising*, Chicago and New York: A.W. Shaw Company. (Reprint of the 5th Printing 1927, New York: Arno Press.)

—— (1927), 'The merchandising function in industrial marketing: shifting market conditions demand corresponding changes in products and policies', *Advertising and Selling*, 16 November, 21, 46, 48, 50–53, 54 and 56.

—— (1929), 'Marketing', in Hoover ([1929a] 1966a), pp. 321–424.

—— (1931), 'Some present-day problems in distribution', *Harvard Business Review*, 9 (3), April, 299–310.

—— (1958a), 'Arch W. Shaw', *Journal of Marketing*, 22 (3), January, 313–15. (Also, in Wright and Dimsdale (1974), pp. 129–31.)

—— (1958b), *And Mark an Era: The Story of the Harvard Business School*, Boston and Toronto: Little, Brown and Company.

—— and Learned, Edmund P. (1933), *Merchandising of Cotton Textiles: Methods and Organization*, Business Research Studies – No. 1, Boston, Massachusetts: Harvard University.

Copley, Frank B. ([1923] 1969), *Frederick W. Taylor: Father of Scientific Management, Volume II*, New York: Harper & Brothers Publishers. (Reprint, New York: Augustus M. Kelley Publishers.)

Corley, T.A.B. (1987), 'Consumer marketing in Britain', *Business History*, 29 (4), October, pp. 65–83.

—— (1993), 'Marketing and business history', in Tedlow, Richard S. and Jones, Geoffrey (eds), *The Rise and Fall of Mass Marketing*, London and New York: Routledge, pp. 93–115.

Cornell, William B. (1928), *Industrial Organization and Management*, New York: The Ronald Press Company.

Cowan, Stuart D. (1927), 'Scientific marketing management: a review of Percival White's new book', *Bulletin of the Taylor Society*, 7(4), August, 457–64.

Cox, Reavis and Alderson, Wroe (eds) (1950), *Theory in Marketing: Selected Essays*, Chicago, Illinois: Richard D. Irwin, Inc.

Craig, David R. and Gabler, Werner K. (1940), 'The competitive struggle for market control', *The Annals of the American Academy of Political and Social Science, 209, Marketing in our American Economy*, May, 84–107.

Crowther, Samuel (1923), *John H. Patterson: The Romance of Business*, London: Butler & Tanner Ltd.

Dahl, Robert A. (1957), 'The concept of power', *Behavioral Science*, 2, 201–15.

Dameron, Kenneth (1939), 'The consumer movement', *Harvard Business Review*, 17 (3), Spring, 271–89.

Davisson, Charles N. (1954), 'Automobile', in Clewett, Richard M. (ed.), *Marketing Channels for Manufactured Products*, Homewood, Illinois: Richard D. Irwin, Inc., pp. 83–112.

Day, Clive (1907), *A History of Commerce*, N.Y.: Longman, Green, and Co.

Decker, William S. (ed.) (1962), *Proceedings of the Winter Conference of the American Marketing Association, December 27, 28, 29, 1962, Pittsburgh: Emerging Concepts in Marketing*, Chicago: American Marketing Association.

Dennison, Henry S. (1920), 'A statement of the problem', *Bulletin of the Taylor Society*, 5 (5), October, 200–202.

—— (1926), 'Balancing manufacturing and distribution: how merchandising managers coordinate factory and sales department', *Bulletin of the Taylor Society*, 11 (2), April, 81–2.

—— (1927a), 'Scientific management in manufacturer's marketing: in which a sharp distinction is drawn between merchandising and selling', *Bulletin of the Taylor Society*, 12 (6), December, 526–35.

—— (1927b), 'Merchandising – the coordinator of selling and production', *Printers' Ink*, 15 December, 109–10.

—— (1929), 'Management', in Hoover [1929] 1966, pp. 495–546.

[US] Department of Commerce (1913), *Thirteenth Census of the United States Taken in the Year 1910, Volume X, Manufactures 1909*, Washington: Government Printing Office.

—— (1923), *Fourteenth Census of the United States Taken in the Year 1920, Volume X, Manufactures 1919*, Washington: Government Printing Office.

—— (1927), *Fifteenth Annual Report of the Secretary of Commerce, 1927*, Washington: Government Printing Office.

—— (1928), *Sixteenth Annual Report of the Secretary of Commerce, 1928*, Washington: Government Printing Office.

—— (1935), *Census of American Business: 1933, Wholesale Distribution, Volume I Summary for the United States*, Washington: Government Printing Office.

—— (1937), *Census of Business: 1935, Wholesale Distribution, Volume I United States Summary*, Washington: Government Printing Office.

—— (1942a), *Sixteenth Census of the United States: 1940, Census of Business: 1939, Volume II, Wholesale Trade*, Washington: Government Printing Office.

—— (1942b), *Sixteenth Census of the United States: 1940, Census of Business, Volume V, Distribution of Manufacturer's Sales 1939*, Washington: Government Printing Office.

—— (1943), *Sixteenth Census of the United States: 1940, Census of Business: 1939, Volume I, Retail Trade: 1939, Part 1*, Washington: Government Printing Office.

—— (1975), *Historical Statistics of the United States: Colonial Times to 1970, Parts I and II*, Washington: US Government Printing Office.

[US] Department of Commerce and Labor, Bureau of the Census (1907), *Manufactures 1905, Part I, United States by Industries*, Washington: Government Printing Office.

Devinat, Paul (1927), *Scientific Management in Europe*, International Labour Office, Studies and Reports Series B (Economic Conditions), No. 17, Geneva, London: P.S. King & Sons, Ltd.

Dholakia, Nikhilesh, Firat, A. Fuat and Bagozzi, Richard P. (1980), 'The de-Americanization of marketing thought: in search of a universal basis', in Lamb, Charles W. and Dunne, Patrick M. (eds), *Theoretical Development in Marketing*, Chicago: American Marketing Association, pp. 25–9.

Dixon, Donald F. (1979), 'The origin of macro-marketing thought', in G. Fisk and R.W. Nason (eds), *Macro-Marketing: New Steps on the Learning Curve, Proceedings of the Third Macro-Marketing Seminar*, Boulder, Colorado: University of Colorado, pp. 9–28.

—— (1982), 'The historical origin of the channel concept', in Taylor, Ronald D. et al. (eds), *Progress in Marketing Theory and Practice, Proceedings of the Southern Marketing Association*, pp. 146–51.

—— (2002), 'Emerging macromarketing concepts: from Socrates to Alfred Marshall', *Journal of Business Research*, 55, 737–45.

Dobbs, R.D. (1911a), 'How N.C.R. gets 100 per cent efficiency out of its men', *Printers' Ink*, 29 June, 3–6; 6 July, 3–6; 13 July, 17–20; 27 July, 34, 36–8 and 40.

Donald, W.J. (ed.) (1931), *Handbook of Business Administration*, New York and London: McGraw-Hill Book Company, Inc.

Doody, Alton F. (1965), 'Historical emphasis: its contribution to marketing education', in Smith, L. George (ed.), *Proceedings, December 28–29, 1964, Sheraton-Chicago Hotel, Chicago Illinois, Reflections on Progress in Marketing*, Chicago: American Marketing Association, pp. 555–65.

Drucker, Peter F. (1969), 'The shame of marketing', *Printers' Ink Marketing/Communications*, August, 60–62 and 64.

—— (1973), *Management: Tasks, Responsibilities, Practice*, New York: Harper and Row Publishers, Inc.

—— ([1985] 1993), *Innovation and Entrepreneurship*, New York: Harper & Row, Publishers. (Reprint, New York: HarperBusiness.)

Drury, Horace B. (1915), *Scientific Management: A History and Criticism (Studies of History, Economics and Public Law, Vol. 65, No. 2)*, New York: Columbia University.

Duddy, E.A. and Revsan, D.A. (1953), *Marketing: An Institutional Approach*, 2nd ed., New York: McGraw-Hill Book Company, Inc.

Duncan, C.S. (1919), *Commercial Research*, New York: Macmillan Company.

—— (1922), *Marketing: Its Problems and Methods*, New York and London: D. Appleton and Company.

Duncan, Delbert J. (1954), 'Selecting a channel of distribution', in Clewett, Richard M. (ed.), *Marketing Channels for Manufactured Products*, Homewood, Illinois: Richard D. Irwin, Inc., pp. 367–403.

Editors of Advertising Age (1988), *Proctor & Gamble: The House that IVORY Built*, Lincolnwood, Illinois: NTC Business Books.

Edwards, Corwin D. (1937), 'The struggle for the control of distribution', *Journal of Marketing*, 1 (3), January, 212–17.

El-Ansary, Adel I. (1975), 'Determinants of power-dependence in the distribution channel', *Journal of Retailing*, 51, Summer, 59–74 and 94.

—— and Stern, Louis W. (1972), 'Power measurement in the distribution channel', *Journal of Marketing Research*, 9, February, 47–52.

Elder, F. Robert (1932), 'Product design for the market', *Mechanical Engineering*, 54 (8), August, 543–6 and 565.

—— (1940), 'Merchandising', in Alexander, Ralph S., Surface, Frank M., Elder, Robert F. and Alderson, Wroe, *Marketing*, Boston: Ginn and Company, pp. 115–32.

Ely, Rchard T. (1886), 'Report of the organization of the American Economic Association', *Publications of the American Economic Association*, 1 (1), March, 5–32.

Emerson, Harrington (1908), 'Efficiency as a basis for operation and wages', *Engineering Magazine*, 35 (6), 909–20.

Emerson, Richard M. (1962), 'Power-dependence relations', *American Sociological Review*, 27 (1), February, 31–41.

Engeström, Yrjö (1987), *Learning by Expanding: An Activity-Theoretical Approach to Development Research*, Helsinki: Orienta-Konsultit.

—— (1999), 'Activity theory and individual and social transformation', in Engeström, Yrjö et al. (eds), *Perspectives on Activity Theory*, Cambridge: Cambridge University Press, pp. 19–38.

Engle, Nathanael H. (1954), 'Development of marketing channels in the United States since 1920', in Clewett, Richard M. (ed.), *Marketing Channels for Manufactured Products*, Homewood, Illinois: Richard D. Irwin, Inc., pp. 65–78.

Enright, Michael (2002), 'Marketing and conflicting dates from its emergence: Hotchkiss, Bartels, the "Fifties School" and alternative accounts', *Journal of Management*, 18, 445–61.

Fayol, Henri (1917), *Administration Industrielle et Generale*, Paris: H. Dunod et E. Pinat, Editeurs.

—— (1949), *General and Industrial Management*, trans. by Storrs, Constance and Urwick, L., London: Sir Isaac Pitman and Sons.

Fehling, August Wilhelm (1926), 'Collegiate education for business in Germany', *The Journal of Political Economy*, 34 (5), October, 545–96.

Feldman, Laurence P. (1971), 'Societal adaptation: a new challenge for marketing', *Journal of Marketing*, 35 (3), July, 54–60.

Felton, Arthur P. (1959), 'Making the marketing concept work', *Harvard Business Review,* 37 (4), July–August, 55–65.

Fieux, S. (1913), 'Are chain stores a menace to advertisers?', *Printer's Ink*, 17 April, 12–13.

Fisk, James S. (1916), *Retail Selling*, New York and London: Harper & Brothers Publishing.

[Fisk, George] (1982), 'Editor's working definition of macromarketing', *Journal of Macromarketing*, 2 (1), Spring, 3–4.

[Forbes] (1930), 'Modern designs sell', *Forbes*, 15 August, 20–21.

—— (1934), 'Best-dressed products sell best', Forbes, 1 April, 13.

[Fortune] (1930a), 'Color in industry', *Fortune*, 1 (1), February, 85–94.

—— (1930b), 'Bel Geddes', *Fortune*, 2 (1), July, 51–57.

—— (1931), 'The package as merchandiser', *Fortune*, 3 (5), May, 76–81.

—— (1933a), 'Blue chip', *Fortune*, 6 (3), September, 45–49, 102 and 104–107.

—— (1933b), 'The baby radio', *Fortune*, 8 (1), July, 64–5.

—— (1934), 'Both fish and fowl', *Fortune*, 9 (2), February, 40–43, 88, 90, 94 and 97–8.

—— (1935), '1,250,000 out of 4,200,000 US radio', *Fortune*, 11 (2), February, 74–9, 164, 166, 168, 170 and 173.

—— (1938), 'Radio III: a $537,000,000 set business', *Fortune*, 17 (5), May, 118 and 120.

—— (1939), 'Chevrolet', January, 39–40, 46 and 103–104.

—— (1944), 'Radio, refridgerators, and radar', *Fortune*, 30 (4), November, 115–21, 232, 234, 236, 238, 241 and 243.

—— (1945), 'Commander McDonald of Zenith', *Fortune*, 31 (6), June, 140–43, 209–10, 212, 214 and 216.

Forty, Adrian (1986), *Objects of Desire: Design and Society 1750–1980*, London: Thames and Hudson Ltd.

Frederick, J. George (1912), 'Applying the scientific management to selling', *Industrial Engineering and the Engineering Digest*, 12 (5), November, 204–5.

—— ([1919] 1978), *Modern Salesmanagement: A Practical Handbook and Guide*, New York and London: D. Appleton and Company. Reprint, New York: Arno Press.

—— (1928), 'Is progressive obsolescence the path toward increased consumption?' *Advertising & Selling*, 5 September, 19–20, 44 and 46.

—— (ed.) (1930), *A Philosphy of Production: A Symposium*, New York: The Business Bourse.

Freeland, Willard E. (1920), 'Coordination of Sales with Scientific Management', *Bulletin of the Taylor Society*, 5 (5), October, 202–7.

—— (1926), 'Progress towards science of marketing: application of scientific method in sales research, organization, budget in operations, physical distribution and advertising', *Bulletin of the Taylor Society*, 6 (4), October, 207–13.

—— (1934), 'The importance of the product in the recovery period', *Mechanical Engineering*, 56 (5), May, 277–8.

French, Jr., J.R.P. and Raven, Bertram ([1959] 1966), 'The basis of social power', in Cartwright, D. (ed.), *Studies in Social Power*, Ann Arbor, Michigan: The University of Michigan, Reprint version, pp. 150–67.

FTC: Federal Trade Commission ([1933a] 1985a), *Chain Stores: Chain-Store Manufacturing*, March 13, 1932, 73d Congress 1st Session, Document No. 13, Washington, D.C.: Government Printing Office. Reprint, Buffalo and New York: William S. Hein & Co. Inc.

—— ([1933b] 1985b), *Chain Stores: Chain-Store Private Brands*, September 26, 1932, 72d Congress 2d Session, Document No. 142, Washington, DC: Government Printing Office. Reprint, Buffalo and New York: William S. Hein & Co. Inc.

—— ([1939] 1983), *Report on Motor Vehicle Industry*, Washington D.C.: U.S. Government Printing Office. Reprint, Tokyo: Gozan-do.

—— (1945), *Report of the Federal Trade Commission on Resale Price Maintenance: Submitted to the Congress, December 13*, Washington, D.C.: U.S. Government Printing Office.

Fukuda, Keitaro (1929), 'Development of studies on *Haikyu* in America', *Journal of Economics and Business Administration* [*Kokumin Keizai Zasshi*], November, 85–112 (in Japanese).

Fullerton, Ronald (1987a), 'A poverty of ahistorical analysis: present weakness and future cure of American marketing thought', in A. Fuat Firat, N. Dholakia and R.P. Bagozzi (eds), *Philosophical and Radical Thought in Marketing*, Lexington, MA: Lexington Book, pp. 97–119.

—— (1987b), 'Historicism: what it is, and what it means for consumer research', in Wallendorf, M. and Anderson, P. (eds), *Advances in Consumer Research, Volume XIV*, Provo Utah: Association for Consumer Research, pp. 431–34.

—— (1988a), 'Modern Western Marketing as a historical phenomenon: theory and illustration', in Nevett, Terence and Fullerton, R. A. (eds), *Historical Perspectives in Marketing: Essays in Honor of Stanley C. Hollande*r, Lexington, MA: Lexington Books, pp. 71–89.

—— (1988b), 'How modern is modern marketing? marketing's evolution and the myth of the "production era"', *Journal of Marketing*, 52 (1), January, 108–25.

Furo, Tsutomu (1966), 'Product planning and marketing management: focusing on the debates of the features of managerial marketing', *Journal of Kobe University of Commerce* [*Shohdai Ronshu*] 51, October, 111–26 (in Japanese).

—— (1968), *Behavioural Theory of Marketing Channels*, Tokyo: Chikura-shobo (in Japanese).

Gardner, David M. (1994), 'Marketing/entrepreneurship interface: a conceptualization', in Hills, G.F. (ed.) *Marketing and Entrepreneurship: Research Ideas and Opportunities*, Westport, Connecticut and London: Quorum Books, pp. 35–54.

Gardner, Edward H. (1945), 'Consumer goods classification', *Journal of Marketing*, 9 (3), January, 275–6.

Gaski, John F. (1984), 'The theory of power and conflict in channels of distribution', *Journal of Marketing*, 48 (3), Summer, 9–29.

Geddes, Norman Bel ([1932] 1977), *Horizons*, Boston: Little, Brown & Co. (Reprint, New York: Dover Publications, Inc.)

General Electric (1952), *The Sixty First Annual Report*.

Gibbs, E.D. (1911a), 'How N.C.R. gets 100 per cent efficiency out of its men', *Printers' Ink*, 29 June, 3–6; 6 July, 3–6; 13 July, 17–20; 27 July, 34, 36–8 and 40.

—— (1911b), 'How N.C.R. gets 100 per cent efficiency out of its men', *Printers' Ink*, 24 August, 9–11.

Goldman, Arieth (1978), 'Institutional changes in retailing: an updated "wheel of retailing" theory', in Woodside, A.G. et al. (eds), *Foundations of Marketing Channels*, Austin, Texas: Lone Star Publishing, Inc., pp. 189–211.

Gon, Yasukichi (1970), *Development of Business Organisation Thought: A Critical Review on American Idea of Business Organisation*, Kyoto: Minerva-shobo (in Japanese).

Gregory, Paul M. (1947), 'A theory of purposeful obsolescence', *The Southern Economic Journal*, 14 (1), July, 24–45.

Greif, M (1975), *Depression Modern: The Thirty Style in America*, New York: Universe Press.

Greyer, Stephen A. (ed.) (1963), *Proceedings of the Winter Conference of the American Marketing Association, December 27–28, 1963, Boston, Mass., Toward Scientific Marketing*, Chicago: American Marketing Association.

Haber, Samuel (1964), *Efficiency and Uplift: Scientific Management in the Progressive Ear 1890–1920*, Illinois: The University of Chicago Press.

Hall, S. Ronald (1924), *The Handbook of Sales Management*, New York: McGraw-Hill Book Company, Inc.

Halsey, F.A. (1891), 'The premium plan of paying for labor', *Transactions of the American Society of Mechanical Engineers*, 12, 755–80.

Harada, Hideo et al. (2002), *Basics of Distribution and Commerce: Learning Theory and the Structure by Observing Facts*, Tokyo: Yuhikaku (in Japanese).

Haring, Albert (1940), 'Wholesaling and wholesalers', *The Annals of the American Academy of Political and Social Science, 209, Marketing in our American Economy*, May, 39–45.

Hashimoto, Isao (1966), 'Birth and development of marketing', in Morishita F. and Arakawa Y. (eds), *Systematic Thought of Marketing Management*, Tokyo: Chikura-shobo, pp. 3–34 (in Japanese).

—— (1975), *Establishment of Marketing Thought*, Kyoto: Minerva-shobo (in Japanese).

Hay, Richard C. (1929), *Sales Management Fundamentals*, New York and London: Harper & Brothers Publishers.

Hayes, E.P. and Heath, Charlotte (1929), *History of the Dennison Manufacturing Company*, Cambridge, Massachusetts: Harvard University Press. (Reprint from the *Journal of Economic and Business History*, I, November 1929 and II, November 1929.)

Haynes, William (1949), *American Chemical Industry, Volume VI, The Chemical Companies*, Toronto, New York and London: D. Van Nostrand Company, Inc.

Hayward, Walter D. (1926). *Sales Administration: A Study of the Manufacturer's Marketing*, New York and London: Harper and Brothers Publishers.

Heath, Julian (1913), 'Works of the Housewives League', *The Cost of Living, The Annals of the American Academy of Political and Social Science*, 48, July, 121–6.

Hébert, Robert F. and Link, Albert N. (1988), *The Entrepreneur: Mainstream Views and Radical Critiques*, 2nd ed., New York: Praeger Publishers.

Herrick, Cheesman A. (1917), *History of Commerce and Industry*, New York: The Macmillan Company.

Heskett, John (1987), *Industrial Design*, London and New York: World of Art.

Hess, Herbert W. (1913), 'Advertising and the high cost of living', *The Cost of Living, The Annals of the American Academy of Political and Social Science*, 48, July, 238–43.

Hewitt, Charles Mason (1956), *Automobile Franchise Agreements*, Homewood, Illinois: Richard D. Irwin, Inc.

Hills, Gerald F. (1994), 'Marketing and entrepreneurship: the domain', in Hills, G.F. ed. *Marketing and Entrepreneurship: Research Ideas and Opportunities*, Westport, Connecticut and London: Quorum Books, pp. 5–10.

—— and LaForge, Raymond W. (1992), 'Research at the marketing interface to advance entrepreneurship theory', *Entrepreneurship Theory and Practice*, 16 (3), Spring, 33–59.

Hirose, Arthur (1936), 'The new phase of electric refrigeration', *Advertising & Selling*, 26 March, 28, 60, and 62–4.

Hoagland, William and Lazer, William (1960), '*The Retailer's Manual* of 1869', *Journal of Marketing*, 24 (3), January, 59–60.

Hofstadter, Richard (1955), *The Age of Reform: from Bryan to F.D.R.*, New York: Knopf.

Holden, Alfred C. and Holden, Laurie (1998), 'Marketing history: illuminating marketing's clandestine subdiscipline', *Psychology and Marketing*, 15 (2), March, 117–23.

Hollander, Stanley C. (1960), 'The wheel of retailing', *Journal of Marketing*, 24, Summer, 37–42.

—— (1962), 'Retailing: case or effect?' in Decker, William S. (ed.), *Proceedings of the Winter Conference of the American Marketing Association, December 27, 28, 29, 1962, Pittsburgh: Emerging Concepts in Marketing*, Chicago: American Marketing Association, pp. 220–30.

—— (1964), 'Nineteenth century anti-drummer legislation in the United States', *Business History Review*, 38, Winter, 479–500.

—— (1966), 'United States of America', in Yamey, B.S. (ed.), *Resale Price Maintenance*, London: Weidenfeld and Nicolson, 1966.

—— (1986), 'The marketing concept: a déjà vu', in George Fisk (ed.), *Marketing Management Technology as a Social Process*, NY: Praeger Publishers, pp. 3–29.

—— and Germain, Richard (1992), *Was There a Pepsi Generation before Pepsi Discovered it? Youth-based Segmentation in Marketing*, Lincolnwood, Illinois: NTC Business Books.

—— and Rassuli, Kathleen (1993), 'Introduction', in S.C. Hollander and K.M. Rassuli (eds), *Marketing, Volume I, The International Library of Critical Writings in Business History*, Aldershot, UK: Edward Elgar, pp. xv–xxxiii.

Hollingworth, Harry L. ([1913] 1985), *Advertising and Selling*, New York and London: D. Appleton and Company. (Reprint, New York and London: Garland Publishing, Inc.)

Hoover, Herbert (chairman) ([1929] 1966), *Recent Economic Changes in the United States*, Volume I, New York: McGraw-Hill Book Company Inc. (Reprint, New York: Johnson Reprint Corporation.)

Hopkins, George W. (1931), 'Sales promotion', in Donald 1931, pp. 214–47.

Hotchkiss, George Burton (1938), *Milestones of Marketing: A Brief History of the Evaluation of Market Distribution*, New York: The Macmillan Company.

Hotta, Kazuyoshi (ed.) (1991), *Methodology of Research in Marketing*, Tokyo: Chuo-Keizai-sha (in Japanese).

—— (2003), *Study of Advertising in the History of Marketing Thought*, Tokyo: Nikkei Advertising Research Institute (in Japanese).

—— (2006), *The History of Marketing Thought: A Genealogy of Meta-Theory*, Tokyo: Chuo Keizai-sha (in Japanese).

Howard, John R. (1957), *Marketing Management: Analysis and Decision*, Homewood, Illinois: Richard D. Irwin, Inc.

Howe, Frederic C. (1917), *The High Cost of Living*, New York: Charles Scribner's Sons.

Hoyt, Charles W. (1913), *Scientific Sales Management: A Practical Application of the Principles of Scientific Management to Selling*, New Haven, Connecticut: George B. Wilson & Company.

Hunt, Shelby D. (1976), 'The nature and scope of marketing', *Journal of Marketing*, 40(3), July, 17–28.

—— (1977), 'The three dichotomies model of marketing: an elaboration of issues', in Slater, Charles C. (ed.), *Macro-marketing: Distributive Processes from a Societal Perspective*, Boulder, Colorado: University of Colorado, pp. 52–65.

—— and Burnett, John J. (1982), 'The macromarketing/micromarketing dichotomy: a paradigm displacement perspective', *Journal of Marketing*, 46 (3), Summer, 11–26.

—— and Goolsby, Jerry (1988), 'The rise and fall of the functional approach to marketing: a paradigm displacement perspective', in Nevett, Terence and Fullerton, Ronald A. (eds) (1988), *Historical Perspectives in Marketing: Essays in Honor of Stanley C. Hollander*, Lexington, MA: Lexington Book, pp. 35–51.

Hurd, Charles W. and Zimmerman, M. (1914a), 'Why advertisers must give chain-store growth their serious attention', *Printers' Ink*, 14 September, 3–4, 6, 8, 10 and 12.

—— (1914b), 'Why advertisers and dealers see danger in chain stores', *Printer's Ink*, 17 September, 63–4, 67–8 and 71–73.

—— (1914c), 'Why advertisers and dealers see danger in chain stores – III', *Printer's Ink*, 24 September, 22 and 25–7.

—— (1914d), 'How the chains are taking over the retail field – IV', *Printers' Ink*, 8 October, 36–8 and 41–2.

—— (1914e), 'Taking the chains by fields and their number in each – V', *Printers' Ink*, 15 October, 71–2, 75–6, 78–80 and 83–5.

—— (1914f), 'Concentration of ownership and direction in other fields – VI', *Printers' Ink*, 22 October, 60–64 and 66–8.

—— (1914g), 'Chain store advantages in organization and financing – VII', *Printers' Ink*, 29 October, 72–4 and 77–81.

Hyde, C.K., '"Streamlined America": an exhibit at the Henry Ford Museum, Dearborn, Michigan', *Technology and Culture*, 29 (2), 125–9.

Ichiba, Yasuo (1977), 'Freon, a product by organizational research', *Innovation*, 74 (8), August, 38–41 (in Japanese).

[IEED (Industrial Engineering and the Engineering Digest)] (1914), 'The scientific handling of salesmen', *Industrial Engineering and the Engineering Digest*, 14(10), October, 385–91.

Inamura, Tsuyoshi (1985), *Fundamental Issues on the History of Management Thought*, Kyoto: Minerva-shobo (in Japanese).

[(The) Iron Age] (1933), 'Artist joins engineer in the design of the industrial product', *The Iron Age*, 28 December, 25.

Ishihara, Takemasa (1969), 'A critical study on channel selection theory', in Study Group of Modern Marketing (ed.), *Marketing Behaviour and its Environments*, Tokyo: Chikura-shobo, pp. 119–43 (in Japanese).

Iwao, Yasuzumi (1972), *Study of Management Techniques*, rev. ed. Tokyo: Chuo University Press (in Japanese).

—— (1974), *Business Economics*, Tokyo: Maruzen (in Japanese).

James, Edmund J. (1901), 'Relation of the college and university to higher commercial education', *Publication of the American Economic Association*, 3rd Series, 2 (1), pp. 144–65.

James, Gorton (1931), 'Choice of marketing channels', in Donald (1931), pp. 102–26.

Japan Society for the Study of Marketing History (ed.) (1993), *History of Marketing Thought: USA*, Tokyo: Dobunkan (in Japanese).

—— (ed.) (1995), *Marketing in Japan: Introduction and Development*, Tokyo: Dobunkan (in Japanese).

—— (ed.) (1998), *History of Marketing Thought: Japan*, Tokyo: Dobunkan (in Japanese).

Jelinek, Mariann (1980), 'Toward systematic management: Alexander Hamilton Church', *Business History Review*, 54 (1), Spring, 63–79.

Jones, D.G. Brian (1987), 'Edward Davis Jones: a pioneer in marketing', in Nevett, Terence and Hollander, Stanley C. (eds), *Marketing in Three Eras, Proceedings of the Third Conference on Historical Research in Marketing*, East Lansing, Michigan: Michigan State University, pp.126–34.

—— (1995), 'George Burton Hotchkiss: a voice that carried well', in Rassuli, Kathleen N. et al. (eds), *Marketing History: Marketing's Great Empirical Experiment*, East Lansing, Michigan: Michigan State University, pp. 83–94.

—— (1998), 'Milestones of Marketing: a milestone in marketing', *Journal of Macromarketing*, 18 (2), Fall, pp. 179–82.

—— and Monieson, David D. (1990a), 'Early development of the philosophy of marketing thought', *Journal of Marketing*, 54 (1), January, 102–13.

—— and —— (1990b), 'Historical research in marketing: retrospect and prospect', *Journal of the Academy of Marketing Science*, 18 (4), Fall, 269–78.

—— and Shaw, Eric H. (2002), 'A history of marketing thought', in Weitz, Barton A. and Wensley, Robin (eds), *Handbook of Marketing*, London: SAGE Publishing, pp. 39–65.

—— and —— (2006), 'Historical research in the *Journal of Macromarketing*, 1981–1925', *Journal of Macromarketing*, 26 (2), December, pp. 178–92.

Jones, Edward D. (1905), 'The manufacturer and the domestic market', *The Annals of the American Academy of Political and Social Science*, 25, January, 1–20.

Jones, Hohn G. ([1917] 1922), *Salesmanship and Sales Management*, Modern Business Texts Vol. 6, New York: Alexander Hamilton Institute.

Kajihara, Masakatsu (1980), 'Marketing thought in Germany', in Nakamura, Tsunejiro et al. (eds), *Management Thought in Current Germany*, Tokyo: Dobunkan, pp. 197–218 (in Japanese).

Kamawada, Tsutomu (ed.) (1984), *The History of Design*, Tokyo: Jikkyo Shuppan. (Collaborated with the Ministry of Education, in Japanese.)

Kaplan, Roger (1987), 'Entrepreneurship reconsidered: the antimanagement bias', *Harvard Business Review*, 87 (3), May–June, pp. 84–9.

Kato, Hisa'aki and Kurata, Yasuhiko (1978), 'The history of refrigerators and changes in design, part 1', *Invention* [*Hatsumei*], 75 (7), July, 61–7 (in Japanese).

Kawazoe, Noboru (1969), 'The domain of design', in Kawazoe, N. (ed.), *The Domain of Design, A Series of Current Design, Vol. 4*, Tokyo: Fuhdo-sha, pp. 9–50 (in Japanese).

—— (1979), *Theory on Design*, Tokyo: Tokai University Publisher (in Japanese).

Keeble, S.P. (1992), *The Ability to Manage: A Study of British Management, 1890–1990*, Manchester: Manchester University Press.

Keir, J.S. and Dennison, H.S. (1929), 'Merchandising standard', in Taylor Society 1929, pp. 163–74.

Keith, Robert J. (1960), 'The marketing revolution', *Journal of Marketing*, 24 (1), January, 35–8.

Kelley, Eugene J. and Lazer, William (1967), *Managerial Marketing: Perspectives and Viewpoints, A Source Book*, 3rd ed., Homewood, Illinois: Richard D. Irwin Inc.

Kellogg, W.K. (1911), 'Manufacturer's right to fix the price', *Printers' Ink*, 7 December, 3–4.

Kelly, Leon (1936), 'Outmoded durability', *Printers' Ink*, 9 January, 59.

Keppel, Frederick P. (1933), 'The art in social life', in *Recent Trends in the United States: Report of the Presidents Research Committee on Social Trends*, New York and London: McGraw-Hill Book Company, Inc, pp. 958–1008.

Kimball, Abbott (1931), 'A design engineer – every business needs one today', *Printers' Ink*, 16 April, 105.

King, Robert L. (1965), 'The marketing concept', in Schwaltz, George (ed.), *Science in Marketing*, New York: Wiley & Sons, Inc., pp. 70–97.

Kirzner, Israel M. (1979), *Perception, Opportunity, and Profit: Studies in the Theory of Entrepreneurship*, Chicago and London: The University of Chicago Press.

Knight, Frank H. ([1921] 1957), *Risk, Uncertainty and Profit*. Boston and New York: Houghton Mifflin Company. Reprint, London: The London School of Economics and Political Science.

Knoeppel, C.E. (1937), *Managing for Profit: Working for Profit Planning and Control*, With the collaboration of Seybold, Edgar G., New York and London: McGraw-Hill Company, Inc.

Kobayashi, Kiraku (1931), *Labour Relationships in Business*, Tokyo: Toyo Shuppan-sha (in Japanese).

Kohara, Hiroshi (1987), *A Historical Essay on the Birth of Marketing in the USA*, Tokyo: Zeimu Keiri Kyokai (in Japanese).

Kometani, Masayuki (1974), 'A review on development of channel theory in the United States', *Yamaguchi Journal of Economics, Business Administration and Laws* [*Yamaguchi-Keizaigaku Zasshi*], 22 (3–4), January, 74–101 (in Japanese).

—— (1978), 'The relationship between marketing and R&D', in Mori, Toshiaru et al. (eds), *Theory and the Framework on R&D*, Tokyo: Maruzen Kabushiki Kaisha, pp. 114–27 (in Japanese).

Kondo, Fumio (1988), *A Study on Marketing in its Early Stage*, Tokyo: Chuo Keizai-sha (in Japanese).

Koontz, Harold and O'Donnell, Cyril (1959), *Principles of Management: An Analysis of Managerial Function*, 2nd Edition, New York: McGraw-Hill Book Company, Inc.

—— (1974), *Essentials of Management*, New York: McGraw-Hill Book Company, Inc.

—— (1976), *Management: A System and Contingency Analysis of Managerial Functions*, 6th ed., New York: McGraw-Hill, Inc.

Kotler, Philip (1972), 'Generic concept of marketing', *Journal of Marketing*, 36 (2), April, 46–54.

—— (1983), *Principles of Marketing*, Englewood Cliffs, New Jersey: Prentice Hall, 2nd ed.

——— (1997), *Marketing Management: Analysis, Planning, Implementation, and Control*, Englewood Cliffs, New Jersey: Prentice Hall, 9th ed.

——— (2000), *Marketing Management, The Millennium Edition*, Englewood Cliffs, New Jersey: Prentice Hall, 10th ed.

——— (2003), *Marketing Management*, Englewood Cliffs, New Jersey: Prentice Hall, 11th ed.

——— (2005), *FAQs on Marketing: Answered by the Guru on Marketing*, Singapore: Marshall Cavendish Business.

——— and Levy, J.S. (1969), 'Broadening the concept of marketing', *Journal of Marketing*, 33 (1), January, 10–15.

——— and Keller, K.L. (2006), *Marketing Management*, 12th ed., Upper Saddle River, New Jersey: Pearson Education, Inc.

Krogh, Gerg von, Nonaka, Ikujiro and Nishiguchi, Toshihiro (eds) (2000), *Knowledge Creation: A Source of Value*, MacMillan Press Ltd.

Kumcu, Erdgan (1987), 'Historical method: toward a relevant analysis of marketing systems', in Firat, A. Fuat, Dholakia, Nikhilesh and Bagozzi, Richard P. (eds), *Philosophical and Radical Thought in Marketing*, Lexington, Massachusetts and Toronto: Lexington Books, pp. 117–33.

LaLonde, B.J. and Morrison, E.J. (1967), 'Marketing management concepts yesterday and today', *Journal of Marketing*, 31 (1), January, pp. 9–13.

Lambert, S.C. (1916), 'How Proctor & Gamble base sales policies on actual market conditions', *Printers' Ink*, 27 April, 3–4, 6, 8 and 10.

Larrabee, C.B. (1936), 'Convenience packages', *Printers' Ink*, 9 January, 45 and 48.

Lave, Jean and Wenger, Etienne (1991), *Situated Participation: Legitimate Peripheral Participation*, Cambridge: Cambridge University Press.

Lazer, William (1979), 'Some observations on the development of marketing thought', in Ferrell, O.C., Brown, Stephan and Lamb, C.W., Jr. (eds), *Conceptual and Theoretical Development in Marketing, Proceedings of a Conference Held in Phoenix, Arizona, February 7–9, 1979*, Chicago: American Marketing Association, pp. 652–64.

——— and Kelley, Eugene J. (1962), 'The systems approach to marketing', in Lazer, W. and Kelley, E.J. (eds), *Managerial Marketing: Perspectives and Viewpoints*, Revised Edition, Homewood, Illinois: Richard D. Irwin, Inc., pp. 191–8.

Leavitt, Robert K. (1933), 'Gallery ... Ralph Starr Butler: No.1 advertising manager', *Advertising & Selling*, 6 June, pp. 22–2 and 47–8.

Lebhar, Godfrey M. (1930), 'Chain store developments and what they mean to the manufacturer', *Consumer Marketing Series*, 1, New York: American Management Association, 3–12.

——— (1933), 'The manufacturers' selection of channels of distribution', *Consumer Marketing Series*, 12, New York: American Management Association, 19–28.

——— (1959), *Chain Stores in America: 1859–1959*, New York: Chain Store Publishing Corporation.

Levin, Marilyn and Archdeacon, Thomas J. (1989), 'The role of historical method for marketing research', in Hirschman, Elizabeth C. (ed.), *Interpretive Consumer Research*, Provo, UT: Association for Consumer Research, pp. 60–68.

Lewis, E. St. Elmo (1916a), 'The six principles of scientific salesmanship, I. investigation – the problem of distribution', *The Engineering Magazine*, 51 (6) (September), 837–42.

—— (1916b), 'The six principles of scientific salesmanship, part II – investigation – studying the market', *Industrial Management: The Engineering Magazine*, 57 (1), October, 10–15.

—— (1916c), 'The six principles of scientific salesmanship, part III – organization', *Industrial Management*, 52 (2), November, 225–30.

—— (1916d), 'Applying the scientific method to sales management: organization – functional – analysis', *Industrial Management*, 52 (3), December, 289–98.

—— (1917a), 'Applying the scientific method to sales management, V – records – operation, statistical and other data', *Industrial Management*, 52 (5), February, 684–96.

—— (1917b), 'Applying the scientific method to sales management, VI – standards – purpose, performance, and policies', *Industrial Management*, 52 (6), March, 869–78.

—— (1917c), 'Applying the scientific method to sales management, VI – (continued) standards – purpose, performance, and policies', *Industrial Management*, 53 (1), April, 65–74.

Lichtenthal, J. David and Beik, Leland L. (1984), 'A history of the definition of marketing', in Sheth, Jagdish N. (ed.), *Research in Marketing: Research Annual*, Greenwood, Connecticut and London: JAI Press Inc., pp. 133–63.

Lief, Alfred (1958), *"It's Float": The Story of Proctor & Gamble*, New York and Toronto: Rinehart & Co., Inc.

Litterer, Joseph A. (1959), 'The emergence of systematic management as shown by the literature of management from 1870 to 1900', unpublished Ph.D. thesis, University of Illinois.

—— (1961a), 'Alexander Hamilton Church and the development of modern management', *Business History Review*, 35 (2), Summer, 211–25.

—— (1961b), 'Systematic management: the search for order and integration', *Business History Review*, 35 (4), Winter, 461–76.

—— (1963), Systematic management: design for organization recoupling in American manufacturing firms', *Business History Review*, 37 (4), Winter, 369–91.

Little, Robert W. (1970), 'The marketing channel: who should lead this extra-corporate organization?' *Journal of Marketing*, 34 (1), January, 31–8.

Locke, Robert R. (1985), 'Business education in Germany: past systems and current practice', *Business History Review*, 59, Summer, 232–53.

Lockley, Lawrence C. (1950), 'Notes on the history of marketing research', *Journal of Marketing*, 14 (5), April, 733–6.

Long, Wayne (1983), 'The meaning of entrepreneurship', *American Journal of Small Business*, 8 (2), Fall, 47–56 and 59.

Lorentz, Christopher (1986), *The Design Dimension: The New Competitive Weapon for Business*, London: Basil Blackwell Limited.

Lynd, R.S. (1933), 'The people as consumer', in *Recent Social Trends in the United States: Report of the President's Research Committee on Social Trends, Volume II*, New York: McGraw-Hill Book Company Inc., pp. 857–911.

Lyon, Leverett S. ([1926] 1978), *Salesmen in Marketing Strategy*, New York: The Macmillan Company. (Reprint, New York: Arno Press.)

Macbain, A.L. et al. (1905), *Selling: The Principles of the Science of Salesmanship; Methods and Systems of Selling in Various Lines*, Chicago and New York: The System Company.

Maclaurin, William Rupert (1949), *Invention and Innovation in the Radio Industry*, New York: Macmillan Company.

Macpherson, David (1805), *Annals of Commerce, Manufacturers, Fisheries, and Navigation, with Brief Notices of the Arts and Sciences Connected with Them*, London: Nichlos and Son et al. (Microfilm).

Mallen, Bruce (1963), 'A theory of retailer-supplier conflict, control, and cooperation', *Journal of Retailing*, 39 (2), Summer, 24–32 and 51.

Marco, Luc (2006), 'L'arborescence de l'histoire du marketing', *Market Management: Marketing & Communication, Le Centenaire du Marketing*, 2, 4–19.

Marcosson, Issac F. (1948), *Whenever Men Trade: The Romance of the Cash Register*, New York: Dodd, Mead & Co.

[Marketing Bulletin] (1977), 'Editorial', *Marketing Bulletin* (A free synoptic information service from the *European Journal of Marketing*), i–vii.

Marshall, L.C. (ed.), (1928a), *The Collegiate School of Business: Its Status and the Close of the First Quarter of the Twentieth Century*, Chicago: The University of Chicago Press.

—— (1928b), 'The American collegiate school of business', in Marshall 1928a, pp. 3–44.

Matsushita, Mitsuo (1982), *United States Antitrust Law*, Tokyo: University of Tokyo Press (in Japanese).

Mayo, James M. (1993), *The American Grocery Store: The Business Evolution of an Architectural Space*, Westport, Connecticut and London: Greenwood Press.

Mazur, P.M. (1925), 'Is the cost of distribution too high?' *Harvard Business Review*, 4 (1), October, 7–16.

McCammon, Bert C. Jr. and Little, Robert T. (1965), 'Marketing channels: analytical systems and approaches', in Schwartz (ed.) (1965), 321–85.

McCarthy, E. Jerome (1960), *Basic Marketing: A Managerial Approach*, Homewood, Illinois: Richard D. Irwin, Inc.

McCrea, Roswell C. (1935), 'The collegiate school of business in our American economy', *Journal of Educational Sociology*, 8 (9), May, 520–28.

McGarry, Edmund D. (1950), 'Some functions of marketing revised', in Cox, Reavis and Alderson, Wroe (eds), *Theory in Marketing: Selected Essays*.

McKay, Edward S. (1954), 'How to plan and set up your marketing program', in *Marketing Series, 91, Blueprint for an Effective Marketing Program*, New York: American Management Association, pp. 3–15.

McKendrick, Neil (1960), 'Josiah Wedgwood: an eighteenth-century entrepreneur in salesmanship and marketing techniques', *The Economic History Review, Second Series*, 7 (3), 408–33.

——, Brewer, John and Plumb, J.H. (1982), *The Birth of a Consumer Society: The Commercialization of Eighteenth-century England*, London: Europe Publications Limited.

McKinsey, James O. (1922), *Budgetary Control*, New York: The Ronald Press Company.

McNair, Malcom P. (1931a), 'Department store rentals. II', *Harvard Business Review*, 9 (3), April, 339–47.

—— (1931b), 'Trends in large scale retailing', *Harvard Business Review*, 10 (1), October, 30–39.

Meikel, Jeffrey (1979), *Twentieth Century Limited: Industrial Design in America, 1925–1939*, Philadelphia: Temple University Press.

Mitsuzawa, Shigeo (1966), 'Fundamental features of merchandising in the 1930s', *Business Review [Keiei Kenkyu]*, 85, September, 81–95.

—— (1973) 'Development of marketing', in Morishita, Fujiya (ed.), *Economics of Marketing*, Part II, Kyoto: Minerva-shobo, pp. 41–61 (in Japanese).

—— (1975), 'Taylor-system and marketing thought: the features and problems in the marketing management thought in the 1920s', *Journal of Osaka University of Economics (Osak Keidai Ronshu)*, 108, November, 86–102 (in Japanese).

—— (1977), 'The structure of A.W. Shaw's thought', *Dohsisha Business Review [Dhoshisha Shogaku]*, 28 (5–6), 205–32 (in Japanese).

—— (1980), *Birth and Development of Marketing Management*, Kyoto: Keibun-sha (in Japanese).

—— (1984), 'The concept of marketing by R.S. Butler', *Dohsisha Business Review [Dhoshisha Shogaku]*, 36 (3), October, 74–96 (in Japanese).

—— (1987), *Development of Marketing Management*, Tokyo: Dobunkan (in Japanese).

—— (1990), *The Origin of Marketing Thought*, Tokyo: Chikura-shobo (in Japanese).

Miura, Makoto (1951), 'A consideration on Shaw's Some Problems in Market Distribution', *Journal of Business Administration [shogaku Ronshu]* 1, December, 77–100 (in Japanese).

—— (1958), 'Birth and development of marketing thought', *Journal of Business Administration [Sangyo Kenkyu]*, 25, 33–58.

—— (1971), *The Structure of Marketing Thought*, Kyoto: Minerva-shobo (in Japanese).

Mohri, Shigetaka (1965), *General Theory in Business Administration*, 2nd ed., Tokyo: Chikura-shobo (in Japanese).

Moody's Manual (1932), *Moody's Manual of Industrials*, New York: Moody's Investors Service.

—— (1936), *Moody's Manual of Industrials*, New York: Moody's Investors Service.

Moore, Truman E. (1972), *The Traveling Man: The Story of the American Traveling Salesman*, New York: Doubleday & Company, Inc.

Mori, Takashi (1976), *Essays on the History of American Capitalism*, Kyoto: Minerva-shobo (in Japanese).

Morishita, Fujiya (1959a), 'The modern nature of managerial marketing, No. 1', *Business Review [Keiei Kenkyu]*, 40, February, 1–29 (in Japanese).

—— (1959b), 'The modern nature of managerial marketing, No. 2' (in Japanese), *Business Review [Keiei Kenkyu]*, 41, June, 1–28 (in Japanese).

—— (1960), *Modern Economics of Commerce*, Toyko: Uhikaku (in Japanese).

—— (1968), 'The fruitlessness of literal translation of marketing', in Study Group of Modern Marketing (ed.), *Farewell to Literal Translation of Marketing*, Tokyo: Seibun-do Shinko-sha, pp. 8–23 (in Japanese).

Murchison, Claudius Temple ([1919] 1968), *Resale Price Maintenance*, New York: Columbia University Press. (Reprint, New York: AMS Press, Inc.)

Myers, Kenneth H. and Smalley, Orange A. (1959), 'Marketing history and economic development: a report and commentary on two recent conferences concerning the need for a history of marketing in the United States', *Business History Review*, 23 (3), autumn, 387–401.

Nadworny, Milton J. (1955), *Scientific Management and the Union, 1900–1930, A Historical Analysis*, Cambridge, MA: Harvard University Press.

Nagata, Ken'ichi (1982), 'Making "design" ubiquitous and everyday life: a consideration from the aesthetic point of view', *Science and Philosophy* [*Kagaku to Shiso*], 43, Winter, 107–124 (in Japanese).

—— (1983), 'Design', in Shibata, Shingo (ed.), *Theory on Artistic Labour*, Part I, Tokyo: Aoki-shoten, pp. 221–57 (in Japanese).

Nakamura, Seiji (1983), *Research on the Automobile Industry*, Tokyo: Yuhikaku (in Japanese).

Nakano, Yasushi (1965a), 'Retailers in the period of the NIRA', *Annals of Economic 2 Studies Kagawa University* [*Kenkyu Nempo*], 5, 195–244 (in Japanese).

—— (1965b), 'Some problems on retail distribution in the 1930s in the USA, part one', *The Kagawa University Economic Review* [*Kagawa Daigaku Keizai Ronsan*], 38 (4), October, 44–69 (in Japanese).

—— (1966), 'Some problems on retail distribution in the 1930s in the USA, part two', *The Kagawa University Economic Review* [*Kagawa Daigaku Keizai Ronsan*], 39 (4), October, pp. 1–47 (in Japanese).

—— (1973), 'Emergence of marketing', in Morishita, Fujiya (ed.), *Economics of Marketing, Vol. 2*, Kyoto: Minerva-shobo, pp. 2–23 (in Japanese).

—— (1975), *Price Policy by Oligopolistic Manufacturers and Retail Merchants*, Kyoto: Minerva-shobo (in Japanese).

—— (1993), 'Establishment of large-sized food retailers in the USA: focusing on A&P, part 3', *The Quarterly Journal of Economic Studies* [*Kikan Keizai Kenkyu*], 16 (3), Spring, 1–29 (in Japanese).

NAMT: National Association of Marketing Teachers (1935), 'Definition of marketing terms: consolidation report of the committee on definition', *The National Marketing Review*, 1 (2), Fall, 148–66.

Nash, Ben (1934), 'How and why of Armour package changes', *Printers' Ink*, 3 May, 57–8 and 60–61.

—— (1937), 'Product development', *The Journal of Marketing*, 1 (3), January, 254–62.

NICB: National Industrial Conference Board (1931), *Budgetary Control in Manufacturing Industry*, New York: National Industrial Conference Board, Inc.

Neale, A.D. (1960), *The Antitrust Law of the United States of America: A Study of Competition Enforced by Law*, Cambridge: The University Press.

Nelson, Daniel (1974), 'Scientific management, systematic management, and labor', *Business History Review*, 48 (4), Winter, 479–500.

Nevett, Terence (1991), 'Historical investigation and the practice of marketing', *Journal of Marketing*, 55 (3), July, 13–23.

—— (1996), 'Exploring the nature of marketing history', pp. 114–28, in Nevett, Terence and Usui, Kazuo, 'Exploring the nature of marketing history: proposition and discussion', *Social Science Review* [*Shakai Kagaku Ronshu*] (Saitama University, Japan), 88, July, 113–35.

—— and Fullerton, Ronald A. (eds) (1988), *Historical Perspectives in Marketing: Essays in Honor of Stanley C. Hollander*, Lexington, MA: Lexington Books.

—— and Nevett, Lisa (1987), 'The origins of marketing: evidence from classical and early Hellenistic Greece (500–300 B.C.)', in Nevett, T. and Hollander, S.C. (eds), *Marketing in the Three Eras, Proceedings of the Third Conference on Historical Research in Marketing and Marketing Thought*, MI: Michigan State University, pp. 3–12.

—— and Hollander, Stanley C. (1994), 'Towards a circumscription of marketing history: an editorial manifesto', *Journal of Macromarketing* 14 (1), Spring, 3–7.

Nishimoto, Yoshiyuki (1974), 'Marketing thought in the 1910s: historical features of A.W. Shaw's theory comparing with R.S. Butler's'. In Takamiya, S., Iwao, Y. and Moroi, K. (eds), *Current Tasks of Modern Theory on Business Administration*, Tokyo: Yuhikaku-shobo, 89–105 (in Japanese).

Nishizawa, Tamotsu (1987), 'The higher commercial education movement around the turn of the century: with particular reference to Iida, Seki and Fukuda' (in Japanese), *Journal of Economics* (*The Keizaigaku Zasshi*), 88 (1), May, 57–78.

—— (1988), 'Towards the organization of higher commercial education in England', *Osaka City University Economic Review*, 23, March, 61–82.

—— (1991), 'The organization of economics and commerce education by Ashley and Marshall: with particular reference to the Faculty of Commerce at Birmingham University' (in Japanese), *The Economic Review* [*Keizai Kenkyu*], 42 (2), April, 153–74.

—— (1994), 'Re-examining the Decline of the British Economy: Intellectual and Industrial Rigidities' (in Japanese), *The Economic Review* [*Keizai Kenkyu*], 45 (4), October, 343–63.

Nonaka, Ikujiro (1994), 'A dynamic theory of organizational knowledge creation', *Organization Science*, 5 (1), February, 14–37.

—— and Takeuchi, Hirotaka (1995), *The Knowledge-Creating Company: How Japanese Companies Create the Dynamics of Innovation*, New York and Oxford: Oxford University Press.

Nystrom, Paul H. ([1914] 1986a), *Retail Selling and Store Management*, New York: D. Appleton-Century Company. (Reprint, Osaka: T.M.C. Press.)

—— (1915), *Economics of Retailing*, New York: The Ronald Press Company.

—— ([1917] 1986b), *Retail Store Management*, Chicago: La Salle Extension University. (Reprint of 1923 Version, Osaka: T.M.C. Press.)

—— ([1932] 1986c), *Fashion Merchandising*, New York: Ronald Press. (Reprint, Osaka: T.M.C. Press.)

Ogburn, W.F. (1933), 'The family and its functions', in *Recent Social Trends in the United States: Report of the President's Research Committee on Social Trends, Volume I*, New York: McGraw-Hill Book Company Inc., pp. 661–708.

Otterson, John W. (1924), 'An experiment in distribution: The Winchester-Simmons Company', in Clerk, F.E. (ed.), *Readings in Marketing*, New York: The Macmillan Company, pp. 328–35.

Ozaki, Kunihiro (1990), 'The elimination of middlemen and theory of selecting the type of channels', in Suyama, Keisuke and Takahashi, Hideo (eds), *Marketing Channels: Management and its Results*, Tokyo: Chuo-Keizai-sha, pp. 3–25 (in Japanese).

Packard, Vance (1960), *The Waste Makers*, New York: David McKay Co.

Palamountain, Joseph, C., Jr. (1955), *The Politics of Distribution*, Cambridge, Massachusetts: Harvard University Press.

Parlin, Charles Coolidge (1914a), 'Why and how a manufacturer should make trade investigations', *Printers' Ink*, 22 October, 3–4, 6, 8, 10, 12, 74–6 and 78–80.

—— ([1914b] 1978), *The Merchandising of Textile: An Address Delivered before the Tenth Annual Convention of the National Wholesale Dry Goods Association*, Philadelphia: The National Wholesale Dry Goods Association. (Reprint, in Henry Assael (ed.), *The Collective Works of C.C. Parlin*, New York: Arno Press.)

—— (1916), 'The manufacturer, the retailer and branded merchandise', *Printers' Ink*, 6 July, 84, 86–8 and 93–9.

Pea, Ray D. (1993), 'Practices of distribution intelligence and designs for education', in Salmon, Gavriel (ed.), *Distributed Cognition: Physiological and Educational Considerations*, Cambridge: Cambridge University Press, pp. 47–87.

Person, Harlow S. ([1929a] 1972), 'The origin and nature of scientific management', in Taylor Society [1929] 1972, pp. 1–22.

—— ([1929b] 1972), 'The new attitude toward management', in Taylor Society [1929] 1972, pp. 23–34.

Pevsner, Nikolaus (1949), *Pioneers of the Modern Design from William Morris to Walter Gropius*, 2nd ed., New York: The Museum of Modern Art.

Plummer, K.C. (1974), 'The streamlined moderne', *Art in America*, 62 (1), January–February, 46–54.

Polanyi, Karl (1966), *Dahomey and the Slave Trade: An Analysis of an Archaic Economy*, Washington: University of Washington Press.

Polanyi, Michael ([1966] 1983), *The Tacit Dimension*, Gloucester, Massachusetts: Peter Smith.

Pollard, Harold R. (1974), *Developments on Management Thought*, London: William Heinemann Ltd.

Pollard, Sidney (1965), *The Genesis of Modern Management: A Study of the Industrial Revolution in Great Britain*, London: Edward Arnold (Publishers) Ltd.

Poor's Manual (1910–1916), *Poor's Manual of Industrials*, New York: Poor's Railroad Manual Co.

Porter, Glenn and Livesay, Harold C. (1971), *Merchants and Manufacturers: Studies in the Changing Structure of Nineteenth-Century Marketing*, Baltimore, Maryland and London: The Johns Hopkins Press.

[Printers' Ink] (1910), 'How Macy's, New York, regards price maintenance', *Printers' Ink*, 4 August, 38–39.

—— (1912a), 'A summing-up of dealer co-operation: what has really been accomplished to date as presented by a committee of the A.N.A.M.', *Printers' Ink*, 12 September, 72–3, 76 and 78–85.

—— (1912b), 'Manufacturers' co-operation from the dealer's standpoint: continuation of the A.N.A.M. report on relationship of manufacturer and retailer', *Printers' Ink*, 19 September, 42–4 and 46–7.

—— (1912c), 'Manufacturers' co-operation from the dealers' standpoint: conclusion of the A.N.A.M. report on relationship of manufacturer and retailer', *Printers' Ink*, 26 September, 69–70, 72, 74–7 and 80.

—— (1913a), 'Fixing of resale price attacked by government: significance of suit against Kellogg Toasted Corn Flake Company', *Printers' Ink*, 2 January, 17–20 and 25.

—— (1913b), 'The Supreme Court decision against price maintenance: the highest tribunal hands down an epoch-making ruling in Sanatogen Case', *Printers' Ink*, 5 June, 3–4, 6, 8, 10 and 12.

—— (1913c), 'When price control is legal', *Printers' Ink*, 4 December, 4, 72–3.

—— (1914a), 'Manufacturers favor new price maintenance legislation', *Printers' Ink*, 2 April, 64–6 and 68–70.

—— (1914b), 'How manufacturers regard private brands', *Printers' Ink*, 21 May, 61–2 and 67–8.

—— (1914c), 'Kellogg's fight on chain stores', *Printers' Ink*, 17 September, 23–4.

—— (1915), 'The Macy argument for price-cutting', *Printers' Ink*, 8 April, 64–5.

—— (1916), 'Story of "Crisco" as told by Proctor & Gamble', *Printer's Ink*, 5 October, 73–4, 77–8 and 80.

—— (1918), 'Procter & Gamble accused of price maintenance', *Printers' Ink*, 28 November, 47.

—— (1928), 'Why merchandising is more than marketing', *Printers' Ink*, 26 April, 140 and 143.

—— (1932a), 'What is merchandising?' *Printers' Ink*, 4 February, 33.

—— (1932b) 'No product is too old to be changed', *Printers' Ink*, 10 November, 75–6.

—— (1932c), 'How 10-cent package has created a place for itself', *Printers' Ink*, 15 December, 60–63.

—— (1932d), 'The merchandising manager's jobs', *Printers' Ink*, 22 December, 52–3.

—— (1933a), 'New design opens new outlets', *Printers' Ink*, 6 April, 51–2.

—— (1933b), 'Radical changes in food package', *Printers' Ink*, 14 December, 42 and 44–5.

—— (1936), 'Merchandising', *Printers' Ink*, 2 January, 39–41.

—— (1937), 'Too much styling', *Printers' Ink*, 3 June, 77–81.

—— (1939), 'Magazines: 1914–1921, advertising revenue during World War was up through linage dropped, study shows', *Printers' Ink*, 29 September, 66–70 and 72.

—— (1958), 'New marketing concept at Westinghouse: decentralize and study the consumer', *Printers' Ink*, 24 January, 33–5.

[Procter & Gamble] (1944), *Into a Second Century with Proctor & Gamble*, Cincinnati: Privately Printed by the Proctor & Gamble Co.

[Product Engineering] (1936), 'Activities and trends in product design', *Product Engineering*, 7 (11), November, 406–7.

—— (1937), 'Trends in engineering design', *Product Engineering*, 8 (11), November, 422–3.

Pyle, John Freeman (1942), *Marketing Management*, Ypsilanti, Michigan: University Lithoprinters.

Rae, John B. (1965), *The American Automobile: A Brief History*, Chicago: The University of Chicago Press.

Redlich, Fritz (1957), 'Academic education for business: its development and the contribution of Ignaz Jastrow (1856–1937), in commemoration of the hundredth anniversary of Jastrow's birth', *Business History Review*, 31, Spring, 35–91.

Reed, Vergil D. (1929), *Planned Marketing*, New York: The Ronald Press Company.

Reekie, W. Duncan (2006), 'Marketing behaviour and entrepreneurship: a synthesis of Alderson and Austrian economics', in Wooliscroft, B., Tamilia, R.D. and Shapiro, S.J. (eds), *A Twenty-First Century Guide to Aldersonian Marketing Thought*, Boston, Dordrecht and London: Kluwer Academic Press, pp. 351–64.

Reilly, William J. ([1929] 1978), *Marketing Investigation*, New York: The Ronald Press Co. (Reprint, New York: Arno Press.)

Richmond, H.A. (1931), 'Merchandising: adaptation of the product to the market', in Donald, W.J. (ed.), *Handbook in Business Administration*, New York and London: McGraw-Hill Book Co., Inc., pp. 68–90.

Ridgeway, Valentine F. (1957), 'Administration of manufacturer-dealer systems', *Administrative Science Quarterly*, 1 (4), March, 464–83.

Risse, W. (1972), 'Der Begriff des Marketing und seine Stellung im System der Betriebswirtshaftslehre', *Zeitschrift für Betriebswirtschaft*, 42 (5), May, 337–60.

Ritzer, George (1996), *The Macdonaldization of Society: An Investigation into the Changing Character of Contemporary Social Life*, Thousand Oaks, California: Pine Forge Press, Revised Edition.

Robinson, Eric (1963), 'Eighteenth-century commerce and fashion: Matthew Boulton's marketing technique', *The Economic History Review, Second Series*, 16 (1), August, 39–60.

—— (1986), 'Matthew Boulton and Josiah Wedgwood, apostles of fashion', *Business History*, 28 (3), July, 98–114.

Robinson, Webster (1925a), 'Functionalizing a business organization', *Harvard Business Review*, 3 (3), April, 321–38.

—— (1925b), *Fundamentals of Business Organization*, New York, McGraw-Hill Company, Inc.

Rosenberg, Larry J. (1974), 'A new approach to distribution conflict management', *Business Horizon*, 17, October, 67–74.

—— and Stern, Louis W. (1971), 'Conflict measurement in the distribution channel', *Journal of Marketing Research*, 8, November, 437–42.

Rostow, R.R. (1990), *The Stages of Economic Growth: A Non-Communist Manifesto*, Cambridge: Cambridge University Press, 3rd edition.

Russel, Frederic A. (1922), *The Management of the Sales Organization*, New York: McGraw-Hill Book Company, Inc.

Ryan, Franklin W. (1935), 'Functional elements of market distribution', *Harvard Business Review*, 13 (2), January, 205–24.

Salmon, Gavriel (ed.) (1993), *Distributed Cognition: Physiological and Educational Considerations*, Cambridge: Cambridge University Press.

Savage, Charles J. (1914), 'The issue between the advertiser and the private-brand manufacturer', *Printers' Ink*, 6 August, 32–4 and 37–8.

Savitt, Ronald (1980), 'Historical research in marketing', *Journal of Marketing*, 44 (3), Fall, 52–8.

Schär, Johann Friedrich (1911), *Allgemeine Handelsbetriebslehre*, I. Band, Leipzig: Verlag von G.A. Glockner.

Schumpeter, Joseph A. ([1934] 1961), *The Theory of Economic Development: An Inquiry into Profits, Capital, Credit, Interest, and the Business Cycle*, Cambridge, Massachusetts: Harvard University Press.

Schwaltz, George (1963), *Development of Marketing Theory*, Cincinnati: South-Western Publishing.

—— (ed.) (1965), *Science in Marketing*, New York, London and Sydney: John Wiley & Sons, Inc.

Scott, Walter Dill ([1903] 1985), *The Theory of Advertising*, Boston: Small, Maynard & Company. (Reprint, New York and London: Garland Publishing, Inc.)

—— ([1908] 1978), *The Psychology of Advertising*, Boston: Small, Maynard & Company. (Reprint, New York: Arno Press.)

Searle, G.R. (1971), *The Quest for National Efficiency: A Study in British Politics and Political Thought, 1899–1914*, Oxford: Basil Blackwell.

Seligman, Edwin Robert Anderson (1927), *The Economics of Installment Selling*, Volume I, New York: Harper and Brothers.

[US] Senate (1910a), *Report of the Selected Committee on Wages and Prices of Commodities, Part 1*, Presented by Mr. Lodge, June 23, 61st Congress 2d Session, Report No. 912 Part 1, Washington: Government Printing Office.

—— (1910b), *Report of the Selected Committee on Wages and Prices of Commodities, Part 2*, Presented by Mr. Johnston, June 23, 61st Congress 2d Session, Report No. 912 Part 2, Washington: Government Printing Office.

Shaw, Arch Winslow (1904), 'The factor of system', *System*, 5 (2), February, 142.

—— (1905), 'The morgue of figures', *System*, 7 (3), September, 308.

—— (1911), '"Scientific management" in business', *The American Review and Reviews*, 43, March, 327–32.

—— (1912), 'Some problems in market distribution', *The Quarterly Journal of Economics*, 26 (4), August, 703–65.

—— (1914a), 'Wanted: a Government Bureau of Business Practice: an editorial by A.W. Shaw', *System: the Magazine of Business*, April, 444–8.

—— (1914b), 'More about a Bureau of Business Practice', *System: the Magazine of Business*, 25 (6), June, 665–72.

—— (1914c), 'Trust legislation and the average business man', *System: the Magazine of Business*, 26 (1), July, 109–12.

—— (1914d), '"Trust legislation and the average business man"', *System: the Magazine of Business*, 26 (2), August, 221–4.

—— (1914e), 'The European war and the average business man"', *System: the Magazine of Business*, 26 (3), September, 333–6.

—— (1914f), '"Scientific management" in business'. In Thompson (1914a), pp. 217–25. Reprint of Shaw (1911) with some omission.

—— ([1915] 1951), *Some Problems in Market Distribution: Illustrating the Application of a Basic Philosophy of Business*, Cambridge, Massachusetts: Harvard Business Press. (Reprint, Cambridge, Massachusetts: Harvard Business Press.)

—— (1916), *An Approach to Business Problems*. Cambridge, Massachusetts: Harvard University Press.

—— (1924), 'Simplification: a philosophy of business management', *Harvard Business Review*, 1 (4), July, 417–27.

—— (1928), 'Is this why the over-production bogy-man is a bogy-man?' *The Magazine of Business*, September, 263–5.

Shaw, Eric, and Jones, D.G. Brian (2005), 'A history of schools of marketing thought', *Marketing Theory*, 5 (3), September, 239–81.

Shawver, Donald L. and Nickels, William G. (1978), 'A rationalization for macro-marketing concepts and definitions', in G. Fisk and R.W. Nason (eds), *Macro-Marketing: New Steps on the Learning Curve*, Boulder: University of Colorado, pp. 29–45.

Sheldon, Oliver ([1923] 1965), *The Philosophy of Management*, London: Sir Isaac Pitman & Sons, Ltd. (Reprint, London: I. Pitman.)

Sheldon, Roy and Arnes, Egmont ([1932] 1976), *Consumer Engineering: A New Technique for Prosperity*, New York and London: Harper and Brothers Publishers. (Reprint, New York: Arno Press.)

—— (1925), 'The development of scientific management in England', *Harvard Business Review*, 3 (2), January, 129–40.

Sheth, Jagdish, Gardner, David M. and Garrett, Dennis E. (1988), *Marketing Theory: Evolution and Evaluation*, New York: John Wiley & Sons.

Shima, Hiroshi (1979), *Studies on Scientific Management*, Enlarged (ed.), Tokyo: Yuhikaku (in Japanese).

Shively, Nilas Oran (1916), *Salesmanship*, 4 vols., Chicago and San Francisco: Shively Service Bureau.

Silk, Alvin J. and Stern, Louis William (1963), 'The changing nature of innovation in marketing: a study of selected business leaders, 1852–1958', *Business History Review*, 37 (3), Autumn, 182–99.

Simpson, Roy B. (1911), 'The private brand problem', *Printers' Ink*, 25 May, 20, 22–4 and 26.

Sloan, Alfred P., Jr. (1963), *My Years with General Motors*, New York: Doubleday & Company.

Smith, Donald B. (1927), 'Planning sales for manufacturing company', *Harvard Business Review*, 5 (2), January, 186–96.

Smith, J.G. (1928), 'Education for business in Great Britain', *The Journal of Political Economy*, 36 (1), February, 1–52.

Smith, L. George (ed.) (1965), *Proceedings, December 28–29, 1964, Sheraton-Chicago Hotel, Chicago Illinois, Reflections on Progress in Marketing*, Chicago: American Marketing Association.

Smith, Ruth Ann and Lux, David S. (1993), 'Historical method in consumer research: developing causal explanations of change', *Journal of Consumer Research*, 19 (4), March, 595–610.

Sorenson, Helen ([1941] 1978), *The Consumer Movement: What It Is and What It Means*, Columbia, Missouri: Institute for Consumer Education, Stephens College. (Reprint, New York: Arno Press.)

Spears, Timothy B. (1995), *100 Years on the Road: The Traveling Salesman in American Culture*, New Haven and London: Yale University Press.

Stanton, W.J. and Buskirk, R.H. (1974), *Management of the Sales Force*, 4th ed., Homewood, IL: Richard D. Irwin, Inc.

Star, Susan Leigh and Griesemer, James R. (1989), 'Institutional ecology, 'translations' and 'grens'-objects: amateurs and professionals in Berkeley's Museum of Vertebrate Zoology 1907–1939', *Social Studies of Science*, 19, 387–420.

Stelzer, Irwin M. (1976), *Selected Antitrust Cases: Landmark Decisions*, 5th ed., Homewood, Illinois: Richard D. Irwin Inc.

Stephenson, James (1924), *Principles of Commercial History*, London: Sir Isaac Pitman & Sons, Ltd.

Stern, Barbara B. (1990), 'Literary criticism and the history of marketing thought: a new perspective on "reading" marketing theory', *Journal of the Academy of Marketing Science*, 18 (4), Fall, 329–36.

Stern, Louis W. (1963), 'Pragmatism and marketing history', in Greyer, Stephen A. (ed.), *Proceedings of the Winter Conference of the American Marketing Association, December 27–28, 1963, Boston, Mass., Toward Scientific Marketing*, Chicago: American Marketing Association, pp. 324–9.

—— and Gorman, Ronald H. (1969), 'Conflict in distribution channels: an exploration', in Stern, L.W. (ed.), *Distribution Channels: Behavioral Dimensions*, Boston: Houghton Mifflin, 156–75.

——, Sternthal, Brian, and Craig, C. Samuel (1973), 'Managing conflict in distribution channels: a laboratory study', *Journal of Marketing Research*, 10, May, 169–79.

Stewart, John B. (1959), 'Problems in review: planned obsolescence', *Harvard Business Review*, 37 (5), September–October, 14–15, 18, 21–2, 24, 26, 28 and 168–74.

Stewart, Paul W. and Dewhurst, J. Frederick (1939), *Does Distribution Cost Too Much? A Review of the Costs Involved in Current Marketing Methods and a Program for Improvement*, New York: The Twentieth Century Fund.

Strasser, Susan (1989), *Satisfaction Guaranteed: The Making of the American Mass Market*, New York: Pantheon Books.

Streichler, Jerry (1963), 'The consultant industrial designer in American industry from 1927 to 1960', unpublished Ph.D. thesis, New York University.

Sturdivant, Fred D. (1965), 'Approaches to the use of historical materials in marketing education', in Smith, L. George (ed.), *Proceedings, December 28–29, 1964, Sheraton-Chicago Hotel, Chicago Illinois, Reflections on Progress in Marketing*, Chicago: American Marketing Association, pp. 579–88.

Sugiyama, Chuhei and Nishizawa, Tamotsu (1988), '"Captain of Industry": Tokyo Commercial School at Hitotsubashi', in Sugiyama, Chuhei and Mizuta, Hiroshi (eds), *Enlightenment and Beyond: Political Economy Comes to Japan*, Tokyo: University of Tokyo Press, pp. 151–69.

Surface, Frank M. (1940), 'Choice of distribution channels', in Alexander, Ralph S. et al. (eds), 1940, pp. 377–94.

Suzuki, Takeshi (1976), *Introduction to German Functional Theory in Commerce*, Kyoto: Minerva-shobo (in Japanese).

Swinney, John B. (1917), *Merchandising*, New York: Alexander Hamilton Institute, Modern Business Volume 19.

Syllas, De (1969), 'Streamform: images of speed and green from the thirties', *Architectural Association Quarterly*, 1 (2), April, 32–41.

Takeuchi, Yasukazu (1977), *Origin of Japanese Management*, Kyoto: Minerva-shobo (in Japanese).

—— and Miyamoto, Mataji (eds) (1979), *A Genealogy of Business Philosophy: An International Comparative Study*, Kyoto: Doho-sha (in Japanese).

Tamura, Masanori (1971), *Systematic Thought on Marketing Behaviour*, Tokyo: Chikura-shobo (in Japanese).

Taniguchi, Akitake (1984), *Studies on the Earlier Established Trusts: A Prologue to American Monopolistic Capitalism*, Osaka: Osaka University of Economics (in Japanese).

Taylor, Frederic Winslow. (1895), 'A piece-rate system', *Transactions of the American Society of Mechanical Engineers*, 16, 856–903.

—— (1903), *Shop Management*, N.Y.: Harper & Row. (Also in F.W. Taylor, *Scientific Management: Comprising Shop Management, The Principles of Scientific Management, Testimony Before the Special House Committee*, N.Y.: Harper & Brothers, 1947; Reprint, Westport, Connecticut: Greenwood Press, 1972.)

—— (1911), *The Principles of Scientific Management*, N.Y.: Harper & Row. (Also in F.W. Taylor, *Scientific Management: Comprising Shop Management, The Principles of Scientific Management, Testimony Before the Special House Committee*, N.Y.: Harper & Brothers, 1947; Reprint, Westport, Connecticut: Greenwood Press, 1972.)

—— (1912), *Taylor's Testimony Before the Special House Committee*, in F.W. Taylor, *Scientific Management: Comprising Shop Management, The Principles of Scientific Management, Testimony Before the Special House Committee*, N.Y.: Harper & Brothers, 1947. (Reprint, Westport, Connecticut: Greenwood Press, 1972.)

[Taylor Society] (1920a), 'Comment', *Bulletin of the Taylor Society*, 5 (6), December, 229–30.

—— (1920b), 'Abstract of a Preliminary Report of the Committee on the Questionnaire, Presented at the Annual Meeting of the Taylor Society, New York, December 3, 1920', *Bulletin of the Taylor Society*, 5 (6), December, 231–4.

—— (1920c), 'Abstract of a Preliminary Report of the Committee on the Organization and Functions of the Sales Engineering Department, Presented at the Annual Meeting of the Taylor Society, New York, December 3, 1920', *Bulletin of the Taylor Society*, 5 (6), December, 235–7.

—— (1920d), 'Abstract of a Preliminary Report of the Committee on the Organization and Functions of the Sales Operating Department, Presented at the Annual Meeting of the Taylor Society, New York, December 3, 1920', *Bulletin of the Taylor Society*, 5 (6), December, 238–43.

—— (1920e), 'A Sales Executive Section', *Bulletin of the Taylor Society*, 5 (6), December, 244.

—— (1921a), 'Abstract of a Preliminary Report of the Committee on the Questionnaire, Presented at the Annual Meeting of the Taylor Society, New York, December 3, 1920', *Bulletin of the Taylor Society*, 6 (5), October, 202–4.

—— (1921b), 'Abstract of a Preliminary Report of the Committee on the Organization and Functions of the Sales Engineering Department, Presented at the Annual Meeting of the Taylor Society, New York, December 3, 1920', *Bulletin of the Taylor Society*, 6 (5), October, 205–7.

—— (1921c), 'Abstract of a Preliminary Report of the Committee on the Organization and Functions of the Sales Operating Department, Presented at the Annual Meeting of the Taylor Society, New York, December 3, 1920', *Bulletin of the Taylor Society*, 6 (5), October, 208–13.

Taylor Society ([1929] 1972), *Scientific Management in American Industry*, New York: Harper & Brothers. (Reprint, Easton: Hive Publishing Company.)

Teague, Walter D. (1932), 'What he does and how he works', *Product Engineering*, June, 245–7.

Tedlow, Richard S. (1990), *New and Improved: The Story of Mass Marketing in America*, New York: Basic Books, Inc.

—— (1993), 'The fourth phase of marketing', in Tedlow, Richard S. and Jones, Geoffrey (eds), *The Rise and Fall of Mass Marketing*, London and New York: Routledge, pp. 8–35.

Teraoka, Hiroshi (1984), 'Problems of petty retailers in the USA and establishment of the Robinson-Patman Act, part 2', *Research in Industrial and Commercial Economy* [*Sho-ko Keizai Kenkyu*], 16, October, 20–34 (in Japanese).

Thompson, C. Bertrand (1914), 'The literature of scientific management', in Thompson, C. Bertrand (ed.), *Scientific Management: A Collection of the More Significant Articles Describing the Taylor System of Management*, Cambridge, Massachusetts: Harvard University Press, pp. 3–48.

—— (1915), 'Scientific management in practice', *Quarterly Journal of Economics*, 29 (2) (February), 262–307.

TNEC: Temporary National Economic Committee (1941), *Monograph, Nos. 1–3, Price Behavior and Business Policy*, Washington, DC: U.S. Government Printing Office.

Toda, Kaiichi (1917), 'Regarding the market of commodities for everyday life', *Economic Review* [*Keizai Ronso*], 6 (5), May, 100–128 (in Japanese).

Tokunaga, Yutaka (1957), 'A historical study on merchandising and its issues', *Meiji University Journal of Commerce* [*Meiji Shogaku Ronsan*], 40 (10), August, 89–104 (in Japanese).

Tosdal, Harry R. (1921). *Problems in Sales Management*, Chicago: A.W. Shaw Company.

—— (1925), *Problems in Sales Management*, 2nd ed., Chicago: A.W. Shaw Company.

—— (1927), *Market Planning, The Manual of Business Management, Volume IV*, Chicago and New York: A.W. Shaw Company.

—— (1930), 'Trends in the manufacturer's choice of marketing channels', *Consumer Marketing Series*, 2, New York: American Management Association, 2–16.

—— (1931), *Problems in Sales Management*, 3rd ed., New York and London: McGraw-Hill Book Company Inc.

—— (1933a), *Introduction to Sales Management*, New York and London: McGraw-Hill Book Company Inc.

—— (1933b), 'Some recent changes in the marketing of consumer goods', *Harvard Business Review*, 6 (2), 156–64.

—— (1939), *Problems in Sales Management*, 4th ed., New York and London: McGraw-Hill Book Company Inc.

—— (1940), *Introduction to Sales Management*, 2nd ed., New York and London: McGraw-Hill Book Company Inc.

Town, Henry R. (1889), 'Gain-sharing', *Transactions of the American Society of Mechanical Engineers*, 10, 600–629.

Tsuchiya, Takao (1970), *History of Business Philosophy in Japan*, Tokyo: Nihon Keizai Shimbun-sha (in Japanese).

Uchida, Hoshimi (1974), *Introduction of the History of the Electronic Industry*, Tokyo: Nihon Keizai Shimbun-sha (in Japanese).

Uchiike, Renkichi (1906), *The Introduction to Science of Commerce*, Tokyo: Dobunkan (in Japanese).

Ueda, Teijiro ([1937] 1975), *General Theory on Economics of Management*, Tokyo: Toyo Shuppan-sha. (Reprint, Tokyo: Daisan Shuppan) (in Japanese).

Updegraff, Robert R. (1929), *The New American Tempo*, Chicago: A.W. Shaw Company.

Urwick, L. and Brech, E.F.L. (1951), *The Making of Scientific Management, Vol. I, Thirteen Pioneers*, London: Sir Isaac Pitman and Sons, Ltd.

Usui, Kazuo (1993), 'Ralph Starr Butler: a forgotten pioneer', in Japan Society for the Study of Marketing History (ed.), *History of Marketing Thought: USA*, Tokyo: Dobunkan, pp. 23–38 (in Japanese).

—— (1995), 'A brief history the rise and fall of macro-level marketing studies (studies of *Haikyu*) in Japan', in Rassuli, Kathleen N. et al. (eds), *Marketing History: Marketing's Great Empirical Experiment*, East Lansing, Michigan: Michigan State University, pp. 155–73.

—— (1997), 'A note on the current features of historical research in marketing in the U.S. and Japan: towards international cooperation for historical research in marketing', *Social Science Review* [*Shakai Kagaku Ronshu*] (Saitama University, Japan) 90, March, 13–44 (in Japanese).

—— (1999), *Study on the History of American Marketing Thought: The Historical Context of Development of Marketing Management* (in Japanese), Tokyo: Ootsuki-shoten.

—— (2000), 'The interpretation of Arch Wilkinson Shaw's thought by Japanese scholars', *Journal of Macromarketing*, 20 (2), December, 128–36.

—— (2001), 'Advantages and disadvantages of Japanese marketing: focusing on marketing by automobile manufacturers and convenience stores', in *2001: A Marketing Odyssey, Academy of Marketing 2001 Proceedings* (CD-ROM Version), Cardiff: Cardiff University.

—— (2005), 'An early version of the "*keiretsu*" retail store: marketing of Western-style sweets by Morinaga before the Second World War in Japan', in *The Future of Marketing's Past, Proceedings of the 12th Conference on Historical Analysis and Research in Marketing (CHARM)*, Eric H. Shaw and Leighann C. Neilson (eds), Long Beach: California State University, 301–11.

—— (2006), 'The science of commerce, studies of "*haikyu*" and the Younger German Historical School in Japan: a historical and comparative study with the USA and the UK', *Social Science Review* [*Shakai Kagaku Ronshu*] (Saitama University, Japan) 119, November, 1–21 (in Japanese).

—— ([2008] forthcoming), *Marketing and Consumption in Modern Japan*, London: Routledge-Curzon Press.

Vanderblue, Homer B. (1921), 'The functional approach to the study of marketing', *The Journal of Political Economy*, 29 (8), October, 676–83.

Veblen, Thorstein (1923), *Absentee Ownership and Business Enterprise in Recent Time: The Case of America*, New York: B.W. Huebsch, Inc.

Walker, Amasa (1913), 'Scientific management applied to commercial enterprises', *Journal of Political Economy*, 21, 388–99.

Weber, Max ([1904] 2001), *The Protestant Ethic and the Spirit of Capitalism*. Trans. by Talcott Parsons, London and New York: Routledge Classics.

Webster, Noah (1832), *A Dictionary of the English Language,* London: Black, Young, and Young.

—— (1836), *An American Dictionary of English Language*, New York: N. and J. White.

Webster, William C. (1903), *A General History of Commerce*, Boston and London: Ginn & Company, Publishers.

Weld, L.D.H. ([1916] 1978), *The Marketing of Farm Products*, New York: Macmillan Company. (Reprint, New York: Arno Press.)

—— (1917), 'Marketing functions and mercantile organization', *The American Economic Review*, 7 (2), 306–18.

—— (1923), 'The progress of commercial research', *Harvard Business Review*, 1 (2), January, 175–86.

Wenger, Etienne (1998), *Communities of Practice: Learning, Meaning, and Identity*, New York: Cambridge University Press.

Westing, J.H. (1974), 'Ralph Starr Butler 1882–1971', in Wring and Dimsdale (1974), pp. 23–6.

Weston, E.F. (1933), 'Low obsolescence becomes a selling point', *Printers' Ink*, 23 November, 12–13.

White, Percival (1921), *Market Analysis: Its Principles and Methods*, New York and London: McGraw-Hill Book Company Inc.

—— (1925), *Market Analysis: Its Principles and Methods*, 2nd ed., New York and London: McGraw-Hill Book Company Inc.

—— (1926a), *Business Management: An Introduction to Business*, New York: Henry Holt and Company.

—— (1926b), *Forecasting, Planning and Budgeting in Business Management*, New York: McGraw-Hill Book Company, Inc.

—— (1927), *Scientific Marketing Management: Its Principles and Methods*, New York and London: Harper and Brothers Publisher.

—— (1929), *Sales Quotas: A Manual for Sales Managers*, New York and London: Harper and Brothers Publisher.

Wilder, R. F. (1932), 'Coodination of research, sales, and production', *Transaction of the American Society of Mechanical Engineers*, 54, 25–39.

Williamson, Harold F. (1952), *Winchester: The Gun that Won the West*, New York: A.S. Barnes and Company, Inc.

—— (1963), 'Application of historical analysis to marketing', in Greyer, Stephen A. (ed.), *Proceedings of the Winter Conference of the American Marketing Association, December 27–28, 1963, Boston, Mass., Toward Scientific Marketing*, Chicago: American Marketing Association, pp. 319–29.

Wood, James Playsted (1961), 'Ralph Starr Butler', *Journal of Marketing*, 25 (4), April, 69–71.

Wooliscroft, Ben, Tamilia, Robert D. and Shapiro, Stanley J. (eds) (2006), *A Twenty-First Century Guide to Aldersonian Marketing Thought*, Boston, Dordrecht and London: Kluwer Academic Press.

Wren, Daniel A. (1979), *The Evolution of Management Thought*, 2nd ed., New York: John Wiley & Sons, Inc.

Wright, John S. and Dimsdale, Parks B., Jr. (eds) (1974), *Pioneers in Marketing*, Atlanta, Georgia: Georgia State University.

Yamamoto, Akira (1977), 'Birth and development of product planning', *Business Review* [*Keiei Kenkyu*], 27 (4–6), March, 51–64 (in Japanese).

Zimmerman, M.M. (1955), *The Super Market: A Revolution of Distribution*, New York, Toronto and London: McGraw-Hill Book Company, Inc.

Zinn, Walter and Johnson, Scott D. (1990), 'The commodity approach in marketing research: is it really obsolete?' *Journal of the Academy of Marketing Science*, 18 (4), Fall, 345–53.

Index